The Fog of Faith

Surviving My Impotent God

A memoir by
Leona Stucky

Prairie World Press
New Mexico

The Fog of Faith - Surviving My Impotent God
A memoir by Leona Stucky
Published by: Prairie World Press
903 West Alameda, Unit 513, Santa Fe, NM 87501
WWW.PRAIRIEWORLDPRESS.COM

ISBN xxxxxxxxxxxx

LCCN: pending

CIP block

All photographs ©

All poems by permission

Edited by

Cover photograph by

Cover design by

Interior design and typography by

Printed in xxxx

First Edition

DEDICATION

For my children, grandchildren, and whole family
And for
women who have experienced intimate partner violence or abuse
And for
spiritual seekers on their own journeys

CONTENTS

PREFACE

I still shudder at my vulnerability. Yet I have known my whole adult life that I needed to write this narrative. The times I tried failed, and avoidance became my motto. But with the years has come courage, and now I invite you into my personal story.

Because of several mistakes with a seventeen-year-old boy, I forfeited the life I might have lived: the functioning farm, peaceful prairie, prayers of praise, raucous rollicking, and non-violent verse. These things would have held me close.

Of course, trouble began before those mistakes. But I started as a thoughtful girl in a quietly rugged world, where I nestled in the contentment, mercy, and innate goodness of a Mennonite family on a Kansas farm. We lived guilelessly on the expansive land, our triumphs and disappointments coalescing into meaning. We laughed and loved, bonded by the naïve honor we practiced, the heartfelt values that won our stern dedication, the earthbound simplicity of raising animals, food, and a succession of children.

Growing up in the 1950s and '60s in a loving, religious context had ample moments of innocence and peace, until trauma intervened and tested our spiritual convictions daily. Jungians say severe trauma is necessarily a numinous experience: it reroutes meaning and belief—often from busy roads to dead ends. What we had been certain about before trauma may be reworked and sifted again through layers of grief-filled doubt.

Immediately after the initial ordeal, I measured faith questions against my reality, while I still believed in song and sorrow, in hope and tomorrow. I kept thinking, *It's going to work out. I have faith. I'm a Mennonite, for Christ's sake.* Literally for Christ's sake. And for mine, too. But prolonged danger and potential death beget a kind of exploration and thinking that can sharpen perception and lead to acute self-honesty. I focused on the often unnoticed contrasts between thoughts and the unconscious imperatives that rule our lives, while love and cruelty pushed my story forward.

My family's purpose, courage, and resilience helped my tenacious personality triumph over skin-crawling nightmares. Later, mining those experiences eventually taught me what I needed to know, enough to share my knowledge by nurturing clients over a thirty-year professional therapy practice, teaching graduate and postgraduate students, and loving a husband, children, grandchildren, and treasured family and friends.

The events of this story are true, but I have changed some names and locations to protect others' privacy. Likewise, I did not create composite characters, but I may have changed details that describe specific characters. I speak from my own perspective and memory, acknowledging that siblings or others who shared aspects of these times in our lives have their own viewpoint.

Come with me on this journey.

– Leona Stucky, 2017

WAKING NIGHTMARE

Boston, 1972

"Please, Ron," I pleaded quietly, hating the sound of my voice. "You're going to make me scream. Please don't twist my arm so tight."

My shoulder felt on the brink of popping out of its socket, but I was more concerned about the knife he held against my back. At twenty– one I knew in my bones, without forethought or reflection, that if I survived, what I will have done would once again be more humiliating than anything he will have done.

Dad and his first daughter, LeAnn

PART I - A TRUE BELIEVER

God sees the little sparrow fall,
It meets His tender view;
If God so loves the little birds,
I know He loves me, too.

– Maria Straub, 1874

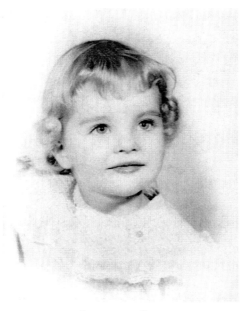

Leona, age four

CHAPTER 1 - ON VIOLENCE

Kansas, August 1966

The problem was my boyfriend, a dominating but shy guy named Ron. I wanted to break up with him. Though not a Mennonite like me, he was a nice enough boy. He seldom said a cross word, he was not mean, he didn't smoke or drink. Yet he thought he owned me, and that felt weird and suffocating. At sixteen I was tired of this and wanted to date others. Again, I resolved to end it, despite knowing that if I broke free, he'd feel I was stealing something from him.

I was scared, but I had the confidence of innocence. With the comforting cloak of Jesus wrapped around me and my whole family keeping me safe and satisfied, fear was only a game I played with my siblings.

As kids, whenever Mom and Dad went to town together and left us alone at the house, we played the danger game. In those hours of childhood fantasy, fear ramped up our imaginations and prepared us for the worst, which we pictured as a bad man coming to our farm to kill us. We picked the best places to hide: the chicken coop or the red barn's hayloft, arranging bales of hay as a fort. We sounded coded tones to warn siblings. We imagined trapping him in the pump house or escaping bareback on our horses. Our playbook was an early farm version of the much later movie *Home Alone*.

In our pretense, we were excited, not scared. We knew we'd win. If all else failed, Mom and Dad would save us. We trusted God and our parents completely, even though Mennonite tenets would not permit them to hurt an intruder.

That "bad men" really existed never occurred to me. Even with Ron, even though I knew *something* was coming, I didn't anticipate violence. So I was not prepared. What my life path indicated and what happened were two different things, too different to hold in one thought, to speak in one breath. In our faith, our childhoods, our farm, our family, and our community, *violence* had a different meaning to us than it did to the rest of the world. We were strangers to that other kind of violence.

Not that violence was absent from our lives: though I was raised a pacifist, I discovered at a young age—oh, probably seven or eight years old—that violence and cruelty thrived in me.

Kansas, Summer of 1958

Those damn birds, sparrows and starlings mostly. They were doing it again, pecking the grains we planted, nurtured, harvested, sold, or fed to the cows and pigs. They stole it off stalks or pilfered it from our grain storage building. They carried it to their young. Wheat stalks waved in the wind like ocean swells, heads protruding forward, grains already well developed by mid-June. Naturally we felt protective of our crop. With most of next year's livelihood burgeoning in those undulating fields, who'd allow sparrows and starlings to steal it?

Scriptural passages about birds of the air and lilies of the fields misled us. Birds could be carefree *because* we worked. It wasn't fair. They paid no regard to my mother's unsteady gait or her shaking hands covering her tears. They wouldn't notice our sacrifices to follow Jesus's message. They were blind to our toil from dawn to dusk that produced food and hopefully purified our souls.

Plenty of these birds would be shot when my ten-year-old male cousins gained birthday BB guns. I took action right along with my pacifist siblings and cousins. Like a snake up a tree, I crawled up the ladder to the highest shelf of the hayloft in the red barn. Those little nestlings, I knew they'd be there, and I plopped those translucent baby birds into a rusted coffee can. I grabbed more babies from hard-to-reach nests dotting the farm. My can stood just as tall and full as my cousins'. Those boys couldn't show me up.

One task remained: splat the baby birds from the can onto the outside planks of our hoary outhouse. When my turn came, I plunged my hand into the coffee can, squeezed my fingers around some squirming, featherless bodies, wound up my arm like a major-league pitcher, and *kabaam*. Dogs jumped up to lick the remains.

I'd watched Dad take his hunting rifle and chase coyotes, followed by neighbors also in hot pursuit. As a point of protective pride, they felt righteous, shooting the devils that tore apart our lambs. Shouldn't I feel as honorable about thinning out bird populations? I didn't care much about birds one way or the other.

But Dad returned and gave me a furrowed-brow look that said *don't ever do it again*. His eyes told me I should act like his daughter, and coffee cans of baby sparrows and featherless bodies splattered against the outhouse were unacceptable. Under his gaze my revelry turned to embarrassment. I looked down and studied the frayed rips in my sneakers.

I had been as dogged as most kids about stomping on stink bugs or trapping lightning bugs until my jar was lit. Dad raised no eyebrow to that. Still, I should have known that killing baby birds was a step too far. At least for a girl.

People who haven't lived on farms don't always get it. I stood up for Dad years later in the Boston College student lounge, when my friends berated farmers who butchered animals with their bare hands. They turned up their noses at butchering, yet they stuffed their faces with cheeseburgers. I didn't tell them what happened when my dad helped with our annual Butcher Day Fundraiser for Hopefield Mennonite Church: sick from killing, he came home green and vomited. I didn't tell these students that some people butcher and hate it.

There's a lot about farm life you wouldn't understand if you didn't grow up on a farm. I didn't tell them that when I was five and Mom and Grandma Schrag butchered a couple of hens, they both laughed till they cried—while I, eyes wild with fright, screamed like a banshee and ran in circles to escape the blood-spurting, headless chicken chasing me.

I didn't tell them about the day my sister Debbie and I tried to surprise Mom with a meal we delivered right to the table— we swung a dull ax against an old rooster's unyielding neck.

I didn't tell them I had the mark of baby birds on me.

I didn't tell them either that God saw the little sparrows fall. He didn't do a damn thing to help them. But according to our songs, *He so loves the little birds*, and therefore I should believe He loves me, too. He watched those birds splat against our outhouse! What kind of love is that?

I didn't tell them because they didn't have eyes to see or ears to hear. Instead, I told those college kids who berated farmers for butchering, "I was raised on a farm where your hamburger comes from."

I should have asked them what they thought about their dads. They went to World War II, didn't they? They killed people, not cows, pigs, or chickens. None of these students approved of the Vietnam War. They had no desire to kill or be killed in Southeast Asia. Still, they didn't put their wartime dads on the same level as brutish farmers. I didn't ask why, because I didn't think of it until several hours later. But given time to ponder, anyone who ruminates would know we all have blood on our hands.

Chapter 2 - FAMILY

By the time I reached my teenage years, Mom had become sick and disheveled. She slumped in her wheelchair, her body loosened from her bones like a sack of dough. Dad put his hands on her shoulders and soothed her tears. Her round, pocked face and wide, watery eyes expressed her enduring need to collapse. Brown clumps of her hair extended into thin spikes that protruded wildly, like a porcupine past its prime.

Dad brushed her hair without taming it into a style. He sat patiently. He gathered from her lap chunks of food that fell from her hands before she could stuff them into her mouth. He talked to her in a low, quiet voice and sought her advice, somehow deciphering the chorus of hollow words she would utter. Could he hear her call his name, Carl? Mom's former heartfelt and purposeful responses had faded with her optimistic energy.

The wideness of Dad's love matched the expanse of his three-hundred-pound, six-foot-tall frame. His buzz-cut dome with its prominent widow's peak, winged ears, and fire-red cheeks topped a muscle-bound thickness that engulfed us kids and camouflaged his faults.

An energetic man on a mission, my dad worked to make good on his family birthright. He owned the land and farmed it successfully to be generous to his community and the world. He embellished integrity like a frog puffed itself up to float in a pond. With little room for pride, ostentatious clothing, and recounting of victories, you sometimes saw him sigh after a job well done.

The sickness unto death that eventually permeated our lives arrived slowly, unnoticed at first. We kept spinning like planets, as if nothing would happen, oblivious to the asteroid on course to collide with us. After all, we were a branch of the Stucky family, inheritors of privilege, substantial people in our tiny sectarian world. We were no strangers to what must be done, hoped for, believed in—neither were our Mennonite relatives and neighbors of Moundridge, Kansas.

For years my mother, Deloris, agonized over her feet refusing to land where she intended. She was surprised by dropping a pot roast before it reached the table. She lost her balance as the top half of her body contorted forward, then backward, while she lurched toward equilibrium.

Perhaps her uneasy feelings began after her first child, LeAnn, was born in 1948. Maybe a twinge of blank spaces interrupted her brain and a flicker of muscles and nerves misfired between her wrists and fingers.

When I came along in 1950, her unsteady gait became obvious to others, although not yet to her. I remember LeAnn and I toddling on either side of Mom while she held our hands. We aimed to keep our white Sunday shoes on the sidewalk, but her gait threw us off. She griped at us for muddying our shoes, leaving us befuddled.

By the time she had her third child, Debra, in 1952, she must have suffered doubts. Do most mothers stab their fingers when pinning a diaper? How many times had she almost caught her arm in the wringer washer? No doubt, she prayed.

Her prayers probably intensified when Dorthy arrived in 1955. Without a spare moment to herself, still helping her husband with milking and still lining up kids to wash hair and polish shoes on Saturday night, I imagine she bargained with God: "If You'll let my fingers open the shampoo lid, I'll sing praises before I close my weary eyes."

She owed God for sure when a son arrived. "Butch"—Donavan Carl—was born in 1959. Finally blessed with a boy, she and Dad beamed. Though this time, her doctor told her more firmly than before that her fragile body couldn't endure the strains of birthing children. But what was she supposed to do? She and Carl decided years earlier not to interfere with God's prerogative to create new life in her body. Now, chastened and fearful, she prayed for forgiveness when she popped her first birth control pill.

By 1961 she quit driving; she knew she couldn't safely steer a car. She now needed her husband to open jars or reach bottles of horse liniment off the bathroom closet's top shelf. Finally she heard a diagnosis from a reflexologist who felt anomalies in her toes. The medical doctors before him weren't certain or courageous enough to deliver the death sentence: multiple sclerosis.

Five children's care requires coping for any mother. Yet, with birth control pills, she still added to her brood. By now, those of us old enough realized Mom was pregnant again when Dad carried a large bowl, a box of saltines, and a glass of water to their bedroom. In late 1962 Lynnett arrived. It seemed as if man could do nothing to hinder God's choices.

A few months after Carla, the last of seven, slid past resistance in 1965, Mom fell when hanging laundry. Perhaps our clothesline, fixed in her dimmed gaze, seemed a few inches closer than it was. That day when she carried clean wet diapers to hang on the line was the last time Mom walked. Our lives changed overnight. Baby Carla seemed to belong to us older children as we fed her bottles of Similac and changed her diapers.

CHAPTER 3 – THE MENNONITE WELL OF FAITH

We looked enough like a normal Midwest farm community that you might not guess we were Mennonite unless you knew our history, motives, thought processes, or noticed our controlled impulses and abundant gentleness. What you couldn't see revealed the most about us. Underneath our disciplined exterior burned passion. We focused it on doing what Jesus wanted.

Our faith, the well from which we drank our identity, defined what our lives should be. We learned how to judge each event and where to place our trust. We knew another world loomed out there, a bad one that often dismissed our re-purposing of Jesus's sermon on the mount. My family didn't touch or taste that world, and seldom did that world intersect ours. Being held in Jesus's love and resting in His arms was poignant enough for us.

My family's Mennonite story began in Swiss-German territories as part of the nonviolent, radical Protestant Reformation in the 1500s. Years after both Catholics and more sophisticated Protestants slaughtered us for our simplistic beliefs, Catherine the Great invited our Swiss-German group to the Ukraine. She allowed pacifism, a fairly literal interpretation of the New Testament, and believer's baptism if we built a farming economy. But a hundred years after Catherine's offer, the Czar demanded military service. We wouldn't comply. The memory of our martyr history helped us endure renewed persecution. We'd rather be burned at the stake than practice infant baptism or kill others. We'd rather be stuffed in a gunnysack, tied to rocks, and drowned than pledge allegiance to a tradition that obstructed our direct path to Jesus with priests, theologians, kings, or queens. We'd rather be driven from our homes and forced to give up our earthly goods than pick up a sword or gun on behalf of an earthly leader. No king, czar, dictator, or government could make us close our ears to Jesus.

So, led by Elder Jacob Stucky in the 1870s, my Mennonite ancestors homesteaded in Kansas on land the United States government had taken from Native Americans. They forged a New Testament community: simple, disciplined, and devoted. When sensing His presence, they became uplifted, expansive, and full, like a quiet lake after spring rains.

My people stepped in a straight line behind Jesus, each person willingly carrying His cross. Whatever was required, we put our hands to. The rest of the world might be cultured, but we chose to be fools for Christ. In tune with Jesus, we were happy. No amount of suffering could dispel that happiness. The world failed to grasp blessings we knew intimately. Thus we abandoned that world's lurid temptations.

In the 1950s our community of General Conference Mennonites approved some pleasures of modern life: electricity, motorized vehicles, and regular clothing—though nothing flashy or unseemly for women. For Grandpa Stucky's taste, our skirt hemlines hugged our lower shins and we shunned jeans or shorts, except at home where Mom and Dad allowed jeans for working outside. The time Grandma and Grandpa Stucky drove into our yard unannounced, we girls shimmied up the balcony poles while Mom and Dad engaged them with conversation and coffee in the kitchen. We came downstairs to greet them in dresses. A few years later, after they had passed, we noticed that shorts for children were becoming acceptable in our community. We participated in that change, especially at home where regulating with clothes was our defense against the discomfort of weather. Grandma Schrag allowed pink lipstick for her adult daughters, but red was an abomination.

Industrious, frugal, and faithful, we prospered and bought land. My Stucky grandparents owned quite a bit of it, enough to give each of their four living adult children a farm or something close to that. We inherited a half-section—three hundred and twenty acres—and a large three-story farm house they built. It sported two basements, carved mill wood, decorative paintings on walls and ceilings, a main floor, upstairs, and attic, large and numerous rooms, and several porches, including an upstairs balcony.

Perhaps because we stayed away from the world, when we met it, we were deeply influenced by it, for better or worse. You might imagine that, when my separatist family met the real world, sparks would fly or a cataclysmic scene would erupt. But that's not what happened the first time I experienced the "outside," when I was eleven and Mom and Dad took us to the circus. We had a blast—more fun than our favorite outdoor hide-seek-and-chase game of "gray wolf" with our cousins.

The main tent was huge. Exotic animals we had seldom seen even in picture books peered through their cages. Each event thrilled us as only a first experience could. Clowns made a face and we laughed; their gut-splitting antics drew us breathless into the present moment. Could you imagine elephants standing on their hind legs? Who would dare enter a pen with tigers? Cows with horns scared us. Look way up there on those high-flying swings—those were real people. Judas Priest! There were even women up there—women in bathing suits, no less. They looked so brave and graceful. They were in sync with their partners. How daring!

For the first time in my life I knew something glamorous that women could do and still be respected. They were not teachers, mothers, nurses, or missionaries. They were amazingly talented and part of the real world. My sisters and I yearned for a dazzling future. Later at home we practiced tricks on the crossbars in a grain elevator room. The metal bars lent themselves to "skinning the cat," or tightrope walking, or swinging upside down with our hands gripping tight. If we fell, we landed on the wheat below.

Unwelcome intrusions into my fantasies created a different kind of circus, though. I fantasized climbing to the highest platform: the curtain dropped, and I began my act with a bow, and—oh, no! My family, friends, and community were in the audience. They saw me wearing a bathing suit. I'd capitulated to pressures from the world. They frowned and turned their faces away.

In the next version, I climbed to the highest platform. The curtain dropped, and I began my act with a bow. The audience booed. I was wearing a long-sleeved blouse with jeans. My grandparents approved of this attire only because they realized that a dress in this position would be far too revealing.

No compromise would appeal to both my extended family and the general audience. Neither would budge an inch, even in my imagination! Pleasing them all might be impossible in real life. But surely I could discover a way in my fantasies. I tried and tried. My world and the other world sat in opposite corners and glowered at each other.

CHAPTER 4 - LAMBING TIME

Up on my own around 4:30 and half blind in the dark, I shuffled down the stairs. Dad and I carved out a strong relationship, starting especially when I became Dad's most reliable helper. My sisters and I worked together in summer and often in winter after school, but I'm the child of the three oldest who rose early to chores before school and the one who did much of the field work.

"Dad," I whispered into their dark bedroom. "Can you help me with fractions?"

"I'll be there."

I turned on the light in the kitchen and saw the boxes next to the floor furnace. Two cute little lambs' heads stuck out. I discovered two more, asleep. I petted curly wool and made sucking noises to get their attention.

"I bet you're hungry," I said, laughing at the one pushing at the box.

With overalls on and a splash of water on his stubbles, Dad sat next to me at the table and stared at the workbook.

He helped me understand, yet I still stumbled over problems. "I wish I didn't have to go to school. I'd be glad to help you all day long if I could stay home."

"You'll get something good out of school. Anyway, you have to go."

I said with increasing emphasis, "I wish, I wish, I wish, I wish, I wish!"

When I finally finished my homework, I eagerly turned to my farm chores. We each grabbed two lambs and tucked them under our arms. We stepped off the chore room threshold into wind.

"When did you last check on the new lambs?"

"About two this morning," he said. "It's too cold to leave them long. They'd freeze."

My chest swelled. Dad could do anything that must be done.

Dad lifted the chain out of the notch and pushed the gate open. He locked it behind us. We walked towards the white barn, on the frozen mush below our feet. I didn't drop below the frozen crust, but Dad's boots sank with every step. He opened the white barn door. I rushed in to escape the wind and handed my lambs to him. He placed them in the pen with their mothers.

We searched through the flock looking for new births, hoping for twins as a bonus. We found a ewe licking the birth sack off her baby. Dad picked it up and held it close to his belly to warm it. Then he used it to draw the ewe toward another pen. I walked behind the ewe and redirected her if she veered off Dad's path. We repeated this pattern four times. With the newest lambs and their mothers safely in a pen surrounded by cushy layers of hay, we attended those we brought from the house.

Snow and bitter cold never stopped us. Bundled up, we started the Five Star tractor and hitched up the silage trailer and parked it directly under the silo chute. We both climbed up and Dad pitched one shovelful. While he refilled, I pitched another shovelful with my muscled ten-year-old arms. We moved in rhythm. I sang, *Jesus wants me for a sunbeam, to shine for Him each day,* but I soon gave way to heavy breathing. Aware that Dad took pride in my work, I gave my best effort.

He counted on me. His smile flashed a kindness so rich I could barely absorb it. He deserved and needed help—so much work to do, so many kids, and a sick wife. Already Dad assumed some of Mom's duties. Once we finished here, Dad would melt butter to cook milk gravy and wake the kids while I would clean myself and change clothes for school.

My five-year-old sister popped into my mind. Without editing, I said, "I think Dotsy has the most beautiful legs I've ever seen."

"What makes you think that?"

"I don't know. I just do think that. I think Dotsy will be a beauty when she grows up," I said, embarrassed to bring up a subject that seemed dangerously close to forbidden vanity.

"She's only five years old now. We'll have to wait a while before we know how she'll look as an adult."

"Maybe so," I said, working my fingers and toes open and closed to keep blood flowing. "But I bet she'll be beautiful!"

Dad hid a smile when I looked up. "Maybe so," he said.

My fingers felt like ice cubes with nerve endings. "Lonie," Dad said, using the first part of my nickname, Lonie Baloney, "why don't you run on in? You can warm up for a bit. I'll bring the lambs in. Then we'll feed the cows."

I jumped at the chance and ran toward the house. With fingers too stiff to open the chained metal gate, I scrambled over the fence, cresting the top like a cup that runneth over.

Mom, always tired from her perpetual tasks—those she could still manage—became part of the backdrop of my daily existence. She didn't push through with abrasive clarity or a strong, demanding personality. I relegated her to the wallpaper of my mind.

In her twenties, she impressed friends and family as a warm, fun-loving, and engaging young woman. But a tide of patriarchal practices limited Mom's personal power and presence. She couldn't keep her own name and identity when she married. While Dad and probably most Mennonite men were loving and respectful toward their wives, she was expected to love, support, nurture, and obey the man in her life, not outshine or compete with him. She conformed to his guidance, his style of living, and his desires. If this wasn't enough to overshadow her innate animation, the continuing challenges of birthing and raising children kept her focused on what *others* needed, on those too young to remember all she did for them. Like a phantom, she performed an angel's bidding, vanishing into a back room to nurse the next baby before she could be noticed for the tasks she already completed.

Still, her love inspired us when my sisters and I played house or drove our tiny tractors in the backyard on a nest of aromatic needles. I felt it when we helped her roll out dough, slice it in squares, and fill the squares with a cottage cheese and egg mixture before sealing the edges to make *kase beroggi*. I smelled it in her homemade *knepp* and cherry *prie* pudding. Her love permeated grainy bricks of lye soap. I discovered it in the worn sheet she spread under the ripe mulberry trees we shook. The sounds of our laughter echoed a now ancient symphony of smiles that, when we were babies, danced in her eyes.

Mom's father died when she was thirteen. Her mother, Grandma Schrag, raised four children with little money. She farmed, and our mother, who was the oldest, helped the younger children. In spite of hardships, Mom attended Bethel College, our General Conference Mennonite school, for one year during World War II, and studied teaching. Later she rode a horse to her one-room school and carried wood to fire the stove before the children arrived. In that small space she taught all eight grades.

Focusing within her small Mennonite community, she married her second cousin, Carl J. Stucky, in 1947, in spite of his recent release from prison and third-degree burns that still erupted in open sores on his legs.

In my early years, Mom assisted Dad with outside chores as well as housework. She sometimes played on the piano hymns for us at home and for Hopefield worship services, until it all changed, until she couldn't, until multiple sclerosis unhinged mental commands from her hands, fingers, and eyes.

Chapter 5 - FARM GIRLS

Though we seldom left the farm, like most kids we believed in fun. We built play houses in worn-out combine bins, explored the old haunted house across the road, or built a dam across the pasture creek. When we were hot we chased the cows away and plopped into their circular metal water tank. We pretended we could swim, and arose from the water covered in mossy green.

On rare occasions we found a bloated, dead cow in the barnyard, before Dad dragged her away with one of our two tractors to a pit grave beside the wheat field. We lined up to jump on her belly. Like on a trampoline, we bounced and shot off in different directions, trying not to land in the gooiest mush or too close to her cavities where maggots congregated.

Sometimes our play turned serious. One morning we challenged each other to catch frogs, and I was earnestly racing around until I noticed my bucket wasn't as full as it should be. Debbie and Dotsy had dumped the frogs from my bucket and from LeAnn's bucket into theirs. When questioned, Debbie denied it and fabricated an elaborate story.

I looked Dotsy straight in the eye and told her that I knew Debbie was lying, and that I knew she wouldn't lie. I asked what Jesus would do in her situation. She burst into tears and confessed the whole story, saying how sorry she was. When

Debbie finally realized the dead weight of her fibs, she couldn't understand why her little sister wouldn't keep their secret.

LeAnn and I forgave Dotsy. Beyond being found out, the only punishment was a solid warning that Debbie had better not do it again—as if our rigid judgment could halt her adventurous spirit!

Another time, my sisters and I took turns in our two-holed outhouse, after we dealt death blows to the spiders and wasps that shared it with us. We wouldn't venture into the house to do our business; Mom might ask us to help her. The summer day was blisteringly hot. Noticing the tall stalks, we ran into the cool and inviting field.

"Let's play hide and seek in here," I suggested. "Dotsy can be on my team."

Our play turned from hide and seek to making mansion-sized houses by tromping down the silage. Dotsy and I jumped into the tall stalks and rode them down. "This is like magic!" I yelled at Debbie and LeAnn, as I showed them how we rode down the descending stalks. As weightless as fluttering angels, we destroyed more silage.

Suddenly Debbie sensed someone near us. "Oh!" she said, alarmed. "Hi, Dad. You're back!" Without another word, our jumping and falling stopped. Quickly we saw that, in our glee, we'd damaged part of Dad's field. He seemed to have stood there long enough to enjoy our make-believe games. He nodded approval of our angel rides a little while longer and then dished out afternoon chores.

As a family, we laughed at pain and pleasure alike, and bucked up under everyday lessons. Slapstick hilarity erupted when one of us stubbed a toe on a metal kitchen chair leg and hopped around yelling *suffering sassafras* or *darn it again*. We cut loose when we spilled a bowl of strawberry Jell-O in a lap or caught our belt loop on a loosened nail-head that jerked us back when we took a step.

We hooted the time Mom narrowly escaped Sassy's horns and demanded Dad sell that blasted cow. When our ram slammed Dad into the gate, we roared. His wide eyes registered surprise as he scrambled over and started laughing with us. When he dropped a chain hook on his big toe or hammered his finger instead of the nail or stepped on a slanted board that ricocheted to his backside, we had to sneak around the barnyard corner to keep from wetting our pants.

Debbie kept us laughing with antics she embellished from school — how one of the boys turned the clock forward and confused the teacher. Spastic moves were a real treat, like the time Butch stumbled on a tree root, veered sideways into the tree, and dumped the bucket of feed he was carrying as he flailed his arms to catch his balance.

Dad buckled into breath-defying cackles when he turned on the electric fence and heard me scream. Shrieking in shock, literally, I ran into the barn. The wild surprise on my face made him laugh harder. With arms gesticulating, I lectured him. "How dare you pull that switch when I'm handling the wires!" He thought I had already finished tying wires together so the cows wouldn't break through. What was taking me so long?

We joked about what it took to put a smile on our faces. Proud to be tough, we enjoyed the benefits of laughing when others might have cried.

Baby Carla's vigorous desires provided typical entertainment. She would jump at the chance to go outside, saying, "Me go. Me go!" She tagged along with me to hang up a load of laundry and played in the dirt next to the lines for a while, then wandered a few feet away. I heard her scream and poked my head around the sheets to see our most aggressive goose, Nervous, chasing her. Carla's chubby little legs, which until then had only known a waddle, stretched out fully, her muscles taut, her face registering determination and terror. I grabbed Carla and chased Nervous, laughing as she skirted away. Dad snickered when I told him. I suggested we sell Nervous because she was mean. He shook his head. "Carla doesn't know it, but Nervous is her best friend. Her fear of Nervous stops her from going outside without one of us."

"You're right," I nodded. "There'd be nothing Mom could do."

We both smiled, knowing our proclivity for odd advantages that few would understand. Daily vigor and wit pulled us through. Perhaps God smiled with us.

CHAPTER 6 – PRECARIOUS TEEN YEARS

November 23, 1963

When I was thirteen, Jay, one of several workers we hired after they were released from prison, came back to our farm. Dad liked to assist these grateful new releases. By the time he rounded our driveway, a hundred yards from the shed, Dad said, "I knew it. That's his swagger." I looked up, excited to see a different face. Both Dad and I were enthusiastic to taste morsels from more worldly plates.

Dad continued straightening a metal hitch vise-gripped to the workbench. Jay stepped into the shed and pointed up to missing corrugated metal pieces. "Looks like you've got more light."

Still hammering, Dad said, "Yeah, a few wind storms since you've been here."

Soon Jay and Dad walked side by side, jawboning. I traipsed along, fetched five-gallon buckets, pulled the hose across the yard, and grabbed the plastic handle on the electric fence to hook it after they passed.

I scrambled up the hayloft ladder and threw several bales to the outside pen while they clipped baling wires and distributed hay slices among four feeders Dad had made from scrap metal.

They came into the barn and told me to throw down bales for the Holstein calves. When they stopped barking orders, I stuck my head through a bale-drop hole to hear the juicy parts of their talk.

"Mark my words," Jay said. "If it's a conspiracy—and I'll bet it is—those bastards have to kill Oswald before he talks."

"What makes you think they'd do something so risky?"

"Because they've got to. I've been inside the Dallas City Jail. They've got torture tools in that place. You can bet they'll use 'em in a time like this."

I envisioned pitchfork prongs sticking out from cell walls. Dad nodded.

"Conspiracy groups know about torture," Jay said. "They ain't gonna let Oswald talk. I know how they operate. They'll find a way."

Dad pulled off his glove to rub his forehead. He looked at Jay straight on. "I won't argue your conspiracy theory, but I don't see how they could kill again with cops swarming--"

"You wait and see, man. You wait and see."

I waited. And it took only eighteen hours after Jay's prediction for Jack Ruby to shoot Lee Harvey Oswald in front of police and cameras for all to see.

Eight days later Jay fell flat on his back on our linoleum kitchen floor while attempting to make a call from our walnut box phone. Mom screamed. We raced to the scene. She splashed water on his face. Jay revived and said he didn't know why the phone came out of the wall and knocked him over.

Some hours later we found an empty rubbing alcohol bottle under a pile of dirty clothes on the bathroom closet floor.

A year or so later Jay swaggered to our farm again. After several weeks of work and conversation, he turned the key in our Plymouth and rolled it in a ditch just south of Wichita.

After another few years we commented that Jay had not shown up. "Maybe he's too embarrassed to show his face again," we said, but we didn't believe that. Silently, we guessed he might have died from injuries sustained in his roll. Or perhaps he found another farmer willing to trade a car for a little adult conversation.

For some years now, guilt more than gravity pulled Dad down. I could see defeat in the way his shoulders dropped down and his neck bowed forward, like an old man leaning over the table to read his Bible, and I knew he felt responsible for not providing better.

None of us girls could guess what we needed in our troubled teen years, though both Debbie and LeAnn spoke louder than I did. When their desires bumped against Dad's stubbornness, he often acquiesced, but not before a verbal tug of war.

When LeAnn wanted suits for her high-school debate tournaments, she pleaded her case, cornering Dad by his old International pickup. "Dad, I have to have some decent clothes. At least two different suits. I'm doing the best I can in debate. A dress is not good enough."

"We bought you several good dresses at the start of the school year. That's more than the rest of the kids got. I don't see how a suit will help you that much more," Dad said. He leaned against the fender and heated up. The rest of us scampered away but stayed within earshot. Taking on Dad was big news.

"It will. Those judges look at you!" LeAnn said with her hands on her hips, standing squarely three feet away.

"I don't know where I would get the money."

"Grandma says you have it! You just won't spend it on us," LeAnn said, aware that she verbalized a rift about which no one spoke, except us kids, to each other.

"I don't believe Grandma has seen my checkbook lately," Dad said.

Their repartee continued until LeAnn hit her boiling point and tears rolled.

"LeAnn, you know damned good and well that I care about you! Who cooks you breakfast every morning? Who takes you to school for your debate events? Who helps you with homework?" Dad paused, caught his breath, looked to the ground, and shook his head. "When is your next tournament?" He agreed to take her to town soon.

LeAnn turned and marched into the house without another word.

Rather than appreciating her courage and self-determination, I silently boiled under the elm tree about twenty yards from the pickup. Dad caved? I broke twigs in my hands and tossed them off. Why isn't *she* out here working?

By the end of my chores I'd be exhausted. I often fell asleep before I opened a book. Whatever I learned from school came mostly from teachers' lectures and my notes. I had little time to read at home, except when I read fairy tales from the Grolier Book of Knowledge to my youngest sisters, Lynnie and Carla.

Debbie and I rebelled during the early days of my freshman year. We jockeyed to force Dad to modernize so we wouldn't have as many labor-intensive chores. Our ideas for change puffed up in an inverse ratio to the descent of our language, from dog-gone to shit and, within a few days, the F word. We wanted to concentrate on school and have time for extra-curricular activities rather than help Dad.

After a week of refusing to do chores, Deb still maintained her resistance, but I caved. Dad bought a feeder so we didn't need to carry as many sacks to the pigs, but it was the hurt in his eyes that overwhelmed me. He needed my assistance, and that was more important than any after-school activity. I had made myself invaluable to Dad; now I stayed the course, believing the strength of hard work would carry me through.

For a quiet fifteen-year-old farm girl with little maternal modeling, Cowgirl Kate was my idol. LeAnn must have read that favorite young adult book to us fifteen times, and each time we clamored for one more. Our roughhousing cowgirl, who frequently outwitted the boys, on the last page would put on a dress and transform herself into a ravishing beauty at the top of their stairs, looking down on a mesmerized young man.

However, dolling up my petite figure and dating were not in my skill set. My masculine work habits inhibited girlish flirtations. Make-up usage required a hard-won confrontation with Dad, who insisted I was beautiful without embellishments. A bag of hammers could have trumped his smarts when it came to real-world dating. Initially I took eye shadow at its word, "shadow." I applied it *under* my eyes.

My clothes were hand-me-downs or sales items Dad bought, and most didn't fit my slender body, or my taste. On rare occasions Dad gave LeAnn a little money and allowed her to drive us to a neighboring town, McPherson, where we shopped for jeans that fit. Once we caught an Elvis Presley movie. An entirely new world barreled at us—exciting and surreal, something we might someday explore if we became immoral enough to resemble the women in that movie—it was nothing like the world we knew.

I was pleased as a cow in a late-fall wheat field when, during my sophomore year, my girlfriend from outside the Mennonite community invited me on a blind date with her boyfriend and his buddy, a football player from a neighboring high school. My date, Ron, was sixteen years old, wasn't Mennonite, and didn't smoke or drink. Painfully shy and slow to engage, we avoided looking at each other, fearing an expectation of words. We double-dated infrequently before we attempted our solo experience.

He didn't complain that I went out rather late Saturday nights, after chores were done. He wanted to see me again, time after time! We continued to bowl, eat at truck stops, and sometimes catch a movie. We discussed high-school drudgery, dingbat social events, and his battles with his parents. He was cute enough: curly blond hair and a muscular five-foot-ten physique. His crystal-blue eyes pierced through his hesitancy, suggesting a little more than his sparse words. He stood firm but with an agile and graceful quickening under the surface. I didn't know enough about nationalities to grasp his Irish ancestry. We were not intimate.

Uninspired after dating for a few months, I called it quits. Later we started again, and that spring I shamelessly begged my father to hire Ron and his friend Sam to work for us during the summer. Dad resisted the notion for several days. His resolve weakened as he realized he would be granting something I really wanted. Perhaps he thought it wise to get to know my special fellow. Perhaps he wondered if he could help the kids from the wrong side of the tracks, a dream of his reflected in his hiring of ex-cons. Hard work with good-hearted people built character. More farm hands meant more girls in the house to help Mom. Summer harvest tended to use all available help, including Uncle Elvin and his boys, who helped us like we helped them. Whatever the reasons, mercy softened his worry furrows. He offered the boys a minimal hourly rate.

We girls challenged Ron and Sam to Tarzan swings on the hayloft rope. We taught them to jump over gates by running, grabbing the middle rung with two hands, twisting the torso upward, pushing, and pole-vaulting over. We jumped on air pockets trapped between layers of dried manure in the barnyard. We wagered they couldn't stay on our Arabian horse for five minutes. Foolishly they took the bait. When the bull snake that lived in the east wall of the red barn startled them, we laughed.

Because we laughed at our stupid mistakes, mishaps, and minor pain, we made most farm incidents a time of raucous glee. Seldom did hours go by without a homemade excuse for crack-ups—the bucket handle broke and splashed water down our pant legs into our shoes or the pig escaped before the gate could be slammed. The boys joined in, joked about our tough-girl stances, and enjoyed it all as much as we did.

Long after his friend quit the farm, Ron kept working. The slapstick humor initially abated pressure from our dating relationship. After supper I would walk with him outside to say goodbye. As the weeks wore on, goodbyes took longer and longer. We rode together in his Opel each night. The sub-stratosphere of sexual tension thickened. We became less shy with each other and my sexual resistance weakened gradually. "I can't let that happen" faded against the compelling mystery, the uprising in our bodies.

After the sexual first encounter I saw my mistake. Fascination departed, and my sense of guilt hit the Richter scale. To appease my feeling of iniquity, we talked about forever, made promises, and he gave me a ring to signify the permanence of our relationship. Surely sex couldn't be as wrong in a committed relationship with a diamond to show for it? Suddenly my sunbeam-self wasn't shining so bright.

The more Ron focused on sex, the more I disliked the subtle yet profound vibes between us. I insisted on compromises—besides ailments, headaches and pregnancy fears, I claimed Dad was getting suspicious—but my interest vanished before summer ended.

When Ron implied I owed him, I realized he thought I *belonged* to him. To me, there was no more repugnant thought. I mustered the courage to break up. One night, again in his Opel, I was determined to call it quits. Tension mounted. And then his eyes rolled up into his head—he couldn't bring them down. I drove him to his parents' house, eyes still stuck in that awful position!

Agitated and flummoxed, I felt more apprehensive about ending our relationship. An incomprehensible but alarming sense that something dreadful would happen ripped into my consciousness. Finally, I did the unthinkable—I told Dad that I must see a counselor. Surprised, Dad asked why I didn't confide in him. But I insisted. As introverts, Dad and I seldom discussed difficulties; the word *sex* didn't exist in our shared vocabulary. Our closeness wasn't established with words but by doing and being together. Saying more than we must—having to justify oneself to the other—might indicate mistrust. Perhaps we didn't understand each other's unexplained decisions, but we banked upon each other's integrity.

Getting to a counseling appointment was an ordeal. What would he do with Mom and the two little kids when he drove me to the Prairie View clinic in Newton? Could he leave them at home when all the bigger kids attended school? Mom, now in a wheelchair, couldn't change diapers, much less catch the kids if they refused to come, or pick them up if they were hurt.

Fearful as days piled up before the appointment, I couldn't concentrate in school. With no idea what to expect from the session, the day finally arrived. I stepped into the professional office: a degree posted on the wall, a couple of arranged chairs with nondescript end tables, and a tissue box. With doors closed, I blurted out that I wanted to break up with my boyfriend, but I sensed something dire would happen.

The counselor asked a few clarifying questions. He agreed that I should end the relationship if I was not happy. Stating that he had no way of knowing what might happen, he didn't ask me to return. Perhaps Dad made it clear when he set the appointment that I would come only once, given the expense and lack of health insurance. Unanswered, my question of *what was about to erupt* weighed more heavily as I left.

It was a crisp, clear mid-December Saturday, cold enough that Dad and I settled into the shed to repair a drill for spring planting. I hated to tell Dad that our counseling effort netted almost nothing. The counselor might have helped if I could have defined my problem, but I had little to report: a dreadful feeling. What could he make of few angry words, little yelling, no drugs, lies, or threats?

Our chatter soon passed into silence, and I sang *Silent Night* and then *O Holy Night*, my mother's favorite.

"Do you see the size of this disc?" he said, pointing to the damaged discs on the back of the drill.

"Yeah."

"Would you go out and see if you can find some replacement discs about this size?"

Dad stored junk around the shed and other farm buildings. Each piece of scrap metal might be a replacement part. If it didn't fit, he'd weld it to make the alteration. Searching could take hours.

"I'll see what I can find."

"You might check there by the tree where the springtooth sets. Seems to me I've seen some there."

A chilly wind penetrated my jacket when I stepped outside the shed. Still, these were the ordinary hours I loved—Dad and me together, fixing something broken, quietly creating something out of nothing. It comforted me to be in sync with Dad's productivity.

From left to right: Donovan, Dorthy, Debra, Leona, LeAnn

PART II - TRAPPED IN TERROR

He vividly recalled Lizaveta's expression as he advanced upon her with the ax and she retreated before him to the wall, with one hand stretched out and a childlike fear in her face.

– Fyodor Dostoyevsky, *Crime and Punishment*

Leona, at her baptism

CHAPTER 7 – LONG, DARK NIGHT

December 1966

Dad and I finished in the shed and moved on to nightly chores, rushing because Ron would arrive by 8:30. Several calves had developed scours—runny, persistent diarrhea—which extended chore time. We broke raw eggs into their mouths and rubbed their gullets till they swallowed. I bounced into the house, cleaned up quickly, and was ready to go by 9:00. Though I dreaded something bad happening, I trusted the counselor who affirmed ending the relationship.

Finally in his car ready to leave, Ron grabbed my purse and rifled through it. I asked him what he was doing, just as he pulled out my high school's pink slip that had excused me from classes.

"Dad took me to see a therapist," I said.

"You went to see a therapist?" I shrank from his voice. His face turned bright red. He grabbed my neck and tightened his grip. He shook me viciously, causing my head to fly back and forth. "What for?"

Shocked, I scrambled my words. "I wanted to see-- I thought-- maybe-- I thought we could make our relationship better," I squeaked. Fright struck my belly like lightning. He had not acted violently before.

"You talked about me?" Blood vessels mushroomed like reddish-purple scars on his face. "What the hell?" With his knees on his seat, he pushed me down, like some giant plunger pressing me into a toilet bowl.

"I was just trying--"

His fists pounded my face, which I shielded with my hands. Searing pain peppered me like short-circuit explosions.

"Please stop! Please stop!" Intense fear collided with absurd numbness.

Seemingly from nowhere, he waved a hunting knife. "You're dead!" he said with conviction. "I know what you were up to. Breaking up with me! Admit it. Go ahead and admit it!"

My mind and stomach were roiling. Should I admit it? Would he stop—or slit my throat? Oh my God! Was I going to die right now? Belief and disbelief clamored for control. This was happening just yards from my front door.

He pushed his knife to my neck. A trickle of blood rolled down. "Honest, I wasn't going to leave you. I wanted to help us. I wasn't doing anything to hurt! I promise."

"You're lying. I know it," he seethed through clenched teeth. "You don't know how much trouble you're in. You're going to die, you fucking bitch!"

Certain that he was capable of murder, I felt tears well in my eyes. But I was too afraid to cry. "Please don't hurt me. Please listen to me. I wanted to help us. I wasn't going to leave you. I promise!"

His weight pinned me to the car seat. I tried to slide down bit by bit. Ever so slightly I moved my neck away from the knife. He kept the pressure on.

"I could slit your throat right now."

"Please, Ron. Please don't." I was pathetic. I couldn't summon anything else, though my life depended on it. I gasped for air.

"You're going to die, you stupid bitch!" he growled. "I'll slice your breasts off, piece by piece. You will feel every slice come off until you bleed to death. And just before you die, I'll put this knife in your vagina. I'll cut your fucking pussy out." His words seemed suspended in air, rumbling like thunder above me. They seemed oddly off the subject. How was leaving him related to breasts and vagina? Was he some kind of pervert?

He lifted the knife up to show his instrument of dismemberment and death. He repositioned himself on his car seat and slammed his Opel in reverse, spraying dirt and sand under his tires as he charged out our driveway.

I disentangled from my cramped position half on the floor, weighing my options. "Please understand--"

He backhanded my cheek. "Shut up!" He sped onto the blacktop road, fishtailing his Opel.

My mind whirled, debating if I should jump. He continued to detail how he would slice off my breasts and throw pieces into ditches for coyotes to eat. Trembling uncontrollably, I crossed my arms in front of my breasts.

I had to do something. But what? We were barreling down Highway 81. If I jumped out and survived the impact, he'd be more furious. He'd probably slam on the brakes, turn around, and drive over me. He might start cutting immediately. But if I don't jump, what? What? A sick smell of fear met my nostrils. *I'm going to die.* And I felt astonished to realize that what I always thought was true, wasn't: that if your life depended on it, you'd come up with the right answer.

Finally it occurred to me: pray. *God, please help me. I don't want to die. Please help! Now!*

For a second I wondered why I didn't pray earlier. Why wasn't prayer my first thought? Why didn't I feel more reassured now? Did I really expect God to do anything? Why hasn't He done it already? *Please, please, God, don't let him kill me!*

"Coyotes will devour you in the ditch. Nobody will know what happened. You will vanish from the earth," he said.

"Ron, I promise I won't leave you. Do you understand? We can be together forever!"

"It is too late now. You're dead."

Death! Was it really death? I remained silent while my mind catapulted from terror to any possible solution. I prayed again and again. We were both silent until he turned onto a dirt road near Newton. Oh my God! Now he would murder me. Being clueless would cost me my life.

"I'm going to fuck your brains out before I slice you up," he said and stopped beside a short driveway into an open field. I scanned the horizon for possible escape. Starlit cropland separated me from potential help. Fighting or running, trying to leave, would further ignite his murderous rage. Fast on his feet, he had won races against me.

He pulled me out on the driver's side. I didn't have time to prepare, so my head and shoulders hit the steering wheel. He threw me onto the wintry ground. "Take off your clothes," he demanded, "and put them by the tire." He pointed to the wheel. He grabbed an old, greasy towel and threw it down. He pulled off his jeans and underwear, and showed himself, as if to say this was his new instrument of death. He slammed me to the ground.

"I didn't mean I would leave you," I said as gently as I could, praying as I went down. *Now I lay me down to sleep.*

Ron's hunting knife waited by his right side as he pulled my legs up and plunged between them. I knew better than to scream, but tears stung my swollen face. The grease-stained towel barely saved me from the gravel underneath. Bruises gestated under fresh red welts. I prayed against Ron's vow to kill me. Filled with the shame of helplessness and absented of my last shred of dignity, without clothes, a choice, or a viable defense, I concentrated on the outcome—the strategy that might keep me alive: soothe and embrace the brute who would kill me.

In my mind I talked to Ron and to God, one after the other. I closed my eyes and called the Lord. *Please help. Please. Please.* Without sound, I spoke to Ron. *I do not breathe while you move your hand toward the knife. I do not cry. I see that my tears whet your appetite.* Out loud, I whispered devotion. "I didn't mean I would leave you, Ron. I will always be true. You can trust me."

Down on the greasy gray towel I prayed, repeating soft assurances to God and to Ron. While he pushed and pounded, I forced my brain to think. *If I should die beside your Opel, right here, right now. If I should die.* . . . His hand closed upon my throat.

"Yes, I love you," I said. "Of course!" He held my throat tight. "Please, Ron, could you move your hand? I can hardly talk."

I struggled to concentrate. *Keep the rhythm, Leona, keep the rhythm or you will die.* . . . "Yes, Ron, I love you. I didn't mean what you thought."

Don't scream, Leona. Say your prayer. Ignore the pain. Suppress it! Let him rest now. Pull him close. I did, and he rested but then started to menace with his knife. *No, don't. I'll turn, I'll bend, I'll surrender my other orifice.*

"I'm so sorry it seemed that way. I would never leave you. Love endures. It always endures." *Please don't take my soul,* I prayed. *Not now.*

The gravel burrowed through the towel into my chest. It dented my chin, my cheeks.

"I would never leave you."

Ron held his knife against my lower lip, forcing my mouth open. The moon lit the blade. I wrapped my hand around his penis and prayed, my breath braced against clenched teeth. *Please don't take my soul.*

I closed my eyes against tears as he pushed his penis in my mouth. Gravel bit into my flesh.

I pray the Lord . . .

Please.

Please.

Please.

Please.

I'll be your sunbeam from now on.

Please.

If I could have moved my head to the side, I would have vomited. I swallowed, gagged, and swallowed again, trying not to choke.

My hands caressed.

I'll be your sunbeam forever.

Finally, exhausted, he laid on top of me, his belly over my face. I could have suffocated. Limp and breathing heavily, he moved down to rest on my chest. I held him close, stroking his back, laboring to calm him. He seemed torn between cutting me into pieces and holding me. My body shivered from cold and fear. Neither of us spoke for a long, long time. His breathing slowed.

Gradually his murderous resolve seemed to weaken. He relaxed more. Had he dozed off or was he thinking? I waited an eternity, perhaps hours, until he raised his head.

"Let's get something to eat," I ventured, feeling like a prisoner facing execution, requesting one last meal.

He laid his head back down and didn't move or speak, but he, too, vibrated with cold. Still I kept my arms around him, gently caressing his shoulders and back.

Finally he pushed away and stood. "Get up and put your clothes on," he ordered. "Hurry up! Get in the car."

He drove to Leonida's Restaurant at the Newton train station. Before we left his Opel, he grabbed his hunting knife and slipped it in his jacket pocket. "If you make any wrong move," he said, "this will go through your heart. Do you understand?" I reassured him.

We settled at a table. Was my face turning black-and-blue? Would I attract attention? What would happen if I did? I doubted he'd be afraid. I imagined he'd jab his knife through my heart or slit my throat. I smiled at him while I conjured a plan.

I rubbed my tummy and sighed. A waitress with drooping eyelids brought menus. We perused the slick pages. "Honey, what looks good to you?" My voice sounded almost normal. I droned on about food choices.

He said nothing and watched me sideways, vengeance slitting his eyelids. When the waitress returned, we both ordered.

I waited a few more minutes, leaned toward him, and told him I needed the bathroom. Fear and anger fired up his eyes.

"Don't worry," I said. "I'll be right back. I just have to go."

He appeared frightened, like he might grab me and bolt out of the restaurant.

"Look," I said emphatically. "We don't want an accident. I've already told you I'm not going to leave you. Plus, the restroom door is right there. You can see it. I just have to go! Let's not make a scene."

To avoid cornering him into a decision, I didn't wait for his consent. I pushed my chair back slightly, got up, turned, and walked to the restroom. I felt hairs on my neck rise up, sensing he might throw his knife. I imagined it gashing into my back.

There was no lock on the door. Tiny mosaic tiles with dirty grout lines snaked around the floor like a whirlwind. I noticed a sealed, grimy window above me, and turned a tall metal trash can over and climbed on top to look out. I banged on the window as a lady walked by. I said as quietly as I could but loud enough to be heard, "Someone is going to kill me. Call the police." She looked bewildered. With no way to open the smoky pane, I moved my finger across my neck.

"Murder!" I yelled quietly. "Call the police!" I gestured with several more fingers across my neck. "Police! Call the police!" I mouthed the words distinctly in case she could lip read. She held up her index finger, turned, and walked away.

I assessed the three toilet enclosures. Which one had the best lock? I quickly chose the middle one. My stomach had been flipping for hours. I prayed that the lady called the police. I flushed and then flushed again. Everywhere I touched hurt. I didn't dare leave the stall to check bruises in the mirror. I stood on top of the toilet seat, waiting for the police. He wouldn't see my feet so he wouldn't immediately know which stall I was in. How could I defend myself if Ron tore the door off? Please let the police come soon!

Then I realized that if he came in, hiding would incite immediate attack. I decided to pull my pants down and sit on the middle toilet. If he barged in I'd tell him my stomach was still churning and would require a few more minutes.

I waited and waited, each moment anticipating Ron's assault. The police still hadn't arrived. Did the lady call them? I poured out my heart to God, tears streaming down my face.

The bathroom door opened and I saw blue pant legs. They didn't belong to Ron! I rushed out of the stall and spilled everything, words tumbling out: the counselor, the pink slip, the beating, the knife, the forced sex and, now, the last supper. I told him about the threat of slicing my breasts off in pieces. I explained how I wanted to jump out of the car but thought Ron would back up and run me over and still slice my breasts and stick a knife down there, too. I'd been terrified. Nothing like this had ever happened to me. I answered his questions about where I lived and where Ron's parents lived. The officer nodded his head and directed me outside to the backseat of the police car and gestured me inside.

I realized—to my horror—that I was sitting next to Ron.

Had they taken the knife away? Would he be more enraged? I quaked at the thought that he might twist my neck, like Grandma used to twist chicken necks, and it would be over. Would the officer drive us to jail? I couldn't imagine why he put me in his car next to Ron.

The nightmare continued. Within minutes we arrived at Ron's house. The officer left Ron and me in the backseat, walked up the path, and knocked on the front door. Oddly, Ron sat still. I was shaking enough to rock the backseat. Ron's dad, Bill, answered the door. The officer motioned Ron and me into the house, then stood outside talking with Bill. Ron's mother called Ron from her bedroom. He stepped over clothes and clutter and closed the bedroom door.

The one-story white bungalow, always before impressively full of antique treasures, now in the dim lamplight of 2:00 a.m. seemed dull, oppressive, and confused.

Ron and his mom, Judy, talked for a few minutes. He returned and asked me to go in. Sitting up in bed, she ordered me to bring a chair around close to her. I moved dirty laundry and sat facing her. She cross-examined me and proclaimed, "I know you're lying."

I was flabbergasted. I wasn't capable of making such things up. "How can you think that?" I asked, feeling like my mind had been splayed open with another impossibility.

"For one thing, I know no man alive could have intercourse four times in a row. The body doesn't work that way."

"It might sound strange, but it did happen exactly like I told you. Perhaps not as fast as it seems."

"You can say a lot of things, but that doesn't make them true," she said, quite unflappable.

I barely grasped what was happening. Why wouldn't she believe me? I'd seen Judy many times. I'd never lied to her.

"What do you want?" she asked.

I slid the ring off my finger and reached my hand toward her, imploring her to take the ring and never let him come close to me again!

Judy did not take the ring. "If you want to break up with him, Leona, you've got to tell him. I'm not taking that ring. That is your business and your job. That's between you and him."

A cold chill rushed up my spine. Scenarios of breaking up with Ron ran through my mind. Without her help, who would stop him from killing me? Ron's dad knocked on the bedroom door. "Let's go," he said. "I'm taking you home."

I stepped out of the bedroom, Ron looked at me and at his dad. "I want to go with you," he said, "I need to make sure she is all right. I might not get to see her for a while."

His dad argued but conceded when Judy intervened.

Again, I sat next to Ron in the backseat of a car. He extended his arm around me, which felt like a slimy suctioning octopus tentacle. My stomach recoiled. I pretended to be impervious to any movement.

We were driving parallel to the ditch into which Ron swore he'd throw slices of my body. Ron slid closer and pulled me towards him. He kissed the side of my head and whispered, "You know I'm sorry for hurting you. I just lost control. I can't stand the thought of you leaving me. I need you so much. I love you, honey. I really do love you. Please forgive me."

I sat there while octopus tentacles were pulling me under. I wouldn't open my mouth. I couldn't breathe.

"Come on, honey. You've got to forgive me. Please believe me. I really am at the end of my rope. I don't know what happened to me. I just went over the edge. That's all I can say. You and I both know I can't deal with breaking up."

We were both silent for a short while. Ron pulled my ear to his lips again and said, "You've got to be a person of your word, Leona. You've got to. I won't be able to stand it if you leave. I would go crazy, Leona. I would not only kill you, I would kill your dad and mom and your whole family. Now you know I love you and your family, but I know I would do it. I wouldn't want to, but I would do it. Just don't ever think about breaking up. OK?"

I let his words sink halfway into my brain. "I understand," I said, finally, in a cold sweat, as Bill drove into our yard. "Thanks for bringing me home," I told Bill. I hurried to the house, gasping for air as if I had been suffocated. My hands slipped off the freezing back doorknob several times before I jerked it open.

My stomach revolted at the thought of telling my parents. Completely overburdened, they didn't need another onslaught. How could I talk about potential murder, slicing breasts, a knife-filled vagina? How could I mention beatings, spread legs, and an eternity of terror? Those were concepts we would never formulate, words we would never speak. How could I break our non-verbal unity with thoughts that could not exist in our lives?

I slipped into the bathroom, wetted a washcloth, and gently dabbed my puffy face. In the mirror I studied the swollen areas and budding black-and-blue marks. I washed the cut on my neck. Nothing looked as hideous as I felt, though my face appeared oddly distorted, as if reflected by a warped carnival mirror. I sat on the toilet and sobbed so ferociously that gasps for air seemed to pull my guts into my throat. I rocked back and forth, sick from raw vulnerability. I felt unbearable dread. No way could I tell my parents, but I must.

Without turning on any lights, I walked to their open bedroom door. I found a straight-back chair and set it in the doorway. Dad snored and sucked in air like someone starting a siphon. I called softly, "Dad. Mom. You guys need to wake up. I have something to tell you." I waited and gently called again, trying to not wake baby Carla, who was sleeping between them. Dad turned over and rubbed his eyes. A pasty moon shone through their window, casting a film of silvery light. I heard Mom rustle her head high enough to see over Dad without waking Carla. Then I realized Lynnie was sleeping there, too, and neither Mom nor Dad could move much without disturbing the little ones.

"What's wrong?" Dad asked with alarm in his voice. It occurred to me that from the age of remembering I had not asked them to wake up in the middle of the night.

"I've had the worst night of my life. I don't know how to tell you," I said and paused for a long moment, swallowing an acidic vomit taste. "Ron went crazy." I told them the story, leaving out details and the fact that he had threatened to kill the whole family. They asked a few questions, and I responded forthrightly.

After utterances of horror they asked if I was OK.

"As OK as I can be. I don't have any broken bones. My face is just starting to get black-and-blue."

Dad's already sad eyes drooped further. "Is there any way we could help you right now?"

"No. I just wanted you to know what happened. I'm exhausted. I'm going to bed. I'm sorry to burden you with this."

"We're so sorry," Mom said in garbled tones. I could barely understand her. "Are you sure there's nothing we can do right now?"

"No. Don't wake the kids. I have to go to bed anyway. I'm exhausted."

I struggled up the stairs, craving a bath, but I fell into my bed, exhausted. Shivering under cold sheets and wincing from the tender areas that quilted covers touched, I wept until sleep overran my agonizing, shocking recounting.

Chapter 8 - AFTERMATH: WAR, GOD, AND PRISON

My body separated from me, like a maple tree hacked from its roots and stripped of its branches, lying there, leaking sap. The next few days blurred with foggy dreams of running and crying. When asked what they might do for me, I told my parents I wanted a puppy. I pictured a mid-sized mutt with shaggy brown hair who happily tagged along.

Even if I had wanted to, I couldn't go to school—the kids would see bruises on my face. Dad called Moundridge High. I would miss final exams and would face a heavy load to catch up after Christmas break.

I spent day and night on the couch. Dad worked by himself. I didn't know what Mom or Dad told my siblings, but they gently put their hands on me, rubbed my head, or asked how I was feeling. They brought a glass of water or a plate of salted hamburger with ketchup and buttered potatoes. Their eyes communicated love and compassion.

A few days after that longest night, Dad answered the phone and told Ron I was not in much shape to talk. I imagined Ron falling over himself with apologies. He would keep calling until I went out with him. I knew it. If I didn't respond, he'd do worse. Maybe the worst ever.

At sixteen, already damaged goods and an idiot to have a boyfriend who would do terrible things, I didn't know I could sink lower. Defeated, I cringed like a songbird punctured by the grasping talons of a hawk.

Though a part of me wanted to kill Ron, I knew I wouldn't. And I wouldn't ask Dad to do it, either. That would go against his core beliefs. He had paid the consequence of prison for his nonviolent stance during World War II. I wouldn't ask him to reverse his most resolute decision.

It wouldn't be feasible anyway. If he decided to protect us with his shotgun, he wouldn't have a hope of guarding all of us all of the time. Ron could come when Dad was gone or at night or anytime and kill all of us. He could hide anywhere and take us by surprise. If we could call the police, they would arrive too late.

We didn't have keys to our house, and it wouldn't help if we did. We went in and out all day. We would lose the keys. Someone would forget to lock the doors. We'd get locked out. Physically protecting ourselves was not feasible. We couldn't hide from him. We couldn't keep him away from us. We couldn't and wouldn't defend ourselves from him if he attacked.

Nothing short of murder or an act of God could save us. Dad was not capable of murder. If he had been, I wouldn't have told my parents the truth. The last thing we needed was for Dad to be in prison for murder. My entire family would not have survived that fate.

Dad radically opposed violence—including state-sponsored violence. We learned how strongly Dad believed in pacifism the unfortunate day the kids taunted us on the school bus.

"Your daddy's an ex-con," rang repeatedly from the backseat chorus as we stepped aboard the yellow Cloverleaf Grade School bus.

LeAnn, Debbie, Dotsy, and I glanced at each other, mutely asking, did you know about this?

We didn't understand exactly what *ex-con* meant. We quizzed our own memories and then each other for some clue. Nothing registered. Still, we felt certain the kids didn't make up a lie. They heard something from an adult source. Probably from their parents, uncles, and aunts who gossiped between trump plays in a rook game.

The bus tires collided with clods of dirt on the unpaved road. Waves of nausea rolled over me as my mind entered a steel trap, unable to find answers and unable to escape. Could Dad have a secret history? Did he do something wrong? What exactly did I know about him, except that he seemed like a good person? He worked hard. He played with us like he was happy to be with us. He had been on the school board and he had led things at church. What could he have done that was so wrong that he would be an ex-con? Didn't that mean he went to jail or something?

With bent heads we whispered across the aisle to each other, guessing what this *ex-con* refrain meant. We looked at LeAnn, the oldest, as if to say, have you been told anything the rest of us don't know? She shook her head and raised and dropped her shoulders. Clueless, we stumbled into each other's unknowing eyes. None of us knew anything about Dad before he was our dad, except that he lived in this community, in the house we live in now. We disagreed about which upstairs bedroom he was born in. He was a loved child of Grandma and Grandpa Stucky. He went to the same type of school as we did. We thought he went to Bethel College where Uncle Harley taught, just a few blocks from Grandma and Grandpa Stucky's house. And since we saw and smelled the pus that oozed from open sores on his leg when he re-bandaged them, we knew about the tractor explosion that severely burned him when he was seventeen. What was missing?

Hours at school stretched into an eternity of guilty doubts. Wasn't Dad one of the best persons I knew? But how could all

Leona Stucky

those kids lie? They had said nothing like that before. Besides, a statement so bizarre couldn't be a lie. Kids couldn't make it up. Only a nasty truth could have raised Mennonite meanness—we weren't that smart about lies.

Released at the end of our driveway, we bounded down the long stretch to the shed. Dad's stocky six-foot frame was slightly bent over a vise-gripped piece of hot metal. His welding face-guard covered his expression. With wiggling commotions we waited for him to push it up and acknowledge our presence.

"Dad," we blurted out, "are you an ex-con?"

Slowly he put down the welding rod and hammer. He removed his face-guard without looking at us. His face flushed. "Who told you that?" he asked, half admitting their claim.

"We didn't believe them, but kids on the bus were singing, 'Your daddy's an ex-con.'"

"It's true. You might as well believe them."

His words split us open like ripe peaches. Our hopes dribbled out as we shuffled our feet on the gravel floor.

"What do you mean?"

Anger flickered in his eyes, but his voice stayed steady and soft. "I guess I should have told you. I didn't think it would come up."

"What, Dad?"

"I didn't think it was right for the government to tell us that we had to go to war, to kill people. War is like a factory of death. People work at killing other people. And many die while they strive to kill others. The government can't make that right. So I didn't register for the draft."

"You mean you didn't go to war? Did you go C.O.?" We weren't sure exactly what C.O. meant, but we heard about it in relation to Mennonites and World War II.

"No, I didn't go C.O., though lots of Mennonites did."

"What did you do then?"

"I refused to register at all. So they arrested me and put me in prison."

"But why? Why not go C.O.?"

"I just didn't think it was the right thing to do," he said to close the subject, as if no one had a right to question his decision. If we had been older, he might have explained that his position was similar to Tolstoy's opposition to state-organized violence.

Instead, he asked us to hurry with our snack and come back out to chores. We had extra work this evening because the cows were pasturing across the road. We'd have to round them up and chase them down the driveway before we could let the calves nurse. We all had to help with this process, because the cows loved to bust through our human blockade to freedom in the fields beyond the shed. One kid blocked the exit from the yard between the elevator building and the shed. Several others guarded our row of Russian olive trees along the driveway. The kid behind the cows chased them fast, so they'd have little time to ponder escape.

I couldn't have been more puffed up if I had been one of the children Jesus blessed. Dad didn't do anything to be ashamed of! I knew that much. I was not sure what noble effort Dad made that was different from a conscientious objector. I thought that pettiness and jealousy caused our Mennonite neighbors to gossip about Dad's actions against war. Like a cow chewing and re-chewing its cud, I thought and re-thought that if he hadn't bragged about his stand on the side of right, they shouldn't have puffed up their stand and put him down. My young, moralistic mind would not forget this event. It hung in the air like pollen in an eternal allergy season.

So I didn't need to remember the school kids' taunting to know that Dad, in the wake of my terrible experience with Ron, would not resort to violence. I knew it as confidently and unthinkingly as I knew I was his daughter. What I didn't know was what to do. The reality of this situation soaked in gradually for me and, I suspected, for Dad and Mom. I took the first step when I realized I would handle the problem.

Dad wheeled Mom to the sofa where I rested. He pulled up a straight-backed chair. It was time for the dreaded conversation. They asked me what I wanted to do. Their question made it sound like I had a choice.

"I'm terrified to go back with Ron . . . and I'm terrified not to."

Mom said I should not date a man who was cruel to me. She didn't grasp the situation, but I didn't say anything. A long, uncomfortable silence ensued while the moments of decision slipped through my hands like a wet catfish. They didn't understand the whole of it. Telling them the first time didn't clarify it, and I wouldn't tell them again: I was trapped. How could I say no to Ron? I knew what he would do if I didn't keep my promise to stay with him.

I was trapped as surely as those Russian dissidents I had recently learned about. The totalitarian government informed them that if they tried to escape not only would they be captured and killed, their families and loved ones would also be punished. If you loved your family, it was virtually impossible to wiggle free under those terms.

Unlike the Russian dissidents, I felt responsible for bringing this tyranny into our lives. I was the one who brought him to the farm, so I was the one who had to take care of this. "Next time he calls, I'll talk to him," I said, concluding our discussion.

Next time seemed like a hideous but necessary outcome— the only option that didn't bring on violence or death. I was afraid, but thought surely a solution would present itself soon.

As days passed and fear intensified, I considered my situation more carefully. I was not a female prophet or one of those people who had special dreams that could foretell the future. I only knew what I knew. I was not certain how I had recognized that something terrible might happen if I broke up with Ron, but I had been right.

Now I knew the enormity of the threat. He would kill me or my family if I broke up with him. That awareness was not a hunch; it was proven fact. While I hoped he wouldn't kill us, I didn't trust that hope.

Before that long, dark night I, like believers everywhere, didn't distinguish between hope and trust, between belief and knowledge. In its aftermath, the distinction was stark: I couldn't trust what I hoped for. If my hope was wrong, the price would be unbearable.

I would have liked to believe that my muscular, farm-girl strength, the gusto I relied upon every day to work like a man, could physically, forcibly disable him. But I'd wrestled with him, worked side by side when he helped us on the farm, and raced in the pasture. I knew my limitations. I accepted what I knew and didn't bank on hopefulness.

But what about God? God could easily remedy this situation. All He had to do was stop Ron from calling or coming to our house. He could simply put the word in Ron's ear: "Don't go back"; better yet, "Ron, I forbid you to go. If you ever go near them I'll strike you dead." Anything God wanted to do, God could. This particular job was God's easiest. All it required was a little influence to turn Ron elsewhere. God was credited with influencing people to do the right thing in countless situations for thousands of years. Surely He could practice a little influence with Ron. Yet I suspected He wouldn't.

Apparently God was a little stingy with miracles, such as healing Mom or other people suffering from terrible illnesses. But I'd not heard of God being stingy with *influence*. He daily pulled people along in one direction or another, helping us behave better than we otherwise would, helping us love when we might otherwise hate, helping us be brave, strong, or kind.

I didn't trust God! This came as an aftershock following the initial quake, rocking my foundations. In spite of everything I believed, I couldn't deny it: I now expected that entropy would increase, and so would misery. Ron would call again. I'd have to handle it myself, no matter how many prayers I said. I had thought for my whole life that I trusted God, but with this problem, I suspected I was alone.

Dad assumed I needed to see a doctor. He made an appointment with a doctor I had not met. We usually went to Moundridge doctors, but this one practiced in a neighboring town. I figured Dad was attempting to avoid embarrassment. For my part, I couldn't stand the thought of having to tell anyone else what happened.

Sitting in her wheelchair, head hanging low, Mom braved it alone at home with the two youngest as we left. Sure enough, the misery I anticipated was compounding.

When my name was called, Dad came with me to meet the white-haired doctor with a stethoscope hanging from his neck. "My daughter and her boyfriend had a spat. I'd like to be sure she's OK . . . and have you check if she might be pregnant."

I was stunned! Had I heard right? A *spat*? What was Dad saying? The doctor looked at me. I nodded and stared at the floor. Dad left. I followed the doctor's instructions. He threw a piece of a sheet over me. I nearly jumped out of my skin when the icy instrument penetrated.

He told Dad I should have no permanent damage. He would guess that I was not pregnant. Dad paid him.

Driving back, Dad stopped to pick up Similac for Carla and a few groceries. I huddled in our Plymouth and stared out the window into a space so thin it couldn't shield the present from the past. After more silence on the drive home, Dad spoke about Mennonite preferences regarding legal issues. He said Mennonites aimed to avoid courts and police. Sometimes Mennonites had sued each other over inheritance, but that was frowned upon.

It dawned on me that he might have said my boyfriend and I had a spat to keep the world out of our affairs. What might the doctor have done if Dad had said I was beaten, threatened with death, and forced to have sex? Was he required to inform the police? Would they say it's not rape if done by your boyfriend and you've already had sex with him? New torments blossomed. In an investigation, I'd have to admit that I'd had sex with him. No one would care what happened to a slut, especially the police. If I were a respectable girl, I'd not have found myself in this situation. Perhaps *nothing* was the best thing that could be done. No wonder Dad had to avoid the world's intrusion. It would have condemned us and made me more miserable, if that were possible.

Dad's words soothed. He explained that Mennonites didn't swear in court. Taking an oath was different than swearing on the Bible. Rather than swearing you should say, *I do so affirm.* "Leona, you always live up to your word. That is all anyone has to know: that you are trustworthy."

My body stiffened as I questioned: What does it mean that I gave my word to Ron? Does it count that I was forced to give my word?

Dad looked across the seat at me. "I know you're a good person, Leona. I'm so sorry, honey. You didn't deserve this."

I broke down right there and bawled into his jacket sleeve, snot and tears running together, crying the whole way home. He patted my head and pulled me close to him. When I could speak again, I thanked him for doing my chores and for taking me to the doctor. "I'll start working again soon."

Chapter 9 – BARGAINS WITH GOD

Some people come back from near-death experiences dramatically changed, having seen a great light, having found a transcendent energy. I came back devastated, tortured by troubling questions about my faith. Grandma Stucky's faithful endurance haunted my awareness. When her son, my dad, was severely burned in a nearly fatal tractor explosion during refueling and was hospitalized for more than two hundred days, *she* didn't give up. *She* didn't hate God. She prayed, waited, and hoped. She turned her pain over to God. She cried, loved her son, and loved God, too. Somehow she didn't see a contradiction. Her son was only a teenager. His life would be forever marred by those burns. He would endure excruciating pain. He would not have the same options for marriage, work, or success. Still, she loved the one Being who could have prevented the accident. She wrote a poem at that time. Several stanzas expressed her beliefs.

Wait my dear soul yes wait do I hear
Teach me to trust in thy will and not fear
Only to what thou doth consent will befall
On thy dear loved ones yes on one and all

So teach me to trust in the day yet ahead
Even the hairs are counted you said (Luke 12:7)

Why couldn't I be more like Grandma Stucky? Or like Dad, who silently carried his burden? After God granted me a positive answer to my prayer—I didn't die, after all—I still was having trouble trusting Him. Something in me seemed lacking, something I could trace back as far as I could remember.

One Sunday when I was seven, our tribe came to church late. Embarrassed, Dad and we big kids—Mom tended her babies in the nursery—tiptoed into an empty pew at the back of Hopefield Mennonite Church. I was expecting another mind-numbing repeat of the good things we'd heard and said before. Dad pretended to tickle me, and I squirmed and slid down the pew to escape.

"Da-a-ad," I whispered, giving his title three syllables. "We're supposed to be quiet. You're not helping!" Gradually I settled into boredom, until the spoken word about the Biblical David sounded a discordant note.

"What does this mean?" I mumbled to Dad. "David did all those bad things and God helped him? God even made him kill a giant and lots of other people?"

He shushed me, but my thoughts ran wild. Didn't God tell us never to kill anybody? Wasn't that our Church's point? We didn't believe in killing anyone, not even bad people! I was guessing that God was no better than the rest of the evil world, when a safer idea landed—this must be a bad minister who preached bad stories about a bad God. How dare the preacher tell us that God is not as good as Mennonites!

I poked Dad's side and said, "How come our minister says that God does bad things, even killing people?"

"Honey, he's asking us to think about things a little differently."

"It's more than a little different if you say God likes killing! Isn't that what the rest of the world thinks? Those who go to war? I thought we weren't supposed to like killing. That's what the Bible tells us."

Dad's red face sprouted purple lines. Beads of sweat rolled down my back. I stood up, thinking I might run.

"Is what he says about David actually in the Bible?" I continued.

"Yes, it's in the Bible, but in the Old Testament, in a time before Jesus."

"Are you saying that God was mean before Jesus came, but then He got nice?"

"Sort of like that," Dad said, motioning for me to sit down and hush up. I wanted to stomp my foot so bad it ached from holding it back. I sat with my arms crossed, fingers digging into my skin, and glowered at our minister.

But I considered that I was in church and I should be kind. Because . . . Because . . . Jesus wanted me for a sunbeam. I was no dumb bunny. I knew that for sure.

At sixteen, I still was no dumb bunny, but I no longer was His sunbeam. At sixteen, the contradictions were gathering like clouds before the storm. Only what He consented to would be done. Right? God did not consent to my death, and I was alive. Yet did He consent to the violence against me? Did He consent to the forced sex?

If He made Ron stop murdering me, why didn't He do it sooner? Couldn't He have brought Ron to his senses immediately? Ron could have suddenly said, "I think God is talking to me! He doesn't want me to kill you."

Was *I* the one who stopped murder? I endured him until he exhausted himself. I held and calmed him. I suggested the last supper, and I found a way out of the situation by promising never to leave.

Was God present? Was God working through me? If He was, couldn't He have told me how to handle Ron? Didn't I fly by the seat of my pants, literally?

I wished I could be as faithful as Grandma Stucky, but I wanted to rip God out of His heavenly home and show Him a thing or two. I'd make Him walk a mile in my mother's shoes, ride a mile in her wheelchair. *He* could cry and pray without relief for sixteen years and find Himself more debilitated each month.

How could my mother keep her faith? "God could heal me," she must say to herself, "but He won't! I love God. He knows what He is doing, even if I don't understand."

Perhaps I was not as accepting and kind as Grandma or Mom. I had bad thoughts. Where the hell was God when we needed Him—busy counting hairs? Watching the sparrows fall?

Another teaching confused me: I'd heard preachers say one of the proofs of God was that non-believers called on Him when they were in a scary situation or when they were dying. Well, I was a believer, and God was not the first thing that popped in my mind in a horrifying situation. I first thought of everything *I* might do. Only after that did I think of asking God for help. If I actually had trusted that God would help me, wouldn't I instinctively have thought of that first?

When God saved someone from a disease or accident, people touted it as proof that God answered prayer. But who talked about the countless times that God didn't save people from disease, accidents, hunger, poverty, or murder?

Do I have a prayer now? What should my prayer be? *God, will You stop him from killing us if I don't go out with him? Do I have to stay in this relationship or will You handle this one?*

Would God consent to Ron murdering me? If He wouldn't, how should I know that? Has He said it unequivocally some-where in the Bible? He consented for Jesus to be tortured and killed. But He had a big reason for that—so we could all be saved. Does He have a reason, even a small reason, for me to be tormented and killed?

Still, I wouldn't dismiss God. Everyone I knew believed He was their source of comfort and power. If He only helped a tiny bit, I needed that. Once, when I was twelve, He even proved Himself to me.

After school I ran down our driveway and inhaled a jelly sandwich before changing to chore clothes. "OK, God, if You give me this, I'll believe for the rest of my life." I grabbed my horse's bridle off a hook in the pump house. I practically flew over fences and landed in the pasture, heading for the creek.

Never had Chocolady allowed me to walk up and bridle her. Usually she and the other horses ran around the pasture umpteen times when we approached, chased, and penned them. Only Dad could pen the horses, tempting them with an oat mixture.

When I was about forty feet away, I expected Chocolady to toss her head, look at me, and run. She didn't. She slowly raised her head from the grass. She stared at me. "It's OK, girl. Stand still and you'll be fine. And I'll be a doubt-proof believer." I inched toward her, now within ten feet. I kept my voice low and soothing. "I won't hurt you. We just have a little job to do. Just stand exactly where you are."

Much to my amazement, she didn't move. She raised not a single foot off the grass. She allowed the bridle in her mouth. What an incredible feat! She did it! I did it! God did it! "Thank you! Thank you! Thank you, God!" I prayed out loud, simultaneously wondering if this was a fluke.

"No," I said to myself and Chocolady, "I will not think like that!" Without a saddle on her, I walked her to the nearest fence, climbed a few levels up, flung myself onto her back, and glided into a place that held me like a cradle. A glorious breeze rustled from her canter. I could almost reach the heavens. Like Chocolady's spirit was mine also. Like I could run and not tire.

Like I was not limited to human ways. I was a giant among people. I had God on my side!

CHAPTER 10 - BRUISES

A few minutes before Ron arrived, I requested a curfew. That way Dad would know he should search for pieces of my body in the ditches if I didn't show up at that time.

"Are you sure you want to do this?" he asked.

"No. I think I have to do it. I'm scared not to and I'm scared to do it. He'll probably be sorry now and won't do anything too terrible, but I don't know for sure."

"I'll talk to him," Dad said, as if he understood what was needed in this situation.

I grabbed the face powder in my purse and stared at myself in the mirror. To hide the bruises, I patted my face so many times the powder flaked off in chunks, and I started over. I resembled an old doll: fake, empty, and emotionless.

Ron must be troubled, too. He was ten minutes late. When he arrived, Dad met him outside. He probably informed Ron that he had made a terrible mistake, one that deeply hurt me and my family. That he must change his behavior, not allow himself to go over the edge, and that he must promise he would not hurt me again. I imagined Dad implored him with a serious talking-to and that Ron complied with every request, apologized, and promised.

I dreaded the moment I heard his shoes in the chore room. I dreaded the moment I saw his face. I dreaded the moment I made a face that masked my true feelings. And yet that moment came.

With quiet courage I swallowed my rage, hatred, and sorrow. I met his gaze and walked toward him. In this eternal night of calm high alert, I wondered when, where, or how I might piss him off and die. I must be real enough that he knows it is me, and not so real that I reflected the monster he was.

I walked toward his Opel and slid into the passenger seat. Stunned to be sitting in the exact spot where he beat me, I marshalled all my strength to hold myself steady. Ron drove from our driveway, with the radio playing Sonny and Cher's "I Got You Babe." My mind whirled in a wild dance with his words: "I would go crazy, Leona. I would not only kill you, I would kill your dad and mom and your whole family. Now you know I love you and your family, but I know I would do it. I wouldn't want to, but I would do it. Just don't ever think about breaking up. OK?" He took his eyes off the road to look at me, and the car swerved. Returning his attention to driving, he continued, "I wish it hadn't happened. You cannot imagine how horrible I've felt. That first night I couldn't sleep at all. The next week I couldn't go to school or work. Mom wrote an excuse for me. I've been so exhausted I could barely function," he said.

"I understand. I've been devastated, too."

"How can I get you to forgive me, Leona? You must know I wasn't in my right mind. You aren't going to leave me, are you?"

"No, I'm not leaving. But you'll have to give me some time before I can trust you. Right now I'm still scared."

"I know. You're shaking like a leaf. Come here next to me. Let me hold you. That will help you feel better. If we can be close again, you'll be OK."

"I'm not ready for that. Let's just wait."

"I don't see how you're going to get over being afraid until we're close again. You'll see how gentle I can be. I promise I won't hurt you."

"Ron, I hurt all over. Just touching me would be painful." The tension was building. In the looming hours of gentle rejections I knew it would take to preserve myself, would the fragile balance of his hopeful desperation unhinge? Would I know before it happened? Would it end with a beating—or a knife in my vagina? Is this dueling dance around sex also a dance around death? If I won, would I lose?

"You let me know when it hurts too much. We can take it real slow. Oh, listen. Here comes our song." He sang along to Herman's Hermit's, "Can't You Hear My Heartbeat." "Come on," he said. "Sing with me. I know you like this song!"

The instant my mouth opened to sing along half-heartedly, I was over—way over—the magic of heartbeats. I scorned that hateful immaturity. I was different now. The things I participated in a week ago I relegated to the distant past. They were part of the problem. Part of what propelled me to this deadly pretense.

Then Ron repeated something he had said on that long, dark night—something I had not allowed my mind to grasp: "Leona, please understand. *I'm at home when we make love.*"

His meaning burst forth with piercing clarity: his murderous violence met my nonviolence and was tamed not when his hands gripped my neck or his fists pounded my flesh but when he penetrated my body and exhausted his brutal passion. That act and only that act saved my life.

His voice—then and now—had a timorous, pleading quality, yet those words were pleasurable enough to curl his toes and engorge his member. He said it as if magic eked from this revelation, as if he had not known *home* before.

I stayed on the farm for several weeks, seeing only my immediate family and Ron. When the Hopefield youth group threw a New Year's Eve party to bring in a year of faith, hope, and charity, I decided that with enough makeup to cover fading bruises I could go. A childhood friend agreed to transport me.

The party did little to distract me from my troubles; if anything, it intensified them. Craving the understanding that would melt my frozen demeanor and rigid isolation, I asked him on the way home if my makeup did the trick, or if he noticed that my face was bruised. He said he didn't notice.

"I've had a really hard time. I've missed a lot of school and all my finals. I couldn't go because of the bruises," I said.

"Oh, I didn't know you missed."

"Something atrocious happened," I said.

He silently endured.

I briefly explained, sputtering to unstick the words.

"Sounds bad," he said, squirming and paying attention to the steering wheel. He pulled up to the farmhouse and waited for me to leave.

"Good night," I said, feeling foolish for mentioning anything. "Thanks for the ride."

"Bye."

I shivered, slipping into our house. I'd keep my mouth shut from now on. I couldn't tell my friends about that pivotal murderous night or those following when danger seeped through my pores and tormented my body. Or how neither Dad nor I could summon the violence necessary to shut down that ominous, berserk boy. Soundlessly I stomped on my short-lived hope that revealing grim realities might bring comfort or understanding. Now, only Jesus could be my refuge and strength.

Chapter 11 - THE HOME FRONT

Receiving no comfort from others, and unaccustomed to nurturing myself, my compassion flowed toward Dad. I watched him carefully, believing his load was heavier than mine. Dad's shoulders hung low as he manipulated bales with heavy arms, cut wires with pliers, and lugged hay slices to the cow feeders. Events of recent months harassed his spirit and slowed his movements. He trekked through chores as if moving against a rushing river, struggling to maneuver, tired and depleted. Yet he poked me in the ribs to hear me squeal, and I jumped in front of him so he had to sidestep off his path. We pointed to the cloud that looked like a ghost, marveled at the mushroom that popped up yesterday, noted the belly developing on a pregnant cow, and chuckled when the watering hose kinked just before we drank.

Still, troubles overwhelmed. Dad's burned leg periodically swelled and oozed. He crawled to the bathroom or hobbled through his days, not letting up, not giving up, not giving in. He slept fitfully with his leg raised. His mind turned over one problem after another: his oldest daughter missed a semester of school with mono and other ailments and now craved prescription drugs; his wife was losing all capacity to tend her children or accomplish even minimal chores. Tension mounted between the older daughters and their mother. His helper was sad and often without energy or zest. Debbie reacted like a wild child to our miseries and was getting in trouble.

He was mother and father to seven children, tending an invalid wife, shouldering a working farm and a stagnant income that fell short of our needs. Each year buildings deteriorated further. He repaired essentials. Most other farmers in the community worked a day job that offered a wage. They farmed part-time. But adding a part-time job to his daily ritual was as impossible as making spring come on time.

He was losing favor with those who knew him, those who judged he had ruined the family home he inherited. It was a shadow of the grandeur it once represented. His earlier days of playing a mean game of table tennis, of winning challenging debates on the issues of the day, of serving on the school board and helping with Church functions, of dreaming that he would be a success were long forgotten. He would be lucky if he could pull through without losing everything, including the home place. Several sour investments and no black gold when he sponsored a drilling project resulted in his inheritance slipping through his hands like sand in an hour glass. Still he worked from before dawn until he dropped at night, always faced with fifteen or twenty requisites he could not tackle that day and would not accomplish in the future.

He drowned under boxes of papers he wouldn't sort through. He wasn't filing or paying taxes. Carting Mom and the kids to medical appointments when it was absolutely necessary was nearly a full-time job, though the kids, except LeAnn, seldom went. Who could pay hospital costs?

He didn't haul Mom up the church steps in her wheelchair anymore, so the older children hauled the younger ones to church. Friends and extended family who used to stop in and chat now seldom showed their faces. We were not invited to come for supper—nine people with one in a wheelchair were too much to add to the average family's table. And we couldn't reciprocate.

The rift between Grandma Schrag and Dad became more obvious. An argument over where the volleyball landed, in or out, broke up a game at Grandma's house, with all the adults opposing Dad's call. Mom often cried on Sunday afternoons at Grandma's house. Sitting in her wheelchair, she was pushed into Grandma's bedroom where she wept alone while her siblings visited in the living room. Her sadness became a fact of life.

As Mom's body became more dysfunctional, so did her mind, or at least we older girls thought so. We remarked that every other word out of her mouth was *BB brain*. It didn't seem odd that we'd abandoned Judas-priest and now every other word out of our mouths was goddamn, shit, or what-the-F. Even those words inadequately revealed our fierce discontent. We advised each other to laugh it off, knowing she was losing it. We shouldn't listen to the idiotic ideas she imposed on us. Like the time she ordered me to fry two eggs and put them on top of the orange Jell-O salad we were taking to Grandma Schrag's house for Sunday dinner. I informed her I sure-as-hell would not.

Her voice produced uncontrolled screeches, sounding like a siren. "I told you to do it and you have to do it. Now get the fry pan!" Her words, when she was angry, became more intelligible.

"Mom, no way am I frying two eggs to put on top of a Jell-O salad. That's the stupidest idea I've ever heard! I won't do it."

"You are doing it or I'll do it myself!"

"I'm not doing it and neither are you. We are not taking a Jell-O salad with fried eggs on top. That is way beyond the limits of sanity."

"Move over then!" she yelled and tried to wheel herself to the stove.

I grabbed the cast-iron pan and backed away from her.

"Give me that pan!" she screamed.

"Mom, please don't do this. It's not right to put eggs on top of a Jell-O salad!" I put the pan back on the burner as Dad entered the kitchen.

"What's all this commotion about?"

I explained that Mom was ordering me to do something ridiculous.

Dad said calmly, "If your mother tells you to do that, then you must fry the eggs and put them on the Jell-O. Don't make her yell. She doesn't need the aggravation."

"But Dad! You can't think it's right to put eggs on a Jell-O salad. It will look stupid. We'll all have egg on our faces! In front of all our cousins and aunts and uncles!"

"I don't care about eggs. I want you girls to listen to your mother. Now fry the eggs and let's get going. We're already late. Debbie, see if you can find Lynnie's and Carla's socks and shoes. LeAnn, get diapers packed. All of you need to get your jackets. Where's Butch? Tell him I need help getting the junk out of the car."

I fried the eggs and dumped them on the Jell-O salad while Mom glared at me with a vindictive smirk.

We all piled into the old Plymouth, the little kids sitting on bigger laps in the backseat, arguing about who had to carry the Jell-O salad into Grandma's house.

"Hush now," Dad said.

We quit talking. We were silent for a moment and then burst out giggling. We incited each other with soundless gestures, pointing to the one who would carry the Jell-O salad into Grandma's house, mimicking disapproving looks on our relatives' faces. By the time we completed the three-and-a-half-mile drive we were hysterical, tears streaming down our cheeks from laughing so hard.

At night Dad wheeled Mom to their bedroom, helped her change clothes, lifted her onto the bed, and commiserated with her as if they shared the load of raising a family, making ends meet, and figuring how to face the next day.

Once a week a home health aide helped Dad place Mom in the tub. She washed Mom and tended to her health. Dad came back into the house to lift Mom out of the tub. We stopped caring that her hair plastered to her head or jutted out uncontrollably, that her lap was covered with food, or that she was shaking, drooling, or drooping. Sometimes when we heard her crying and praying, we patted her on the shoulder or rubbed the part of her back that pulled forward off the vinyl wheelchair, and sometimes we walked by—as if we had no eyes to see nor ears to hear.

We abhorred any thought of emulating her. Womanhood seemed like endless misery, and being sick on top of that was utterly unbearable. We heard that MS might be hereditary. We promised each other that we'd go behind the barn and shoot ourselves before we became like her.

After the fried-eggs-on-Jell-O-salad episode and several other screaming matches, my sisters and I decided to act. Since I had the closest relationship with Dad, they elected me spokesperson. I gradually built up my courage.

One evening after finishing the regular chores with Dad, we hooked a hind leg of a dead Holstein cow to the back of the tractor. I opened and closed the gates. Dad pulled her out of the pen. I jumped on the tractor with Dad. We motored toward the dumping site. I held onto the fender and yelled above the tractor's roar, explaining that we older girls believed Mom was losing it. She didn't think clearly, wanted us to do stupid things, and often called us mean names. Dad listened. We paused at the site. We unhooked the cow. Dad used an old wooden post to leverage her into the open grave while I pushed against her with my body.

We started toward home on the tractor, and Dad said the problem was not so much Mom as it was us girls. We were sassy. We didn't show enough respect. We didn't understand how hard she tried to work with us before she got so frustrated that she couldn't stand it. We needed to appreciate her more. Be kind to her. She wanted the best for us.

The truth of his words pierced my heart, and I sobbed the rest of the way home. I walked around the house outside for a long time before I set foot in the kitchen. Everyone could see I'd been crying. I announced that I was not hungry and marched upstairs to bed.

CHAPTER 12 - QUESTIONING GOD

What was my relationship to God, His to me? Why did I feel so alone in the world—so far below even the little sparrows who enjoyed His attention?

Some days I believed that God and I had negotiated a truce—a division of labor. It was my job to keep me and my family safe. That of course meant that I must remain in the relationship with Ron and make sure he didn't guess my unhappiness. He must think I wouldn't leave, that I loved him the way he loved me. I must keep my part of the bargain until God lived up to His part—to devise an exit opportunity by influencing Ron to reject me. I had no alternative but to sustain my part until God completed His. But it had been over a year, a year of sexual obedience and degradation, and God had done nothing.

I didn't understand why God let this go on and on. My charade did nothing to glorify Him. Unlike my dad's nonviolent stance—where he testified about his beliefs in court and important Mennonites wrote public letters of support—no one knew of my suffering, and it would never be considered honorable. If I killed Ron I would be a traitor to my nonviolent beliefs and would be locked away in prison. If I practiced my beliefs and didn't return violence to violence, no one but God would know, and I would remain a slut, not a religious hero of some sort. Was there a difference between nonviolent roles for

Mennonite women and Mennonite men? We'd not discussed that in my Church.

There were occasional good days, when I even believed that with time I'd have a future again. Since I'd successfully managed Ron, I sometimes felt strong and courageous. He didn't suspect anything and therefore he didn't become violent. I still hoped, as Scripture said, that my light shone in the darkness, and the darkness had not overcome it.

The truth was I did sometimes strive to love Ron. Maybe if I could love him better than I did, God would heal him and make him a better person. I thought that was how faith worked. That was why people were supposed to love others, so God would make life better for everyone.

As for romantic love, the whole concept seemed unclear. I imagined when Ron held me tight that he loved me in his way. Perhaps I should be thankful that I was loved. Not every girl knew she was loved. At least he was not afraid to admit it. Wasn't love supposed to be a healing force? Like the little placard in my bedroom said, LOVE CONQUERS ALL. But trying to love Ron felt like sowing a breeze and reaping a cyclone.

Each weekday of my senior year, Ron's Opel pulled up to the Moundridge High School at noon. So that he wouldn't come into the building, I hurried outside to meet him. He had already graduated and now worked nights at an aircraft plant in Wichita. He said he needed to see me as often as possible. He missed me so much. In truth, it was all arranged so he wouldn't miss the half-hour rush that serviced his desires as if I was a sexual vending machine. Then, a few minutes before the bell rang, I dashed to the restroom and on to American history class. I hoped my face wasn't blushing too much, my dress wasn't too disheveled, and semen wasn't running down my leg. Panties that didn't hug the thigh tightly could be dangerous. A hideous endurance.

From God's perspective, I supposed I deserved punishment—that first act had been my own choice, my own damn fault. What must I do to atone? Run off another roof?

The sloped, white barn roof was our favorite slippery-slide, and the string roofs—a string of small, old buildings positioned about two feet apart—provided hours of forbidden entertainment. Though Dad told us not to climb on roofs, we didn't think he'd enforce it. While he was still eating, talking with Mom and playing with baby Butch, we escaped the lunch table, ran outside, climbed the oak tree, and slid across its branch to the string roofs. We made superman jumps from one roof to the next. We became airplanes, with our hands outstretched. We played tag—squealed, raced, and darted away.

The screen door slammed. Hands on his hips, Dad stood in front of the porch, staring right at us.

Stricken with guilt, I ran like a jackrabbit escaping tractor wheels. In five steps, the roof no longer under my feet, I crashed into concrete.

My sisters climbed down and sped towards me. Dad ran from the house and arrived first.

"I'm fine. I'm all right." Tears sprang like jet streams.

"Why did you do that?" Dad asked. "You ran straight off the roof!"

Without a clue, I shrugged my shoulders.

"Where does it hurt?"

"Mostly on my heinie. My leg a little, too."

"Can you walk?"

He lent a hand to pull me up. I made tiny movements like a tight bolt forced by a socket wrench. "I'll be fine."

"Look," Debbie said, pointing to the protruding faucet. "You're lucky you didn't hit that."

"Yeah," LeAnn said. "A foot and a half over and you'd be a bucket of guts."

"Cut it out," Dad said. "Get back to your chores. I'll make sure Lonie's OK."

Later that evening, we laughed at my little legs carrying me over the edge of the roof. I laughed, too, but wondered why guilt propelled me. I didn't usually act before I thought, but when guilt was involved, apparently thinking didn't enter the equation.

Questions of faith dogged me. Dad sent me to the silo to start filling our trailer to feed the cattle. Cold, I was shivering as I climbed to the sixth level. I shoveled for a while and then rested to catch my breath. After the top layer of silage was removed, the silage was warmer than the air. I kneeled down in the middle of the warm silage and prayed out loud.

"God, if You're there, please forgive my failings and doubts. Help me be better, especially with my mother. God, please don't let us get hurt. Help me get out of this! Are You putting me through this so I can convert Ron? You convert him! Try striking him blind on the Damascus road!"

I uttered variations frequently—in the red barn while sorting calves, on the swather while cutting hay, or lying in bed before sleep. I wanted to feel blessed and cared for again.

When I was not begging, I was furious with God. While my life depended on Him, I apprehended the ways that God was not dependable. What could possibly be so great about faith if you had to ignore the evidence that God wasn't doing His job? Why couldn't God solve problems for people rather than put them in terrible binds? He knew already whether they were good.

Is forgiveness really that hard for God? Couldn't He just understand that the people He created were screwed up? He should help us more or forgive us more—one or the other.

But I also knew the other side: God did not give us more than we could bear, and so far I had tolerated everything. I had to hope that He would make something good come of this. When His presence soaked into me, I was grateful. I realized that we shouldn't expect an easy life. God didn't promise that. Suffering and being tested was part of the deal. Jesus suffered more than anyone, and I shouldn't push off my cross any more than He avoided His.

I looked for God's hand in everything. In the field where we cut silage, I backed up the tractor to hook the silage trailer to it. Dad stood next to the trailer hitch, holding the hitch pin. He'd drop it in as soon as the trailer and tractor aligned. I glanced backwards to angle the tractor just right. OK, close enough. My foot reached for the clutch. It wasn't there! What the hell had happened? I stretched both feet forward to push the clutch in. In seconds I would back over the trailer. I turned the steering wheel as sharp as I could, and the tractor scraped the front side of the trailer. Oh my God! Where I was backing was the exact spot where Dad was standing! Where was he? Was I driving over him? Where was the clutch? How could I stop the tractor? What happened to Dad? I backed twenty-five more yards before it occurred to me to turn off the key.

Terrified, I looked back for Dad. Oh my God! There he was, walking toward me. I buried my head in my hands.

"What happened, Lonie?" he asked.

"Are you OK?"

"I'm fine. I jumped back in the nick of time. How come you didn't stop?"

"Are you sure you weren't hurt at all?"

"No. I'm fine. Thankfully, I'm safety-conscious."

With a flushed face and stinging eyes I said, "I feel utterly stupid, but I couldn't find the clutch. I tried and tried with both feet. I was losing my mind! It's like the clutch vanished. I know that can't happen, but that's what it seemed like."

Dad checked the platform where the clutch should be. "I'll be darned," he said. "You're right. The clutch isn't here!" He explained how cast iron sometimes crystallized and broke.

"It scared me to death. I thought I had driven over you!"

"Lonie, you were the one in danger. We're so lucky that you thought quick enough to turn the tractor so sharp. If you had backed into that trailer rather than over the trailer hitch, well, that's the stuff of major tractor accidents."

Maybe God saved me from this death, I thought excitedly.

"Come on, Lonie. Let's walk home. In the morning we'll get the other tractor and try it again. It's too dark now."

"Tomorrow morning will you back up the tractor and let me pin the hitch?"

"I don't think two clutches will crystallize on us, but I'll do the driving if you prefer."

The next day we found the missing clutch in the field.

Absolutely everything that Mennonites said, did, or thought had theological implications, and our job was to determine what those implications were. How did God function in the world? What could or should we count on from God? What would God want from us?

I clung to the thought God had spared my life, and it soothed the violent doubts and fears I battled, just as I soothed Ron's violence. Faith resurged. Like a Las Vegas gambler throwing hard-earned money at tables, I bet on God. Like any good gambler, I had grave doubts; nevertheless, thinking it was my best bet—or my only one—I acted on my belief.

"Amazing grace how sweet the sound, that saved a wretch like me," I belted out in fields or when running down the driveway. I sang it in my heart and drummed it into my soul. Repeating hymns, I surmounted my doubts to again internalize hope. On good days, I felt I had been saved and hoped I would be saved in more ways than one.

The leaves were sprouting again. I'd made it through another winter and was almost through my senior year, seventeen years old. God had sufficed for everyone I knew, including the great man Dr. Martin Luther King, who was recently murdered. Because of his faith, Dr. King had moved mountains to end the unjust suffering of his people. I deeply respected his vision and his nonviolent stance. Dr. King laid his life before his Father.

Perhaps I was laying my life before God also. But perhaps God wouldn't save me, either.

Family picture at Leona's wedding inside
Hopefield Mennonite Church

PART III - ENDURANCE WITHOUT FAITH

I said to my soul, be still, and wait without hope

— Four Quartets, T. S. Eliot

Randy, seven months

Chapter 13 - SHAME

I had been counting on God not to get pregnant. I didn't know what else to do but hope for His help. Without God's help, I couldn't avoid getting pregnant. After all, God was the author of life. No one had babies unless God chose that for them.

I accepted that God might need to chastise and punish me. But no one, not even God, had a right to bring an innocent child into this hellish circumstance. A child had done nothing to deserve God's wrath. Nothing! God should not cause innocents to suffer.

But then it happened, what I dreaded. I felt nauseated in the morning, when I couldn't stomach eggs or Dad's gravy. I fainted, for the first time in my life, hitting my shoulder on the edge of the tub. I waited and waited for my period, for the cleansing blood of hope, for the blood that would be my salvation. Finally I explained to Ron that we must find a doctor. He would have to pay for it because I had no money. He seemed relieved, almost happy, that I might be pregnant.

With the embarrassment of the bad teenager I was, I faced the doctor. He pronounced that I was, indeed, pregnant. He might as well have said there was no God. Everything I based my life on for my entire life was a lie—and I would pay for that lie for the rest of my life. *He might as well have said that I had been a complete fool to operate from the religious fantasy of everyone I knew.*

And now everyone I knew would condemn me. Nothing and no one could spare me: I was and forever would be shame incarnate.

I loathed myself and wanted to die; I would have been better off if Ron had killed me on that dark night. My life had pivoted from the biggest living hell to an even bigger living hell. I lost everything in a crap shoot where the dice were loaded and I imagined I had a chance.

I carried my despicable self to Ron's car where he was waiting. I spilled the news, as evenly as I could, with tears slowly emerging. "That's OK," he said, "we'll just get married a little sooner. We were going to get married anyway. It's not a big deal."

Chapter 14 - RAGE

The next day, a Saturday, Dad needed me to springtooth a fallow field.

With implement in tow, I drove the tractor to the outer edge of the field and started the rounds. Heaps of sad and then sarcastic thoughts clamored, vying for attention, compelling me to finally say it, scream it: the meaning of my pregnancy, of God's latest and final failure, was that God did not exist. And I vowed never to be fooled again—never to believe, never to desire breath or a song in my heart.

Against the roar of the tractor, no one could hear me. I drove, stood up, and shook my fist toward the high heavens. "You Bastard, who should be up there but isn't! You goddamned, hateful, lying, sorry excuse for a God! You sleazy Figment of everyone's imagination! You sick Joke! People give their lives for You! And You have the nerve not to exist?

"OK, God, here's one for Your Holy Sickness: knock me off this tractor! Come on, You can do it, can't You? Strike me with lightning, You Wimp! Go ahead, You slimy Chicken-Shit! Make the Five Star explode! I hate You for being the Nothing You are! Give it Your best shot!"

I waited for a while, half wondering if it could happen.

"What? You need me to make excuses for You? Oh, God can't kill me today. He's busy killing everyone in Vietnam. Sorry, no time to kill little old Leona." I shot my fist in the air and extend my middle finger. My mind whirled in despair. Did I really want to die? Did it matter? "You do-nothing, be-nothing Blankness. Can't You hear me above the tractor noise? Can't You read my thoughts? Kill me now. I double dare You!"

Weaving the tractor, I'd gapped the rows and would need to re-do the last two circles. I didn't care. It allowed more time to scream at God, to wrest Him from my soul, to wring Him out of my blood, to pound Him out of my heart. I must do it once and for all. If I left one smidgen of Him inside, He would grow uncontrollably from that mustard seed. With a raw voice, I blasted and blasphemed.

I sat down and jiggled on the tractor seat. At the thought of telling my parents, I burst into tears. How could I tell them I had brought shame to their name, to my whole family, to our community? I failed my faith, duty, and honor.

I wouldn't, though, tell them that we couldn't count on God for anything. I'd shoulder the blame alone. God, good little God? He was not in trouble. God could never be blamed. If something bad happened, people had to accept the blame. You didn't pray hard enough. You were not good enough. You will-fully defied. You were stuck on your own power and devices. You didn't trust enough. You deserved it.

No one but me was willing to point a finger at God. "God does not exist, people! Get that through your needy little souls! God is not, was not, will not be. No God. No Almighty. No Prince of Peace. No Jesus, Son of God. No virgin birth. No redemption. No forgiveness. No love. No life after death. No heaven. No hell. Do you get it? No God!"

I could scream it forever and not one person would be swayed. Before all this happened, I wouldn't have entertained the thought myself. Look what I had to endure to finally rip apart my faith. Look at all the stupid excuses I made for God, all this time.

I had needed God. I had traded my brains for God. I had been a fool for God.

"Did Jonah make it out of the whale and Daniel out of the lion's den? You rely on those whoppers, don't You?" I rifled through miracles. "How many people did You magically help Jesus feed? For some reason You've never been able to feed people since." I shrieked, digging into my flesh, into my bones to yank out the ingrained effervescent hope in His existence, certain it would be easier to die; to remove my foolish faith was to take all of me anyway.

"And what about the Virgin Mary? You didn't want damaged goods, did You? Was it really a choice You gave her?"

Vaguely I understood that a number of women had faced worse. Women who were beaten more than I had been, women who had been murdered. I wondered if they, too, lived through their anguish without hope in God.

"Oh, yes, speaking of brutal—remember the pestilence, the locusts, the dry years, the diseases. You couldn't find a better way to let Your people go? Send a cloud of grasshoppers now!" I had hours to complete this feat. I was amazed. The scales fell from my eyes, and I saw each scene in the Scriptures marching into a moral abyss, falling off the cliff of sanity, or emptying into divine tragedy. I uttered each story clearly, so it couldn't crumble into self-doubt. I sharpened the razor edge of this truth and felt it cut through my life-line. Either He dies to me, or I do.

"Isn't it interesting, God, that You're the One who wins wars? In the early days You helped Israel defeat enemies in Canaan. But for some odd reason the Israelites had to fight, and people still have to fight and die. You could just say, 'This side wins.' But instead You sit back and let the little soldiers entertain You."

Has He ever done anything alone? I considered it carefully. "You always need help from people. We suffer on your behalf, laboring to help You as if You weren't Almighty and couldn't do it by Yourself." I spent hours squeezing God stories until the guts of truth shot out like pus from a pimple. Each time I was amazed to see what I had not seen before—the realities covered by naïve belief, by stories that made no sense yet were believed. I laid them open with venomous sarcasm and mockery.

Finally, I would not go gentle into that good night. I would not accept crumbs and try harder.

"Oh, yes, God, now tell me again about blasphemy. The worst of all sins? The all-knowing, all-powerful, all-wonderful, all-glorious God would be threatened if some little person somewhere said something bad or perhaps disrespectful about You?

"You get riled up about blaspheming! But not starving people. Not the sick, who pray and pray and die by random chance. Not the disillusioned and disheartened. Not babies who can't be helped. Not men dying on battlefields. Not hurricane, volcano, flood, or tornado victims who leave this life terrified. No. You won't trouble Yourself to help them. But if someone calls You names, You're on it."

Nothing happened. God didn't make a move—to my relief and eternal sadness.

Why didn't I think of these discrepancies earlier? Wouldn't it have been amazing if I could have landed here without each painstaking step of disappointment, fear, failure, anguish, betrayal, and finally, unremitting rage? I could have been relieved of my faith, knowing better than an imaginary God what was true.

My mind turned another corner. "You didn't mean for people to create You, did You? Born of uncanny human need, like the rest of us, You had no choice. You can't squirm out of Your position until people let You go. But people won't let You go. They'll cover for You. They'll protect You, even though You won't protect them. They'll trust You. You don't need to do anything. People will do it for You and give You the credit.

They like the lies they created for You! They'll blame others or even themselves. If all else fails, they'll say they can't understand but they know You have a good reason—it will all come to good in the end."

I sat there jiggling, considering the enormity of the lie. "It's a sad story for You as well as for the rest of us. We have craved 'Your' lies."

I wished I could garner some satisfaction from finally knowing I was ultimately alone. I didn't. I felt sad, bereft, enraged, betrayed, and exhausted. I suspected that in cutting God out of my life, I had unwittingly cut out an essential part of myself— the sunbeam part. Now I must deplore her ignorance and eradicate her shining faith. Still, I couldn't imagine living without her curious fascinations, her earnest yet carefree reverence, and her desire to embrace goodness.

CHAPTER 15 - TELLING DAD

The worst was still ahead: telling Dad that I was *with child*. I must speak the unspeakable. I already knew much of what he would indicate: I must publicly confess in front of the people I have known my whole life and ask this nonexistent God for forgiveness, as if He or they were capable of granting it. I must marry the fucker and be his sex slave. I must officially sanction and assent to becoming his obedient wife, taking on his identity and shedding my own. I must continue for the rest of my life to play the same obsequious role with him that I have played for the last two years. And I must raise a child in the midst of this never-ending disaster.

So I ask you, how could I argue with Dad on that evening when I told him? We rode together in the rusted, red International pickup, moving slowly along the gravel road sectioning our farmland from the neighbor's fields. Anguish poured through my pores like milk from a sequestered cow's teats when her calf bellows. I had already rattled off my brief soliloquy about bringing shame to the family, how I hadn't meant to disappoint him, and how I had no idea what to do. Did I want to marry Ron? Not a chance. I said honestly that I hated him more. I never wanted to see him again. I wanted to run away.

Dad said, "But you know, Leona, every child needs a father."

How could I have said anything but *I know*? There was no recourse but to marry.

"Abortion? What's that?" I asked, when Dad gingerly brought up the subject and explained that it was dangerous and illegal.

"Do we do things that are illegal?" I asked.

"Not for things like this." And the subject closed like steel doors slamming shut.

We both were silent for a long while. Looking ahead, Dad maneuvered the steering wheel. I was sitting sideways on the front seat, so I could see him, but I stared at the holes in the seat cover.

"You probably know what you will have to do if you get married in church here."

He brought this up as he drove by Hopefield. I looked up and saw the white, blocky shape through the moonlight, its steeple proudly beckoning.

"I have to publicly confess, right?"

"That will be required. Confessing offers advantages. It lets you announce the pregnancy all at once, so you don't have people whispering. The other advantage is once they've forgiven you, it's supposedly over."

"I know how *over* it will be. Let's just say over the top! Those self-righteous jerks won't forgive me. They'll say so in church, but they'll be waiting with bated breath to tell their friends and neighbors."

"Leona, you certainly are hard on everyone."

"I'm speaking the truth, Dad, and you know it."

"You're taking it to an extreme, honey. You might be surprised how caring people are. They've more to worry about than whether you are what they think you should be."

"I hate everyone, including myself. I wish I could die."

More silence overtook us.

"When you confess, people know you aren't hiding anything, that you handled it with dignity."

"You call that dignity?"

"You know what I mean, Leona. Let's not make this worse than it is."

"What happens after I confess?"

"You can confess one Sunday and be married the next. You probably don't want to confess too early. We can plan the wedding. You can talk with Reverend Schmidt and decide on the Sunday for the public confession and the date for the wedding."

"Dad, I still have a few weeks of high school. I don't want anyone to know before I graduate."

We decided on late July, after harvest, and talked of logistics. The guest list would be a couple of friends, extended family, and the Hopefield congregation. As little cost as possible, since I had five sisters—some who might marry soon.

Stale darkness surrounded us like the secret. Each chug of the engine groaned supplications, turning rage and sorrow into one repetitive tone, until I swung open my door and upchucked into the ditch. Dad braked too late. The jolt jerked my head, and a line of vomit trailed from the world beyond to my chest and back again.

Neither could avoid a snicker, seeing the surprise on our faces through the other's eyes.

"Goddamn it, quit laughing!" I said.

"Let's go home and get you cleaned up," Dad said, wiping away his inappropriate smile.

"As if that were possible."

He turned into the driveway. No matter how hard I tried, I couldn't for the moment keep the corners of my mouth down. I held my nose and admitted that puking was a fitting end to this day.

We said good night. Thankfully everyone else in the house had gone to sleep. Dad had put Mom in bed before we left. If I listened, I would hear her cry, perhaps wail. While her voice was unstable and her words garbled, when she cleared her throat or coughed or sobbed, she had intense volume. I hoped she didn't wake up three-year-old Carla, who would be in bed with her.

I had done the impossible. I said what I could not say. I disappointed the one man I could not bear to hurt. From this moment forward I would pretend I was still me and not the pariah I had become, eating the bone structure out of our family's identity.

Balling up a wet washcloth I found in the sink, I nudged the bathtub dirt, along with a creepy brown spider, down the drain. I ran the bath water so I wouldn't hear Mom crying. I plopped my heaviness into the warmth. Though I still must confess in public and face marriage, leave the farm and the only people I loved, the worst was over. I had cut it off with God, the non-existent One, and I told Dad. I felt like a monstrous caricature of myself, but the tears didn't roll until I realized I was holding myself upright with rage at everyone else. Perhaps I should appreciate the church people more. But I must not weaken with God. I must keep Him in a disillusioned dark corner where a child would toss a magic wand after a few disappointing tries. I must! As I rested in the water and resolved to keep my heart hardened, the memory of His miracle with Chocolady harassed me.

CHAPTER 16 - CONFESSION

I despised what was happening to me. I hated what my life had become. I would not go to college or be anyone, not even myself. I imagined myself in a strange land where I crossed a border to attend a school that didn't speak my language. Few noticed. I didn't belong. I couldn't be understood. In spite of occasional thoughtful engagement and infrequent arguments about historical incidents, I sucked at high school achievement. I would be graduating as an average student.

Perhaps I wasn't smart, but for some crazy reason I had wanted to go to college. I'd imagined I might somehow finesse a fresh start in some college and turn it all around. But my guidance counselor said I wasn't college material. It pissed me off that he thought he knew me. I didn't think we had talked before he called me into his office. In his highfalutin' opinion, I should kiss college goodbye. I did.

After finals and the high-school graduation I slept through, I came to terms with the practical implications of pregnancy and marriage. I ordered wedding invitations. Amid the ever-present effort to appease Ron, I chose flowers and hired a photographer, all as cheaply as possible. I selected a white wedding dress I didn't deserve or desire, but it was the available color. With it hanging in my closet, I approached the confession that overtly made my white dress obsolete.

Early on that dreaded Sunday morning, while throwing bales from the red barn hayloft, I gazed across the pasture at Hopefield Mennonite Church. It stood there in the foggy morning light like a comforting white ark in a sea of golden wheat fields. Solitary and solid, in a few painful hours it would cradle our congregation. It would entice our spirits into heavy contrition that slid, as if the ark tipped, towards yielding forgiveness.

At the appropriate time during the worship service, Rev. Schmidt called Ron and me forward. We stood in front of the congregants and looked at them. Ron gave no indication of discomfort. He knew no one there but my family. He cared not a whit what the congregation thought. He understood this was a prerequisite to security. If he went through this ordeal he could relax in the knowledge that he owned me; that I couldn't escape. I spoke almost those exact words to coax him into confessing with me. Besides, he acquired the bonus of my promise to love and obey. He would be the head of the family. This religion thing wasn't half bad for him—a small price to pay for the driver's seat guarantee.

I, on the other hand, was staring down the long nose of history, my only history, which was entirely with these people. I had not lived in a different place, gone to a different church, or been part of a different community. These people—many of whom were my uncles, aunts, first and second cousins—represented my whole life, my family's entire existence. They knew my grandparents, Julius and Olga Stucky and Martha Schrag and her late husband Ed. If they were old enough, my appearance brought to their minds my great-grandparents. This congregation provided the eyes through which I saw myself. Together we crystallized generations of history in our gazes.

Ironically, I landed in almost the same spot I had stood eight years earlier. It was my family's turn to provide special music at Hopefield. I don't remember who played the piano for me. Perhaps my own mother, if she wasn't already too impaired.

My ten-year-old solo voice rang out to these same people, hitting each note in a verse from John's gospel, about a woman Jesus saved from stoning. Jesus made it clear that only those without sin should cast a stone. None did. Did anyone remember the words I sang then? Would these people forgive my sin?

I was jealous of Ron, who felt little shame. What had he done? Sown a wild oat? Last night when we practiced the ritual words of confession with Rev. Schmidt, I noticed nothing in the litany that would indicate my guilt more than Ron's. Yet I knew that I was the responsible party, the one who should be ashamed.

In front of the congregation, Rev. Schmidt fed us the confession line by line. We repeated each one. We acknowledged that we were sinful, that we allowed passion to mar our judgment, that we failed our commitment to follow God's way. We said we were weak and unworthy, we were bringing an innocent child into a tainted situation, and we were sorry for our deeds. We acknowledged we had no right to mercy except that we knew God was merciful, and we would count on His Son, who died to save us from our sins.

I was so nervous attempting to repeat the lines that their meaning barely registered. I was saying I had sinned. I knew on a scale of one to ten where my sin landed. I was announcing pregnancy before marriage. Thus I had committed the worst sin a young woman could commit, except murder.

I smelled the acrid fear on my body, a smell to which I was accustomed. But why fear now? No one would jump up and come after me. There would be no physical confrontation. No stones would be thrown. Not a sound would disturb this solemn moment. These kind and compassionate Mennonites were at this moment reciting lines of forgiveness, promising to hold us in their circle of love, inviting us back into the fold of committed souls who walked the path Jesus took, the narrow and disciplined path of salvation.

A stunning emptiness bored a hole in my gut, which was churning. If God existed, would He be smiling right now, catching me confessing sin? Would my remorse please Him? Would He put his arms around me and comfort me if I could turn to Him? I'd rather have done that than practice humiliation in this worship charade. Perhaps the charade was mine alone. Perhaps others were worshipping appropriately and sincerely.

After forgiveness was granted, I smiled a thin, defiant half-moon. Under my breath I dared them to talk about me over Sunday dinner. I guessed some people were sad for me. Some might have felt compassion for my family, burdened by shame. In my whirling sensation of unleashed sinfulness, I thought I was foremost on the congregation's mind. Perhaps, as Dad said, they were mostly worried about their own problems, about the price of wheat, their own daughters or sons, necessary repairs, sick relatives, and impossible budgets. But I couldn't escape my own harsh inward gaze; I couldn't imagine escaping theirs.

With a few more repeated lines, we confirmed our commitment to Christ's way. We settled our desire to be reconciled to the flock. I hoped I'd not see these people again, except for my family and the few who would show up at my wedding next Saturday evening. My hemline quivered against my shins. I clasped Ron's hand as if we were in this together. He led me back to our rigid pew. I no longer knew in which row we were sitting. A plastic smile decorated my horrified face. A mass of eyes looked directly at me, as if I might now reveal a deeper dimension of sorrow and regret.

After the service, I bowed out quickly. I went home to hate myself, to feel the emptiness of ritual forgiving, to understand, once and for all, that love did *not* conquer all. Transforming despair into rage, I cursed the five-gallon buckets of water that sloshed on my feet as I carried drink to lambs, clobbered the goddamned faucet that wouldn't open, smashed the miserable latch that stuck, and stabbed the filthy feed sack that wouldn't yield to my tug.

To avoid heaviness in my heart, I teased out more anger with an *it-ain't-fair* routine. I cursed the brothers Harry and Simon, who had not spoken to each other since an inheritance dispute. They didn't have to confess their sin in front of everyone. And what about the ones who had not given a dime to help the poor? Wasn't that a sin in God's eyes? What about those that had said mean things about each other, like I was doing now? Why at Hopefield was public sin and confession about teenage girls having sex?

Hymns of comfort involuntarily played through my mind, like tunes on a player piano. I could easily identify with what a wretch I was in *Amazing Grace*. *How Great Thou Art*, my mom's favorite, slipped out while I chased cattle from the rented pasture across the road. These songs continued while I cursed God, helped Butch milk goats, played with Lynnie and Carla, and contemplated placements for wedding flowers and a guest book.

Why do stale stanzas of comfort keep returning, long after you know they are as unreliable as the second coming?

Chapter 17 - The Marriage Prison

July 20, 1968

I awoke in an especially foul mood on my wedding day. Throughout the morning and afternoon I cried, lashed out at my siblings for dawdling in the bathroom, and strove to mediate Carla's disappointment. She felt slighted because I chose Lynnie to be my flower girl. Carla complained. I told her I'd selected her for an important job—being a bench warmer. Years later she still remembered my last day living at home as a time I lied to her. The longer she sat on the bench—while her sister marched up the aisle, distributing rose petals—the more certain she became that I had purposely hurt and deceived her. On that day I left little Carla with a lie, my parents and siblings with a scowl, and I vowed before God another lie: to love and obey until death. I hoped "until death" was a lie, but feared it wasn't.

I proffered assurances of my happiness to extended family and friends. As soon as possible after the Hopefield ladies kindly served iced sweet tea, cake, and ice cream in the church basement, I pulled Ron outside toward the decorated car. On the front steps, I tossed my bouquet behind me, saying goodbyes to everyone. Out the back window that said "Just Married," I watched as Dad, my sisters, brother, and Grandma

Schrag, among others, waved in the distance. Full of sadness and regret, I whispered an *I-love-you goodbye* that Ron couldn't hear.

Ron was again driving me along highway 81, this time en route to a reserved room at the Wichita Holiday Inn.

Soon Ron and I settled into a three-room apartment in Newton, Kansas. He drove to his factory job in Wichita. Lost, without an identity, I cleaned, decorated, and stormed around the apartment when alone. I swallowed hard to accept and accept, but I found little peace with defeat. Though sullen and withdrawn, I tried to make the best of it.

My eye twitched when Ron came home and quizzed me. Did I leave the apartment at all? Did I speak with anyone? What did I do all day? I wondered if he had some trap set that would let him know if I went outside. If he caught me in a lie, it would have had the same effect as a pink slip in my purse.

I looked forward to getting away on our "honeymoon," a trip to Fort Hood, California, with Ron's siblings and parents to visit his maternal grandmother's family. I had not been outside Kansas since I was a preschooler. Surreal Western landscapes impressed me. I savored each mysterious formation, each unlikely plant that defied imagination. I wished to touch the unadulterated lands, ingest their singular beauty, and feel their expansive free rein.

With me safely on the car seat beside him, Ron relaxed into the long stretch of scenery. The landscapes seemed to have a soothing effect on him, too. He proclaimed our baby would be named after his friend Randy, if it were a boy. I nodded, unwilling to disturb the peace of the journey. Ron thought Randy had gotten a raw deal in high school, often accused of sluffing-off when he tried his best. But he was a stellar character and his name should be carried forward.

Ron said he often felt misunderstood too. He tried so hard to not steal or smoke or drink. He was on-track to take care of me and the baby.

Judy's lively family welcomed us. To avoid embarrassment for Judy and the rest of us, I disguised pregnancy by wearing T-shirts that hung over my unbuttoned pants. Several of Ron's family members drank beer. I declined. I'd not tasted alcohol, and I'd probably sinned enough. I enjoyed their bantering jokes and laughed when I understood. I didn't know how to enter the conversations but I loved staying attuned to them. I soaked up laughter anywhere I could find it. When someone mentioned Judy's brother who died of a heart attack when he was thirty-six, I silently did the math. If that happened to Ron at age thirty-six, it would be another sixteen years from now, nearly double my age.

In three fast days, we hit the road again. All too soon, I was back in lockup, soon to learn that entire institutions supported Ron as my jailer. In case I didn't understand that the man was the head of the household and the woman had to obey, our local bank drove the point home. After depositing Ron's paycheck a week earlier, I walked back one windy afternoon to withdraw a hundred and thirty dollars in cash, almost as much as I had deposited. Though my account card was signed and Ron's was not, the manager refused to let me withdraw the money. It was Ron's money. I must bring a signed statement from Ron showing that he approved the withdrawal.

Indignantly I explained that I was married to Ron. He knew that; it didn't matter. I still had to bring a signed statement from my husband. I waddled out of there, furious with the manager. We needed cash to buy garage-sale baby supplies.

The next day I proudly presented the signed note, as if to say, "How dare you think I'm the kind of wife who would take her husband's money without his permission! I had his permission and now have a signed note to prove it."

Walking home, I struck gold at a garage sale. Along with some necessities for the baby, I bought a twenty-five cent record on a whim. We had a portable record player at home, and a small stack of popular forty-fives. My new record was by an artist I'd never heard of, and the music without words was not familiar. But after a few tries, I embraced it! I listened to Tchaikovsky's Fifth Symphony daily, all day long. It pulsated energy, almost dispelling my sense of confinement.

Sometimes my landlady, Mrs. Cargan, stopped by. We laughed about her exploits and she offered recipes simple enough for beginners and shared cleaning tips, like keeping a small tub of warm water in the sink so I could wash dishes as soon as I dirtied them.

I enjoyed visits with Ron's older sister, already married and with a child. Fun-loving and kind to me, she made me laugh at life's little surprises: a diaper that didn't hold the whole mess or the last quarter that you knew you brought but couldn't find now in the Laundromat—poignant echoes of laughing with my own sisters.

We managed to sell his old Opel and buy a used Saab from his grandpa's junkyard. In addition to the junkyard, his father and grandfather made extra money by buying wrecked Saabs and constructing useable ones. We visited my family or his on weekends. Ron always drove; he forbade me to drive. Nor was I allowed to suggest what we might do. My activities were his choice. I was careful to roll my eyes only when he wasn't looking. Expletives raced through my thoughts but never showed on my face. I poked my middle finger out surreptitiously when holding a dish. When he was away from home, I secretly mimicked him and blasted him with my ideas. I spent hours imagining the release and joy I would feel if he were dead.

In addition to my pregnant belly pouching out, I ate myself into oblivion, quickly gaining forty-five pounds, almost half my body weight, jumping from size three to size twelve.

Sadness tugged me into dreary tiredness, and I slept an inordinate number of hours.

Occupied and controlled by others, I couldn't abide my body's fantastic betrayal. On the farm I had counted on my physical strength, and it pulled through each time—moving impossibly large hay bales, carrying whatever needed to cross the yard, or enduring the breathless run across the pasture. Now my body was not me or my own but an alien and monstrous form that had captured me.

Ron's main concerns remained cars and sex. Undeterred by my enormous girth, Ron insisted on sex. It was my job as a wife to satisfy him. That was the way God prescribed it. Unfortunately, my lack of faith did not alter his. When I resisted, he became agitated. I knew the cost of maintaining my stance, and I was not prepared to pay the price; I submitted. He was right, no matter what the subject. If he felt uncertain, sex usually reacquainted him with power. I, a tough and ready farm girl, felt about as strong as the crumpled Kleenex I kept in my hand to absorb errant tears. If I were not so fat and pregnant, I might have imagined I was a sex slave. But I was not that classy.

Ron did, however, marvel at the changes in my bulging belly. He wanted to feel the kicks as soon as I felt them. He sometimes rested his ear there to hear a second heartbeat. He rubbed ointment on the stretch marks around my breasts.

I needed Ron's permission to walk to medical appointments. Dr. Rimes advised me to lose weight, most of which wasn't the baby. I was now on Ron's insurance from work, but I hadn't been when I became pregnant, so the entire hospital and doctor bills were on our shoulders. I made extra-large payments with each appointment so his bill was paid off before I went to the hospital.

Sometimes I commiserated with Jane in the apartment across the hall, with whom we shared a bathroom, on the occasions when her husband went to work. Jane attended to his needs for a beer, a cleaner apartment, or a meal as well as took care of their baby.

When Mom and Dad stopped by, I ran downstairs to say hi to Mom before they rushed off to doctor appointments. Then Lynnie, Carla, and I enjoyed Kool-Aid, made donuts, and shared farm stories while I sewed Halloween costumes for them.

LeAnn found a nice Mennonite man at college. She married four months after my wedding. She was the oldest and married second—my shameful circumstance made expectations that the oldest marry first difficult for her. On November 16, 1968, I saw relatives and friends from Hopefield Church for the first time since my confession and wedding. I wore a home-sewn pink maternity dress that ballooned like a silo lid.

I realized that shame didn't just disappear. You had to do something to make it fade. Perhaps I could redeem myself by getting rich. S&H Green Stamps wouldn't do it. I couldn't go to school. I had married a clod who wouldn't advance himself. But if we managed to amass a small fortune, then Ron, as a self-made man, might be respected. That esteem would trickle down into my identity. Eventually my sin's reddish glow would dim.

Fortunately, my cousin and her husband presented Amway. We attended several sessions and learned how fast you could accumulate money. You buy the product, sell, and sign up people under you. Wow! Enthusiastically we bought several products and signed up.

Though we attended trainings and our hopes escalated, we didn't know any potential signers. How could I ask someone to buy products that cost more than they would at Alco? Impossible as asking a favor! This fiasco wasn't Ron's fault.

My doctor's office recommended Lamaze classes. Ron wasn't interested. People had babies before they had special classes for it; besides, they might discover our embarrassingly late wedding date.

Mrs. Cargan laughed when she saw my bulging pregnant body standing on the kitchen table and stretching to wipe the top ledge of the millwork above the kitchen window. "It must be about your time, Leona. You're nesting."

CHAPTER 18 - RANDY'S ARRIVAL

I was lying on our mattress and without warning, it was wet. Had I peed without knowing it? Was this the latest pregnancy hiccup? The wet spot had no specific odor. Suddenly pain shocked me. They began coming a few minutes apart. Labor! I informed Ron.

Ron wasn't so sure. We had no phone, so he jumped into his car and drove across town to consult his mother, who sent him on a speedy return trip to get me to Bethel Hospital. The delay meant missing a needed episiotomy and piercing pain. Thankfully, it was a quick delivery. Like a thirsty child stretching toward a water fountain, I pulled my head forward to greet my baby boy. He was healthy!

When they brought Randy for our first nursing session, my heart overflowed. He was so precious and adorable. I loved the funny little wrinkle lines on his arms and legs and the expressions his lips made. His toes and fingers were beyond tiny, though he weighed seven pounds and thirteen ounces. Nestling him in my arms felt redemptive. The way his hand curled around my little finger brought melting joy, shame, confusion, pain, and love in one warm stream of tears.

My heart felt regenerated, though little changed with Ron. I dreaded his visits to the hospital after work. Didn't I realize he had needs, too? Surely my *hand* was not sore from giving birth. He couldn't wait until I came home.

The day after we came home, Ron insisted on penetrating me. No pleading, pushing, or cajoling would stop him. My pain meant nothing to him. I was a need-satisfying object, and now I had a baby's needs to meet, too.

I wished, but didn't know how, to improve my marriage. Most of Ron's impulses seemed peculiar. I learned to anticipate them, to avoid his rage. I stayed on high alert, and usually he only yelled at and pushed me. He hadn't threatened to kill me again. When I questioned his reactions he said, "Get used to it. I'm not Mennonite."

Our lives seemed sad but ordinary. I listened when Ron told me the guys at work were jerks or his mom was faking illness again or his younger brother didn't stand a chance because his parents alternately beat him or let him evade consequences.

I strove to be the right kind of wife for Ron and a good mother to Randy. I had imagined that raising Randy would come as naturally to me as a cow raising her calf. I had tons of milk. While he nursed one side, the other erupted. Randy's coos and sweet nature helped ameliorate my sleep-deprived lethargy.

I learned to make sausage milk gravy, salmon patties, and pineapple upside-down cake. Like a servant who takes pride in her work, I aimed for gracious productivity. I hoped my attempts to love effectively benefited Ron. Evenings, we often watched TV. We snuggled, teased, and enjoyed. Playful teasing, as we had done when he worked at the farm, was the only time my frustrations eked out in his presence.

Sometimes I needed to tame my own rage and hatred that sprang forth when I had time alone to think. I indulged fantasies that Ron was killed in an accident. Many times I awaited the knock on the door: "I'm sorry to inform you, Mrs. O'Brien, your husband was killed . . ." I practiced expressions that would hide my jubilation.

Finances remained woefully inadequate. Paying the hospital bill and the extra expenses for Randy left us dry, so I searched for a job to which I could take Randy. We moved to the bottom floor of a boarding house—I showed and collected rent for upstairs rooms, kept the yard, and cleaned. Eventually we even bought a washer. No more Laundromat runs with dirty diapers.

Randy was as precious as any baby could be. His light and airy blond hair flew about as I carried him in the breeze. His bright eyes gazed into cloudy skies, watched birds flying and trees billowing, and his little mind put two and two together. This toy fits into that one. This ball will bounce. Mom pops back when she plays peek-a-boo. I celebrated his adorable little body by sewing several outfits from scrap material: two pairs of little pants and a matching vest. They fit him perfectly! What a sweetie.

When I took Randy to Dr. Rimes's office for vaccinations or to run an errand, with Ron's permission, I pushed the stroller down the sidewalk under mature oak and elm trees, with afternoon sunlight filtering through. These were glorious days, wandering along the streets and into a dime store or clothing shop, exploring downtown Newton.

Chapter 19 - ESCAPE FANTASY

Other than making these infrequent excursions, I stayed home, fearful of provoking Ron's punishment. But miraculously, a possibility for escape came right through my door.

I heard the knock and shoved strewn blocks, plastic cars, and farm animals out of the middle of the floor as I headed for the front door. The man introduced himself as Jim Quantree and said he was selling sets of books. Could he come in?

Seeing Randy half naked, I quickly excused myself, grabbed my little boy, and diapered him. I had left it off, with Desitin smeared on his heinie, to help heal his diaper rash.

Jim's long arms draped over the cushioned chair, his face a pinkish pallor. His eyes danced with expectation as he pulled out a pamphlet showing the illustrious encyclopedia set that could revolutionize my knowledge base. I announced my complete lack of money. He only had to glance around to see the mismatched furniture. Surely he noticed "garage sale" written on my clothes.

He commiserated with my lack of funds, saying he appreciated my forthrightness, and asked a few penetrating questions. Had I been married a long time? What was my life like? When was I happiest? Did I sense I was capable of contentment?

Though intrigued by his questions, I was cautious with responses. No good wife said bad things about her husband.

Leona Stucky

I had not spoken so frankly with another human being, and certainly not since I was married. No one had asked.

I offered him my one little luxury: soda pop left over from babysitting Ron's little brother. Jim, a surprisingly gifted salesman, accepted a glass of water.

Our conversation veered from books to life. In Jim's philosophy, it all came down to human love. If we could do that effectively, we would be OK. He asked if I had heard of an author named Erich Fromm and suggested a book I must read: *The Art of Loving*. My eyebrows went up. No, really, he told me, it was not a sleazy book—just the opposite.

Randy passed directly between us, whizzing back and forth on his favorite green plastic horse with riding wheels. He threw back his head and giggled when Jim reached to tickle him.

I blurted out that I now understood love cannot conquer all. I said that as if I knew it for sure, but I still hoped every day that the love I tried to muster would help Ron. I told Jim about the three-by-five block of wood inscribed LOVE CONQUERS ALL that I bought at the Moundridge drugstore in my sophomore year. It still decorated my bedroom. But I no longer credited that statement. What did he think? What would this Fromm person say? Did love conquer all?

I guessed I could read the entire book, and if Fromm argued for love's decisive power, I still wouldn't trust it. It had taken me too long to figure it out—and the consequences of my ignorance were too intense. "Whatever you do, don't tell me God is love, because I have an opinion about that, too, and it's not very nice to say."

I told him I'm not particularly fond of beliefs. They were notions that we stubbornly insisted upon although we didn't know they were true. What did he think about free will? I wondered if some of us had more of it than others. What was free will worth to a person in a concentration camp? What should be done when one person's will directly restricted the will of another?

Eventually, realizing we must not say most things, we ran out of things we *would* say. But Jim wanted to leave Fromm's book with me. He said he hadn't had such a good conversation in years. It would be his way of saying thank you. He met a lot of people. This encounter was special.

As he turned to leave, I swallowed hard and pinned my upper lip inside my lower. I wanted to tell him everything. I wanted to ask him to take Randy and me with him. I didn't find him physically attractive, but I could get over that. Connecting with him felt good. I wanted to talk for hours. I wanted to run away with him. He might be just the person who would help Randy and me escape. I shuddered to think how fat and unattractive I was, how estranged from my body. Yet he made me feel worthy for a moment or two.

I thanked him for the conversation and his book and said goodbye. Could he hear my heart pounding, my inner voice screaming, as I closed the door?

I lifted Randy to kiss his cheek and laid him on the sofa to take off his diaper, giving him the open-air treatment again. I wondered if my diaper-changing timing had been off, and I felt guilty without knowing the answer.

For the next two hours, my mind raced. Could I have gone with Jim? What right did I have to involve anyone in my disaster? Ron would kill all three of us if he caught us. If he didn't find us, what would he do to my family?

I fought to calm myself by letting Randy hold my fingers and run me around the house numerous times before Ron came home. I slid the book deep inside the sofa, so if it was found it would appear that it was there long before we bought the second-hand couch. Should I tell Ron that a salesman came to the door? I left the brochure on the counter.

"You'll be proud of me," I told him when he dropped his keys on the end table and sat down. I hung back in the kitchen so he couldn't read my face. "I saved you one hundred twenty dollars. Some guy tried to sell us a set of encyclopedias."

"Yeah, I've seen those guys go door to door. Mom said they stopped at her house."

"Have you seen her lately? I know she wanted you to stop by after work."

We chatted a bit, and I turned our attention to Randy's walking, hoping Ron didn't notice my enigmatic face and shaky hands. I put Randy between us so we could roll his rubber ball to him. Ron seemed proud of Randy's abilities. He thought Randy would be a good football player, like his daddy.

Randy rewarded this attention with his favorite word: "Wuzdat?" He said it while pointing.

I answered, "That's a tree. That's a window. That's a clothes line. That's our front porch. That's a laundry basket. That's a fly." Then I pointed to his nose and said, "Wuzdat?"

He put his hand on his nose to be sure, and said "Nose!"

"Yes," I said, "That's Randy's nose! Where are Randy's eyes?" The moment passed.

For weeks I hoped that Jim would knock on my door again. I willed him to walk up those steps. This time I'd handle it differently. I'd talk him into it. He must go from town to town. We could live in his car. How could Ron find us if we were nomads? Maybe Ron wouldn't kill my family. Could I get away? Please, Jim, come back!

I had ruminated the same way a year earlier, when a nun stopped me on my way to the bank. She must have assumed I was fourteen years old, with a belly bigger than Santa Claus. She offered a home for pregnant girls. I told her I was married. I flushed crimson, and she was taken aback. We smiled at each other and walked on by.

What if I had gone with her? Surely Ron would not think of a Catholic girls' home. Would he have harmed my family? I wondered. I guessed and re-guessed.

CHAPTER 20 – TAMING FAILURE

We had just settled into the car, and I didn't see it coming. Suddenly my eye exploded and I screamed. I shifted Randy to the far side of my lap, shoving his head down in case another fist came flying our way. At first I didn't know if he hit Randy too, because Randy started wailing.

"I'm blind now. My God. I'm blind. It's my right eye! My only good eye." The realization felt like another blow. Would I ever see again? When I was four, doctors noticed I had a bad left eye. Since then I'd tried glasses and nothing had improved it. I was once told I might have *retinitis pigmentosa*. One doctor thought my mother had it and had probably passed it genetically to her children, however that diagnosis was not confirmed because multiple sclerosis caused visual deterioration also.

I waited for a moment, expecting another explosion, but it seemed Ron turned back and faced the windshield. I pulled Randy close to my chest and rubbed his little stiff arms. My eye wouldn't open more than a sliver. A mixture of water and sand seemed to be rolling around where my eyeball should be.

Ron started his Saab and slammed it in reverse, exiting his parking space at the Moundridge public park shelter, leaving my mother's family, the Schrags, behind. They were saying warm goodbyes to each other while joking about the evening chores awaiting them. For some reason the cows didn't understand that today was Sunday. The Schrags carried their picnic accoutrements to their vehicles, ending the 1969 picnic season.

Ron squealed tires, and the Saab flew into forward motion. We catapulted through side streets. Not slowing for intersections, we careened onto Highway 81. Though I couldn't see, I felt the force of the vehicle moving through space and time like a cannonball. Asking him to slow down might have riled him more. Any distraction could splat us across the highway. I heard Randy's cries over the sound of blood pounding in my ears.

Finally I said, "Ron, it will be OK. It's fine. I'm starting to see again."

I could open my eye enough to check the speedometer tilting on the wrong side of one hundred. When we hit a bump our heads smashed into the ceiling. Randy and I crashed into the door or into Ron when he turned. Sometimes the back of the car spun out, like sideways whiplash. With each new gulp of air, horror seeped into my lungs and defied breathing.

He screeched into our driveway, slammed the car door, and bounded into the house. I couldn't guess what he would do next. Would he come out with his knife and kill us? I gathered the casserole dishes we had taken to the park, the diaper bag, and toted Randy in my other arm. I put the items on the back porch and sat there holding Randy, rocking him on the top step, shaking and waiting. At least we wouldn't be in the Saab if Ron decided to go for another hellish drive.

Finally my tears came, streaming down on Randy, who by now had stopped crying and was playing with my long, straight hair, twisting it through his fingers. He couldn't speak more than a few words, yet he already knew something about terror.

I practiced pulling my eyelid up with my fingers until I could open it naturally. Though I commanded them, my limbs wouldn't move. The laundry wouldn't be taken off the line, diapers wouldn't be folded, and nothing would be scrounged for supper. I wouldn't go inside and check if the football game had calmed Ron.

I sat there and wrestled with my first full-fledged failure to prevent violence—the first one since the long, dark night. There had been scrapes, scary moments, demands for sex, and profound control, but this was the first complete setback.

I knew what the trigger had been: I was not quite compliant enough. I made one moderate statement that could have implied something less than complimentary about him. One statement. I said I wasn't the only person who could have kept an eye on Randy.

I bet he felt justified. Hadn't he told me to watch Randy better? Hadn't I promised to obey him in our wedding vows? Hadn't I let Randy crawl underfoot when tables were being moved? Didn't Randy have a bruise on his arm because of it? After all, Ron worked all day and what did I do but hang around at home with a baby and collect rent for Mr. Pinrod's boarding house? A little cleaning and a little cooking—nothing that any dumb broad wouldn't do.

I walked on eggshells for the next few days. I heard a knock while sitting on the couch, popped springs unevenly squeezing beneath me. Randy, attached to my right breast, complained briefly as I shifted him over my left shoulder to burp. Pushing a pacifier in his mouth, I re-hooked my wet bra cup with a soaked pad still in it. I twisted the old cut-glass doorknob, noticing again its rough edges smoothed over time.

I expected to see Dad as I swung open the heavy wooden door, but I was faced with two six-foot men towering above me—Uncle Harley and Dad. They shared the Stucky trademark, a downward slant to the outer side of their eyes, casting an appearance of thoughtful sadness even upon smiling faces, though their smiles faded as they zeroed in on my only functional eye, now puffy and bruised.

Heat spread through my face like an oxygen-deprived fire now blasted with air. Last night I had sworn to myself I would tell Dad everything if he came. But now? How could I convert centuries of Swiss-German stoic silences into gushing, shameful verbiage in front of both of them?

My knees shook. Randy burped in response to the vibrations. I faced the wooden floor planks and waved Dad and Uncle Harley inside. Dad brought Uncle Harley with him to show off his first grandchild. They both marveled at the little blue-eyed, angel-faced blond, but their pride sagged and their awe-inspired tones rang hollow.

I offered them both extra pillows to cushion the unruly sofa springs, but they declined. They wouldn't seek comfort while I was obviously miserable. "I resolved to tell you this time," I said, jumping ahead of their questions. "Anyway, how could I hide?"

"That's a pretty nasty shiner," Dad said.

I nodded. "It happened Sunday, right after the gathering. You know how the stacked table slipped and bruised Randy. Ron berated me in front of everyone. I grabbed Randy and walked around outside, and he was all right. I thought Ron was over his anger. Well, he wasn't."

"You mean this happened Sunday?" he said, pointing to my eye.

I explained how I didn't see his fist coming, my eye exploded, and Ron's driving could have killed us all.

The silence among us evaporated after an extensive yearning for words. "That should not have happened," Dad pronounced. His three-hundred-pound frame slumped against the couch's side arm. His usually red cheeks were now a deep purple. "I think I should talk with Ron. He has to know this is unacceptable. I don't know if it will help. But I have to try."

"If you do, be careful," I said, patting Randy's back and listening for a slow breathing pattern that signaled sleep. "He's apt to take it out on me. Anything you say he'll blame on me. I don't want a repeat performance."

"He usually listens to me. I'll be careful. But I think we need to have a talk."

"He seemed to be in a better mood when he left for work this morning. When will you catch him?"

"Maybe you two could come to the farm Sunday afternoon. We'll do some chores together. I think he's more receptive when we're working together."

My stomach clutched with rage. My life as a farmhand, doing a man's work, had vanished. Somehow I had become a mere female in a world of men who chose, decided, and acted. Ron would have the privilege of helping Dad. He would do my job. I'd have to be in the house taking care of Randy, cooking some hamburgers, and washing dishes. All the time I'd be worrying that Ron was getting mad and would kill us driving home. He wouldn't show it with Dad, but who knew what he'd do to Randy and me?

Sighing, I said, "I guess we can try that. I don't know if he'll be willing to come. I'll have to tell him you were here today. Otherwise he won't come, because he won't want you to see my black eye. I'll have to tell him that I told you the whole story. I hope that doesn't make him too furious."

"Maybe it will slow him down a bit, knowing he has to face me."

"I don't know. I'll try to keep him calm when I tell him."

Uncle Harley's face seemed buried in a dark mist, clouded with surprise and dismay. He saved his comments for a later discussion with Dad.

On the front porch I gave Dad a hug, saying I was sorry to be a problem. He reassured me it wasn't my fault, but we both knew I was the stain on the family name, what remained of it. I was not the only Stucky girl to have experienced raw shame, but I was the only one in the Carl J. Stucky family. I was the loser who got pregnant before she married. Now I confessed in front of Uncle Harley that I had married a monster. Uncle Harley—a pillar of the community, a college dean, a person who wrote books heralding our Mennonite heritage!

I envisioned what Uncle Harley might say to his brother as they shoved into the Buick and drove off. Harley would probably remind Dad that he shouldn't have allowed his daughter to hang out with that low-class kid from a troublesome family. He sure shouldn't have hired him as a farm hand. That had given him too much access to his daughter. Or maybe Harley would keep his mouth shut, knowing that his brother Carl was already overwhelmed and deeply distressed. The damage was already done.

Exhausted, I carried Randy to my bed and rested with him. I felt unreal, like I'd imagined my existence. I'd spoken, but my words were empty, like a thunderstorm that gathered clouds, sputtered winds, and flashed lightning but produced no rain. A hollow echo chimed in my sleepy brain: *you are not who you used to be.* But was I ever who I used to be? I wasn't the boy, the one whose name mattered, the one who would keep the farm productive, the one who would go to college and find his way in the world. If I died, not much would be lost. Poor Randy would have no one, but now he only had an unskilled, fat mama who was swallowed in a sea of darkness. Too tired to think, I closed my eyes and imagined that once I had been real. Once I had been loved.

Chapter 21 - BOSTON: A BEGINNING

Fear gripped me as we drove to the farm the next Sunday, but Dad's way of easing while pressuring enabled Ron to understand. Ron seemed calm on our drive home, though he didn't mention the discussion. However, the effects of the come-to-Jesus meeting were fleeting.

Several weeks later he came home late. He'd been at fault in an accident. In addition to the damage to his car, we were obliged to pay for the other driver's repairs because Ron wouldn't purchase insurance for his Saab. He knew I felt differently, but he insisted his family didn't waste money that way.

I said I was glad no one was hurt, but he noticed the steam escaping my ears and dollar signs flashing before my eyes. He screamed in my face, "You don't have to make the problem worse!" He pushed me backward and I landed hard. I shut my mouth and focused downward. I waited for him to occupy himself with the TV before rising. I was furious! I wanted to rip him apart, but I feigned a vague serenity.

When Ron arrived home early one afternoon to say he got fired, I struggled to quiet my panic and fury. How would we survive? If I said anything or allowed judgment to register on my face, he might explode.

After several days of reassuring him, I convinced him to leave Kansas. A little over a year from my wedding, my sister, Debbie, married a local boy, now a student at Harvard. She surprised her family with this opportunity to leave the farm and move toward a brighter future in Boston, but her gregarious personality made the transition work. Deb and Keith were happy in Boston. I reasoned that Ron and I could make a new start there, too. He could find a job without the firing episode following him.

Privately I clung to the thought that without his parents aggravating him, some maturation and improvement might occur. I also harbored an unspoken hope of divorcing Ron. Of course, the sin of divorce was second only to the sin of pregnancy before marriage. If I could ever escape, it would be best to divorce in a non-Mennonite world—one where Ron would be far from harming my family.

Arriving in Harvard Square, I was startled at the traffic coming at us from all sides, and I couldn't imagine how Ron would navigate the intersections. People looked strange and intriguing here, with long hair, beards, faded clothes, and leather sandals. Who were these people? I wanted to talk with all of them, to find out more. What an exciting new world!

With much gratitude I accepted Deb's and Keith's generous offer to share their apartment for a couple of weeks until Ron found a job. I didn't know how we would have left Kansas without my sister's assistance.

We found a workable situation. I would be a maid and babysitter for a couple who worked at Brandeis University; and Ron would be a janitor there. We moved into an apartment above the couple's garage in Wellesley and propped up hopes for a new life.

I managed the stresses of being a part-time maid and babysitter in a world I could not have conjured. I was utterly astonished every time I entered the home of my employers. The Barnabils had antiques and fashionable accoutrements, a house the size of a mansion, and a yard and lifestyle that seemed better than ideal. I felt fortunate that they seemed to like me. Their girls were delightful.

Nevertheless, I sometimes felt like a failure at my new work. I ruined Cathie's hand-knitted wool sweater in their washing machine; I couldn't fathom anyone using non-washable children's clothing. There were other issues. Randy was entering his biting phase. Containing him when the Barnabil children came home from school demanded serious focus. As much as possible, I preoccupied him with other activities.

Mr. and Mrs. Barnabil felt stressed and angry sometimes, but I didn't understand why. They possessed more belongings than I thought was possible to desire. They even had a second home on Cape Cod, which they generously let us use several weekends. At Christmastime I heard them unhappily discussing why some family members didn't call and let them know the time they would arrive. Mrs. Barnabil simmered a delicious lamb stew. The house radiated Christmas cheer. Why would they need to know the arrival time? If my family could visit me, I wouldn't care if they arrived ten days late. I longed to see them.

Chapter 22 - FLIGHT

By mid-winter Ron's fearsome intensity manifested regularly on Friday evenings. He took us to drive-in terror movies that I couldn't watch. On the way home, he pretended to be the chainsaw murderer or the monster killer. Sleep eluded me after these menacing evenings; his pretense was far too real. I feared Ron deeply and couldn't dispel images of him with glazed eyes, determined, with a butcher knife raised high.

He wouldn't settle for soothing, and he hit me more frequently. The day after a particularly difficult beating, I called Dad, dizzy with dead ends. He must have sensed the desperation in my voice because he immediately offered to pay for a plane ticket home.

As a novice airline passenger, I entered Boston's Logan Airport with Randy and several bags in my arms, asking questions. In which line should I stand? Which of these planes is ours? Where will we board? What is an airplane gate? (I pictured our beat-up barnyard gate.) How will I know what seat to sit in? Can I sit in this section to wait for the plane? Is this the plane that goes to Wichita? Why Chicago? I thought the clerk said Wichita! How will I know which gate to find in Chicago? Are there bathrooms on this plane?

We navigated the planes correctly, but the last stair-step landing further agitated my frayed nerves and upset stomach.

I threw up in a paper bag, while Randy threw up on me. Aunt Ruby picked us up at the airport and drove us to the farm.

Dad and I laughed about my naïve airplane shenanigans before I impressed upon him the whole nightmare of Ron's control and abuse. I no longer felt obligated, as Ron's wife, to protect his image with my father. I explained that I wanted desperately to find a permanent way out but was terrified of three things: Ron could discover my plans and kill me or even Randy and me. Ron might find me after I left and then kill me or us. If Ron couldn't find me, he might come back to Kansas and kill my whole family, as he threatened. Dad thought he could talk Ron down if he came to the farm in a murderous state. I hoped he was right, but Dad had never seen this side of Ron firsthand. He had no clue how irrational Ron could be.

Ron called that night in a panic, apologizing profusely but also stating that if I didn't go back, he would come get me. He guaranteed I'd be sorry if that happened. I said I was too fearful after the last beating. Ron promised peaceful bliss. He would ask Jesus to help him control himself. I knew that dog don't hunt, but I agreed to come back to prevent whatever holocaust would follow his drive to Kansas.

Relieved that his crisis was over, he was still apologetic when he picked us up at Logan. He promised a honeymoon night when we got home. Unstated sarcasm twisted my brain.

Two evenings after I returned, Ron sent me flying toward the bathtub, knocking my head against the side. I passed out and awakened to Randy's cries. He had been sitting on his potty chair and witnessed the violence. His wide eyes were reddening and his sweet face was contorted in fear. I rushed to comfort him, saying I was OK, though that was only a guess. If I had a concussion, it wouldn't be treated. I felt like a prisoner held in shark-infested waters, with a chain and anchor weighing me down.

In late March 1971, Randy was two years old, and I was twenty. We'd lived in Boston for seven months. I didn't see how we would make it through another five months to my twenty-first birthday. My life was a shambles. Being a maid was challenging. I was so bone-tired that the "less" in hopeless depicted the despair of my soul.

When fear and hope battled for the upper hand, my thoughts disconnected and fell into a tangled web like clipped bailing wire. With no clear purpose in mind, I began furtively collecting whatever coins I found in the pockets of Ron's dirty jeans and whatever money I could siphon off after paying bills. I hid it under the carpet in the hallway, knowing if Ron found my stash he'd assume I was saving to escape and would kill me, probably by torture and dismemberment.

Then one morning before I left for work, the radio mentioned a hotline for people with family problems. I called, saying I was in a violent marriage. They recommended I see a social worker, and I made the appointment for a week later, during Ron's work hours and before mine began. Randy and I used the stashed money for cab fare to the counselor's office.

Mrs. Mitchell, an experienced, older professional woman, put me at ease with her kindly face and cheerful demeanor. I poured out my heart. Unlike Ron's mother, she didn't think I was lying. Unlike the police, doctors, and other professionals I had sought help from, she knew that men like Ron existed in the world. Even my father could not wholly grasp the threat Ron posed; no one in the Mennonite community could.

In no uncertain terms she said I must leave very soon or I would be murdered—and she would help me. She would call the welfare office and get immediate coverage. She would find a place for me to stay and would pick me up Friday morning at my apartment, before Ron's lunch hour, in case he became suspicious and drove home.

After he left for work that Friday, I hurriedly packed an old suitcase for Randy's clothes and another for mine. Mrs. Mitchell arrived as planned to take us to our placement, a room in the home of a woman named Maggie. She explained while she drove that a social worker from the public assistance office would call me soon and that they would pay my rent. As she was advising me to set regular counseling sessions as soon as I had settled, I saw Ron's car pass us, going in the opposite direction. Indeed, he had suspected something—and it was still mid-morning.

PART IV - WRESTING FREEDOM

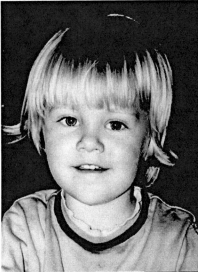

*Randy, age
two-and-a-half*

*Dad and Mom
in Moundridge*

Chapter 23 - PUBLIC ASSISTANCE

Maggie's three boys, curious and interested, welcomed our intrusion into the Wellesley house she and her ex owned. She was a welfare mom, too, in her mid-thirties. Mrs. Mitchell explained that I was in hiding from an abusive husband and would need to keep a low profile. Would Maggie be willing to purchase groceries for me for the first week or two? I would have the public assistance check to pay her back in a few days.

To mitigate the danger surrounding me, I assured them that Ron would be on the road back to Kansas in a couple of days, since he'd assume that Randy and I went home. Maggie let me borrow her phone and pay back the long-distance charges so I could forewarn Dad that Ron would be there soon. I told him Randy and I were safe, that a kind social worker was helping. Dad sighed heavily and said he was so thankful that I found a way out and reassured me that he'd do his best to handle Ron if he showed up on the farm.

I felt shaky and elated. What good fortune! We'd be home free if Ron left my family alone. Only a handful of people knew my whereabouts. We even convinced the public welfare department not to contact Ron for payment, so our location could remain secret.

Wow! Things were working out. We had money coming. A place to stay. We'd met some nice people already. What I had desperately craved for five years was finally coming true, practically overnight. We were still alive! I hugged Randy like I wouldn't let go and told him that we must make the best of this incredible gift. But the fear didn't leave. I thought incessantly, *If only Ron doesn't attack my family.*

Dropping thirty pounds would be a good start at a new life. I concocted a strict diet and exercise program and did it, did it, did it. Maggie offered nutritional advice. After numerous challenges to compete with specific exercises, her boys gave up—they couldn't come *close* to 137 sit-ups! We ran races in their yard. I told them about carrying bales of hay and buckets of water. We watched movies on TV together. Maggie let me listen repeatedly to her *Jesus Christ Superstar* album, especially when she was not home. Mary Magdalene's song, "I Don't Know How to Love Him," captivated me—she was a sexually sinful woman; Jesus was *just a man.*

In our furnished room, Randy and I rolled a big ball to each other and slept in a double bed. I read him stories from hand-me-down books Maggie's sons had outgrown. After my first counseling session, Mrs. Mitchell encouraged us to forage through some donated clothes and toys. Randy, his eyes as big as mine, selected a little truck and several plastic animals, for free! I found a blouse and sweater that would probably fit—if not now, then after I lost another five pounds. After clinging at first, Randy adjusted quickly, showing no sign of missing Ron. We both felt more lighthearted and happy.

I asked Mrs. Mitchell if college was possible. She knew of no option, but she encouraged me. I called organizations and state agencies, looking for loans or scholarships. Several people suggested the state's Vocational Rehabilitation offices. That made no sense, but I followed their instructions and obtained an appointment six weeks away. I sought other resources while waiting.

The friendly rehab counselor had a genuine interest in assisting. He asked if I had health problems. *None.* He asked if I was on any medication. *Only thyroid and birth control pills.* Why thyroid pills? I explained the removal surgery when I was four years old. He suggested I think closely about any other possible medical problems and said I should consider each aspect of my body individually: arms, legs, internal organs, eyes, nose, head, everything.

Something sparked in me when he mentioned eyes. As soon as I said "basically blind in one eye" and "retinitis pigmentosa," his face lit up.

"Bingo," he said. "You'll have to undergo tests with our doctors. If you have a true disability, the state may help with your education. If our doctors agree that you have a disability, we'll test you psychologically and administer an IQ test to see if you have the ability to make use of an education."

"How soon can I be tested?"

"Don't jump to conclusions. The wrong answer at any juncture would halt the process."

"I can't help but get my hopes up. I really, really, really want to go to college! I don't know if I'm smart enough, but I would try my hardest."

"You sure have the spirit."

"If you can help me get there, I'll make it work, even if it takes my last breath."

"I'll put you in the system for testing. Call me in several days. I'll tell you if I was able to schedule your ophthalmology appointment."

I jumped out of the chair. "Thank you so much!" I said, shaking his hand. I wished I could pull him closer and kiss his cheek. He was my hero!

I skipped to the subway. Without a station close, it was a tricky business to get to Maggie's Wellesley home. Sometimes I was able to transfer to a bus and walked a distance. Sometimes I had to hitchhike. Money for a cab was out of the question.

Aside from college, figuring out the world—the real world—topped my agenda. Kids were demonstrating against the Vietnam War. I'd always been against it. But now I wondered, who were these people marching? Could they affect government policies? What about free love? Who said it should be free? Orgies—really? For average people, or just weird people? Communes? Were they for people who like to share?

My personal habits also came into question. My long, straight hair seemed OK, but what kind of clothes did kids my age wear? What was all this about LSD, speed, and grass? I felt like my son when he was one year old, pointing to everything, asking, "Wuzdat?" Maggie, shocked that I hadn't tasted alcohol, suggested I try, especially in the safety of her home. I could handle mixed drinks, but diet and budget prohibited drinking much. Maggie took in another renter, a spaced-out girl who'd used too much LSD. I vowed to avoid that stuff.

Maggie brought me to Parents without Partners events. I was by far the youngest. I became friendly with a man I met there, who was older and wiser. When I was with him I was no longer Ron's property. The relationship budded, but didn't flower.

I was astonished to find that people made few judgments about sexual behavior. While others might not judge, I did. Even though new sexual experiences helped remove the sense of Ron's ownership of my body, I gravitated toward abstinence. I guessed some kind of relationship would be important for me, but I couldn't decide what was OK, what underpinning would ground my decisions. How did one decide without predetermined beliefs?

I approached the counter with my thyroid prescription and showed my card.

"Oh, you, too? You're on welfare?" The pharmacist glared disapproval.

I shuddered to think that everyone behind me heard him and was eying me coldly. I looked young and in good health. They must be thinking, "Lazy, lazy, lazy!" I nodded my head.

"They haven't paid us in months. I swear, we're going to stop accepting these cards. We'll fill your prescription now, but I won't guarantee that we'll refill it. You'll need to find a different pharmacy."

"Is there another one close? I have to walk," I said, flinching.

"It's just a few miles down the road. Straight down the highway."

I shifted my weight from foot to foot. I'd like to pin this man's neck in a cow stall and let him squirm. How many public assistance cards did a prosperous Wellesley pharmacy take? I would die without thyroid pills. He'd rather possess his slick Mercedes Benz than care about poor people. My hot cheeks glowed like morning sun.

He presented the pill bottle and returned the card. I grabbed the package and stampeded the glass door.

It was a frustrating turtle crawl through time to wait for the ophthalmology appointment, and a snail's journey to get results. Would the doctor consider my eyes diseased? Am I hoping for blindness somewhere in the future? Was that my ticket to college? When I finally visited the state's ophthalmologist, I searched for a signal. Definitely something was amiss with my vision. He said little and offered no clues. Several weeks later I received a letter saying I should make an appointment with a particular psychologist who would assess my IQ and psychological readiness. This would take an entire day. Apparently my eye dysfunction met their qualifications. Randy and I celebrated with an ice cream cone at Friendly's.

I asked at Parents without Partners whether I could study for these IQ tests. They shook their heads. I worried I was not college material, as my high-school counselor had pronounced. If the psychologist agreed, I'd have to accept it or find a way to prove them both wrong.

Maggie thought I should wear jeans to the interview. I'd look like a normal college-bound twenty-year-old kid. I wondered if I should wear my dress to show respect for the psychologist. After all, he could cinch my whole future.

Dad telephoned in a dispirited voice. Mom had had a stroke. If she lived, she'd have even more difficulty feeding herself. Dot and Butch actively farmed and managed the household. Before Mom had her stroke, whenever she asked for something, Lynnie and Carla would respond. They crawled up in her hospital bed at home and snuggled with her. They watched her when Dad, Dot, and Butch were out working. Many times they lifted her, placed the bed pan, and cleaned up afterward. But after this stroke, Mom might not be able to pronounce words clearly enough for them to understand her, no matter how many times they asked her to repeat.

Dad hoped I was making it OK. I told him about the slight possibility of going to college, Randy adjusting to our new place, and using the whole house.

"Thank goodness you found a way out," he said. "Maybe things can get better now. Ron hasn't come to the house when we're home, but he comes when we're out. He sifts through papers. When he gives up on finding your address, he'll probably come talk to me."

"I hope he never, ever hurts you guys!"

We were both silent until I asked, "What should I do for you if Mom dies?"

"Leona, there's nothing you can do. Even if you could afford to come here, it wouldn't be safe."

"Please tell Mom I love her. I'll be thinking of her."

I felt odd, like I urgently needed to do *something*. It would be awful if Mom died—and maybe if she didn't. Would the relief of death be greater than the loss? Dad loved her. They looked at each other and they both knew they had that kind of love.

I started babysitting and saving a few dollars here and there for an emergency trip to Kansas, should the situation become safe. Surely Ron would give up on finding me and would fall in love with someone else. Though I'd pity her, I'd be free from the need to hide. Then I could divorce him, after a two-year Massachusetts' residency requirement, and finish off this chapter.

Mrs. Mitchell engaged, guided, and reassured me in our weekly appointments. She took pride in my progress. We appreciated each other. She gave me several small treasures from the donation stash and one from her own home: small glass pitchers. I showed Maggie and placed them neatly on the dresser. Besides clothing, I owned these two decorations. I'd always treasure them.

Allowing extra time for subway mess-ups, I arrived twenty minutes early for the exams, nervous and clammy. Dr. Brown's lovely leather furniture, plush wall-to-wall carpet, stylish lamps and magazines matched his refined, courteous demeanor.

He gave instructions and settled me in an office. I began the IQ tests. He checked in periodically. I hurried through the questions but seldom had time for review. We took an hour lunch break.

The psychological tests started in the afternoon. So far as I could assess, I was answering OK—until he asked open-ended questions. I invented stories for his pictures. Emotion lacerated me. When I saw a young man in the picture, I thought he would hurt someone. I couldn't get those crazy thoughts out of my mind, but Dr. Brown insisted I give my first impression. My stories horrified me, and I feared I was not presenting college material to this psychologist. When I broke down sobbing, Dr. Brown stopped the testing.

He asked what I was experiencing. I told him the truth. I pleaded for the testing to continue. Failing the test would be a nightmare. He said it was best not to test when it evoked trauma. I said I'd experienced traumas in much worse ways before. I'd get over this emotional reaction soon. I'd be fine if he kept testing. He said he didn't need to do the rest of the test.

I left his office, furious with myself. I stepped into the street without checking the light, and a passing car honked. Disoriented, I looked for street signs and guessed at directions. I'd blown my one chance to go to college because of some goddamned tears! Why didn't I abandon this "trauma," as Dr. Brown calls it? I was free of it and yet I couldn't let it go. It was in my past, right?

I dragged myself up the hill to Maggie's house. Randy looked up from his bowl on the kitchen table with pudding splashed across his cheeks and a grimy troll in his hand. I kissed his forehead. At least I capably registered gratitude that Maggie watched Randy for me. I would watch her kids some evening so she could go out.

Maggie read my face. After telling her the details, she didn't think I completely blundered. "A psychologist ought to be able to understand your predicament."

Still feeling like a failure, I welcomed the day ending. Bedtime came none too early. I held Randy close. He ruffled his little fingers around my ear while I told him a happy farm story, and I fell asleep remembering the smell of hay and sound of lambs bleating.

Mrs. Mitchell agreed that I judged myself too harshly. She thought it appropriate for the psychologist to stop the test in those circumstances. It didn't necessarily mean I failed. I should give myself some credit for a good effort, even if I have rough spots in my story.

"Rough spots? Isn't that a bit of an understatement?"

Still, she kindled a hope that sustained me. A few weeks later, the letter came. I picked it up and set it back down on the kitchen table five times before I forced myself to open it. Then I made myself read it, and instantly I jumped up and danced around the kitchen. *Oh my God! I passed it! I get to go to college! I'm approved for the next step! Oh my God!* I didn't understand that psychologist. Maybe he decided to be merciful.

I showed Maggie. I picked Randy up and twirled him around and around, my bell-bottoms flapping in the fray. His giggle was the music we danced to. I hugged him so tight we almost forgot to breathe. I felt expansive, like a wild horse discovering a new meadow. I called Vocational Rehabilitation, asking what to do next.

A flood of pleasant childhood memories enticed me to believe this avalanche of good fortune was bound to happen, that it was as natural as summer harvest when you'd planted winter wheat. I remembered the summer of my tenth grade when I tried to read Dostoyevsky's *Crime and Punishment* and discovered it was Dad's favorite book. And how Mrs. Graber, the Moundridge High School librarian, looked up at me in amazement when I checked out *The History of the Decline and Fall of the Roman Empire, Volume I,* and she noticed that the last person who checked out that book was my own father, twenty-five years earlier.

I found myself identifying with the good fortune of Grandma and Grandpa Stucky—how Grandma Stucky stashed boxes and boxes of clothes they bought new at J. C. Penney's, Hogan's or Litwin's stores in Newton, to ship to impoverished families in Africa or other parts of the developing world. They had plenty to share and they dispersed wisely. I remembered singing our hymn—*Gott ist die Liebe*—with Grandpa playing the harmonica. How my cousins and siblings and I scattered with effervescent anticipation into the pasture or the barnyard and chased rabbits or hypnotized chickens or played gray-wolf.

My lucky break released memory after memory. The Smoky River flashed through my mind—those days when Dad relented about farm work and we joined uncles, cousins, and friends. The kids waded and played water tag while the men poked through underwater brush, bringing up forty-pound catfish that chewed their hands raw. Proud of their bravery, we bellowed Tarzan sounds.

I recalled the day I caught a bunny. Disking a field on the Saturday before Easter, I jammed the tractor into neutral and flew off the machine, landing close to the bunny. Beaming with anticipation, I took it home to Lynnie and Carla for Easter. They adored their little present, and Mom let them hold it while they sat on her lap.

The memory of a little note a judge wrote to me regarding my song in a third-grade singing contest floated up to me. He said that anyone who heard my voice would fall in love with me. That day I skipped down the driveway singing "Twinkle, Twinkle, Little Star," waving a sprig of wild oats, believing I had magical powers and a coveted future. The note from Vocational Rehab made me feel just about the same way.

That night I replayed these memories and more. I went to sleep holding little Randy, his hand still clutching the paper basket we made together.

Chapter 24 - COLLEGE-BOUND

In late August 1971 I turned twenty-one, and the Vocational Rehabilitation people said I could select a college that would admit me. They would process the paperwork by next semester or next year. Painfully aware that I was several years behind my age group, and not wanting to remain on welfare any longer than I had to, I pleaded to start the earlier semester if I could find a college that would take me. They agreed to speed up their process, but they made no promises. Mostly they assumed I couldn't be admitted to colleges that late in the season. Much to my amazement, a number of institutions responded favorably to my application. I ruled out Wellesley, because it was not easily accessible by public transportation, and I thought I'd fit in like a coyote in a pen of sheep. Radcliffe said if I waited a semester they could take me. Boston College agreed to the coming semester, as did Northeastern and Simmons. I must decide quickly.

While riding the subway between schools, I assessed the various brochures like a child unwrapping gifts. An elderly woman in the next seat asked if I was deciding which college to attend. I told her about my options. She offered advice: Boston College was clearly the best school.

"If it's the best, I'll go there."

I was not allowed to live in the dorms with a child, so I answered an ad. Brenda, another welfare mother, wanted a roommate. We talked. She found an affordable apartment in Charlestown, and we rented it. Seeking a community that would fit me better than Wellesley, one with public transportation and other poor people, I was delighted to be in another world with Brenda. And Randy inherited a playmate, her son, Daniel, who was a year younger.

Now I needed to find a babysitter for Randy—someone who'd be willing to take a public-aid stipend. Debbie, my sister, agreed. She lived within a mile of my new apartment. With an hour-and-a-half lead time, I could drop Randy off and make it to BC. I would walk Randy to her house, his hand clasped in mine, then walk to Sullivan Station, make one transfer to the green line, and be on campus!

Just as I had no idea how to prepare myself for these big changes, I had no idea how to help Randy with the adjustment of losing his mama for the day. As his large, round eyes looked up at me with spaghetti-smeared cheeks, I told him that if I go to college, we would someday be better off—that it might be hard now, but it would pay off in the end.

Brenda, Daniel, and Randy—the latter two chasing each other across sidewalks into grass and hiding behind our legs—came with me for registration and to buy my books. We all gawked at the manicured lawns, the spacious commons, and the colossal Gothic buildings. It was definitely a new world for me.

Not only did Vocational Rehab pay for my education, they also bought my books. That little fact was a lifesaver. Just the cost of the books alone would have prohibited my education. I purchased a Smith-Corona typewriter. I ran my fingers over the keys, completely impressed and grateful. I now owned something of value. I nearly failed typing in high school, but now that I owned a typewriter, I'd practice and learn.

CHAPTER 25 - MY FIRST SEMESTER

Brenda and I furnished our apartment with things we collected off the street on garbage days. If we found something that suited us, we toted it home; depending on the size of the object, this feat could be tricky without a vehicle. Sometimes Brenda's ex-husband helped with his Dodge. I cut corners to save money. We used all our government surplus food. The big can of pork tasted pretty good over their rice.

Since we ran out of money before we could purchase a used refrigerator, we walked to some nearby shops and inquired if anyone had an old refrigerator they no longer wanted. Almost like magic, we actually found one and the owner was willing to truck it up to our apartment. With glee in our steps, we skipped back home. Now we could keep milk for the kids!

One day, coming home on the subway from school with my hands full of books and a lamp I picked up along the way, a young man exited at Sullivan Station with me and asked which direction I was going. He was heading that way, too. He'd be happy to help me carry my load. We conversed and laughed as we trudged up the hill to my apartment. He seemed intelligent and handsome.

Dennis helped me lug the items into the apartment as I called for Brenda. Oddly, she wasn't home. We continued talking for a short while. When I said I soon must pick up my son, he suddenly shifted his talk to brutality. He was a fighter. He had hurt people before. He always carried a knife, which he pulled out of his pocket. A cold shiver wired the hairs on my spine as I stared at the blade.

"I want sex right now. I don't want to have to force you. I think you're attracted to me."

I turned white as panic ignited my mind. I was new to this neighborhood. I doubted anyone would come if I screamed. The doors and windows were closed. He was six feet and I was five. If I could escape, I couldn't outrun him or fight him off. How could this be happening again? But it was, and it did.

As soon as he left, I ran to the bathroom and threw up. Nothing helped. Taking a shower didn't clean me. I reran the calamity a thousand different ways. Should I have figured out he was a rapist? What could I have done differently? If I had just thanked him at the door and not let him in, would that have stopped him? With each rerun I felt more inept and stupid. And irredeemable. My eyes yearned to sink below my cheekbone and stay closed.

Wearily, I walked to my sister's house and retrieved Randy. He must have sensed my despair, because hugs were not enough. He wanted to be carried home.

When Brenda returned home, I spilled it, thankful to have a friend who would understand. We repeatedly checked each window through a tiny slit in our curtains. We stared into the dark alleyway, combed our street and sidewalk, and locked and relocked our doors.

I felt hideous. What was it about me that attracted rapists? What was it? Why couldn't I find a decent male human being? Fear and repulsion persistently pumped waves of chemistry through my body until I finally sobbed myself to sleep shortly before dawn.

I stopped seeing Mrs. Mitchell, as I no longer could get to her office using public transportation. I missed her tremendously. A counselor at Boston College, Dr. Joseph Shepherd, took over. He understood that I was not the typical student. I loved my classes and felt honored to have the opportunity to learn, but I had no clue about how to relate to the kids at BC. Students in my class were almost all straight out of high school. Apparently only one other person was married with a baby, and she had money behind her. Almost the whole class was Catholic.

"I didn't realize I was joining such a Catholic institution. I want classes not taught by priests. I've had enough religion for more than a lifetime." I was unaware that the man to whom I was speaking was likely a Jesuit priest. He was not wearing a robe.

"I'm sure you have reasons for wanting distance from religion. Can you tell me how you arrived at your current feelings about faith?" Dr. Shepherd asked.

I laughed out loud. "You have no idea what you are asking." He didn't laugh, and mine faded quickly. I hesitantly told him my religious saga, which was virtually my whole life's story, during our next few sessions. He listened kindly and did not disagree with my assessments. He also thought it would be unwise for me to re-traumatize myself with courses taught by priests. I was uncertain if his advice was more about protecting them or me.

The subway route engraved itself in my mind. After a number of trips, I could relax enough to sometimes doze off yet still wake up right as the train pulled into Haymarket Square, Sullivan Station, or the stop at Boston College. I made my way to classes, excited to hear the next theory, a new insight, or a thought that I would not have otherwise entertained. Several students commented that I was always smiling. They didn't know I was living a dream-come-true.

My mind was full of homework, due dates, courses I was in, or courses I might take. I was mesmerized by the students. Some were brave; they took a strong stand against the war. They knew about politics and famous thinkers. Most of the names, dates, and places were new to me.

Students complained that their parents wanted them home for Thanksgiving, that their *superficial* parents, as they said, would expect them to attend mass. How, they asked, could they tell their parents they no longer believed those silly rituals? Their parents had no idea who they really were, and if they did, they'd be kicked out. Proud of their imperiled status, the students used a little grass to blunt these rejection fantasies.

I didn't miss a class at school. Each one was a challenge. Admitted into the college of education, I took four basic requirement classes: rhetoric and literary forms, Europe since 1500, effective oral communication, and introductory sociology. Each new lecture elicited the wide-eyed exuberance one might expect from a foreign visitor.

But it wasn't a cakewalk. Hardly remembering a lesson from my high-school years, I was deluged with unfamiliar information. I re-read textbook paragraphs two or three times. The words and data swarmed toward me like flies to a sweaty horse. They stung, stuck around for a bit, and flew away. In patches, I seized meaning, and the rest whirled in my head.

Literature class offered a reprieve. We read contemporary authors who wrote about real-world circumstances. Classroom discussions focused on characters and contexts. My experiences and three years past age eighteen grounded a keen understanding. Fortunately, this class lasted for an entire year. I articulated opinions and character analyses that sounded intelligent.

With effort, I was managing good grades. My papers were accepted and praised. I passed tests. Perhaps I was smarter than I thought.

Randy, two-and-a-half, fended for himself more and more. He was strong, with a supple body and buoyant spirit, a capable climber, talked in sentences, and was completely adorable with a blond bowl cut and his quick, searching gaze. He played easily with Daniel and the neighborhood kids. While my mind was preoccupied, I wanted him to be happy and busy with his own creative projects. He was a fairly contented child, but he wanted more of me than I consistently gave. Reading about Summerhill's free-flowing learning environment for my education class reinforced my non-interventionist policy; I encouraged Randy to do whatever he seemed capable of doing and assisted when trouble erupted. He squeezed snakes, balls, and pancakes out of the homemade clay we invented. The kitchen floor doubled as a makeshift table, but, no-no-no, not the covers on his bed.

For reasons I didn't understand, my relationship with my sister broke, and she stopped babysitting Randy. She complained that welfare wasn't paying her on a timely basis. I implored my social worker. She assured me that Debbie would be paid, but I couldn't ask Debbie to reconsider. I searched for an alternative and was elated to find a competent daycare center that offered a loving approach and accepted a public-aid stipend. We used the welfare taxi system to transport Randy to and from the center. He made a smooth transition to this new environment.

Someone (*who?*) reported me to child protective services. More focused on school than on mothering, I apparently did not accomplish what unencumbered and wise mothers would. The investigators didn't find a problem, but they wanted me to take some child development classes at school. Humiliated, I resolved to improve.

Once again bridging two different worlds, I didn't fit either. By day I was a college student with little in common with other students. I didn't participate in campus events, the dorm experience, or extracurricular life because I had a child at home. By night I was a welfare mom, living in a drab apartment with another welfare mom who didn't share my daytime world. Homework and mothering duties often made me unbefitting company.

Still, Brenda and I attempted a social life together. We sometimes went out with her pocket of friends. When they showed up at the apartment, Brenda and I used marijuana with the rest of the group, comfortably relaxing into spacious nothingness. We giggled, told stories, talked about our altered state, ate junk, and slept. I began dating one guy in this group. He smoked pot daily. He was kind and had a job and a vehicle. We saw each other infrequently. While a company of friends was a relief that uplifted, probably none of us would scratch each other's deepest itch. Similar to high-school friendships, I was grateful for inclusion and I fleetingly invested.

On rare occasions Brenda and I negotiated with her sister to babysit so we could paint the town, drink sloe gin fizzes, and enjoy the bar scene common to kids our age. Our nights out were fun and inexpensive. They didn't result in real dates, but we laughed at our attempts—our "wild and free" rush against routine.

Romantic love remained a mystery. My few sexual partners had been unsatisfying and a waste of time. I didn't understand how women benefited from free love. It sold us short, like purchasing a garish sale item that you didn't need and wouldn't use.

"Brenda, guess what I did today!" I said. "God, I was so embarrassed."

"Whad'ja do this time?"

"I walked past a room full of guys. One guy stood in the doorway and asked me if I'd like to join their fraternity. I slowed my stride and said in all seriousness I'd think about it.

Of course a roar of laughter erupted from the room. Then it hit me that fraternities must be only for guys."

Brenda laughed, "Leona, you're too much."

"The other day I pronounced *vignette* as 'vig-net.' Everyone but me laughed."

"You'll figure it out. Just give yourself time."

I ached to relax and feel no pressure, to be with people who loved me without social graces. Christmas break was coming. Unlike other kids in my classes, who nonchalantly resisted going home, I missed my family. I longed to show them that I was making something of my life. And it might be my last time to see my mother. Randy had sprouted inches and abilities since we left Kansas a year and a half ago. They should see him throw a ball across a room or build a tower with blocks. I checked my meager savings and bought a student-rate plane ticket on sale. Randy, not yet three, could fly free, if he sat on my lap. He'd be thrilled.

I hadn't heard much about Ron for eight months. I'd not thought much about him, and in all likelihood he hadn't thought much about me. I hoped he had found a new girlfriend. He wouldn't know that I'd come home. I should be safe.

CHAPTER 26 – THE UNINVITED

Kansas, December 1971

Dad closed the car door and corralled my bags from the trunk. I slid off the seat with Randy in my arms. He woke up. "We're here, honey!" I said and smiled at the excitement registering in his eyes.

"Where are they?" he asked, looking around for his young aunts, Lynnie and Carla.

"They're in the house. Should we surprise them?"

"Yeah!"

"Randy," Dad said, "I didn't tell them you were coming. You're a special surprise."

I gave Randy an extra-strong squeeze. "We're like a special Christmas present to them, and they're a special Christmas present to us!"

Dad opened the chore room door and I stepped up, whispering to Randy, "Get ready to say *surprise!*"

Dad opened the next door, and we entered the kitchen. The kids came running. "Surprise!"

Randy jumped out of my arms to run to Carla and Lynnie. We shared hugs all around. Dorthy and Butch exchanged knowing looks—they had kept the secret.

"Butch and Dot," Dad said, "I could use some help getting groceries out of the car."

I walked to the back room. Lying in a hospital bed, Mom turned her head toward me and smiled. "Hi, Mom," I said, ill at ease. "We made it. I'm so glad to be home. This feels absolutely wonderful! How are you doing?"

She gurgled.

"I didn't quite get that, Mom. What did you say?"

"I'm glad you and Randy are here."

"It seems like forever since we've seen you. So much has happened in these last months. I feel so fortunate to be in college right now!"

Mom smiled and nodded her head. "You beat the odds," she said.

I nodded my head, guessing. "Are you able to sit in the wheelchair and get out of this bed sometimes?"

"When Dad helps me," she said. "I sometimes use his old wheelchair."

Again I guessed. I saw Dad's old caned wooden wheelchair close to her bed. "It's a good thing we kept this all these years. I remember as kids we rolled it around and played 'doctor' upstairs. We gave each other rides in it. It's a wonder we didn't ruin it."

Mom nodded her head.

"I bet you like it because the back tilts down. You can almost lie down in it."

She nodded her head again, too weary to talk. The tears in her eyes stabbed my heart. I fought off my own.

"I wish it weren't so hard for you, Mom."

"It's not so bad," she said. I couldn't understand her warped sounds but recognized the comforting tone. I nodded and looked around for the softer vinyl wheelchair she used before.

Dad came to her bed and said, "Can you believe it? Look who we have here. We've been looking forward to this day, haven't we?"

She nodded. He prepared to move her onto the wheelchair.

"Can I help?" I asked.

"You can help hold her head while I move her to the chair," he said.

"Let me move back here so I can follow her towards you."

He patted her knee and said, "OK, now, I've got you. Just let your legs relax." Dad lifted her up and positioned her backside toward the wheelchair. I held her head as long as I could, bending over her bed until my arms couldn't reach her.

"There we go," Dad arranged pillows and a blanket. "How about coming to the kitchen so we can all be together as we cook supper?"

Mom nodded her head, delighted to be part of the closeness and excitement. Dorthy and Butch were still putting away groceries, and I pitched in. Lynnie and Carla were upstairs, showing Randy their rooms. They'd be down soon; it was cold up there.

I started warm water running and loaded dirty dishes into the sink. Dorthy cleaned the table and set it while telling us how her team took first place in three out of four of their last debate tournaments. She practiced memorizing the data on three by five cards. They had to be proficient at arguing both sides. She was actually against the death penalty, but she could make the case for it.

Dad noticed the red barn light glowing. "Butch, could you run out and turn off the light?"

"Do I have to? I don't want to freeze my butt off. Can't we just leave it on tonight?"

"No. You know about electricity. Now go on."

"I'll go with you," I said. "I haven't run out in the dark here for a long time. I used to complain about having to turn off that light."

"Good!"

I grabbed my coat. Butch and I scampered out the door. "It'll be worse on the way back, because we won't have the barn light guiding us."

"I know," I said.

He flipped the barn light off. We both waited a moment for our eyes to adjust.

"Let's hold hands, so we don't get separated." We plunged into the night's draping dark clouds. We giggled as we stepped off the broken sidewalk.

I was ecstatic. The giddiness in my gut bubbled like a mountain stream. I was finally at home. I belonged where I was. I could let my guard down. I didn't have to learn anything. Here, I knew I was loved, and I loved these people. Here, love wasn't a challenge or an effort—it was the essence of our being together. It existed naturally, like water around fish, so ever-present it wasn't noticed. It was our external environment as well as our internal world. I was happy here. In many ways, in spite of hardship, I always had been.

Dad pulled the Dutch oven out of the bigger oven. He checked the water level on the potatoes and chuck roast. The aroma made our stomachs growl.

"We'll be ready in a few minutes. Kids, go wash up. Butch, would you quickly start a load of laundry?"

Dad adjusted Mom's wheelchair at the table's end. With a safety pin he attached a faded cotton towel around her neck. It covered her front where food cascaded to her lap. He would sit at an angle and assist her. He spooned into her mouth most of what she ate.

I reached into the refrigerator for ketchup and milk. I turned around to place it on the table and my heart stopped.

Ron was standing right in front of me. He had walked into the kitchen unannounced, without knocking. I witnessed the shock on everyone's faces, their mouths gaping open as they stared at him.

"Hi," I said. "How did you get here?" It was a stupid question, but I was buying time. "How are you doing?" I asked in a friendly tone, not hearing a word he said in response. I figured if I started speaking, others would understand that I'd handle the problem.

"Would you like to join us for supper? We're just starting to eat. I imagine we have food for one more," I said, startled that my pattern of soothing and calming him returned so automatically. I hoped he'd follow my friendly tone.

"That would be nice. It smells good and I'm hungry," he said.

The whole family was stunned. No one knew what to say or do. I fetched a flowered Melmac plate and a fork. He grabbed a chair from the chore room. So far he hadn't touched me. I didn't want him to make a scene and scare the kids. He paid no attention to Randy. His focus was clearly on me.

He didn't seem to have a weapon. But I didn't trust that his pockets were empty. Fear rumbled and I lost my appetite. The only way I could get him out of the kitchen would be to go to his car with him, and I was too scared to do that.

Supper was a series of uncomfortable questions. How were his parents, his siblings? *Fine, all fine.* We exchanged inane chatter.

Ron helped us clean up after supper and gradually the troops left. Randy would sleep with Lynnie and Carla. I signaled Dad that I'd handle Ron, so he and Mom could retire.

Ron and I sat on kitchen chairs, talking. I made sure I gave him no information about where I lived or what school I attended. Luckily I was not wearing my Boston College sweatshirt. I racked my brain to reason with him, to have him accept we were separate now. I didn't mean him harm, but I couldn't be with him. He had to live his own life now. Please understand. Our past attempts to be together didn't work.

The clock sounded 2:00 a.m. How could I cajole him into leaving? Sleep pulled down my eyelids. I labored to strike a bargain with him that wouldn't invoke our violent past. Though he kept putting his right hand in his pocket, he hadn't yet pulled out a weapon. He pressed for time with me, and I knew he wouldn't leave without some concession. We finally agreed that I'd spend one evening with him if he'd go home now and if he promised he wouldn't do anything bad when Randy and I left.

When finally he left without incident, I did not feel victorious. The lusty joy I had felt over having a few days with my family slipped away. I was spiraling down to the torment of my past, trading my body and soul to survive, partitioning my brain so I could do what I must and still soak up the goodness of home.

The next night he picked me up in his Saab. I was afraid, but I stayed focused on keeping him calm while talking about living apart. When he brought me back to the farm—quite late—he refused to go home, insisting if I wanted to go back to Boston, I would have to let him stay the night. With no wiggle room and little sleep, I found an inkling of hope in the fact that, for the first time, we were talking about living apart. Or to be more exact, I was talking about it. Was he hearing me? Was he agreeing? Or was he just more placid because he was momentarily satisfied? I was too exhausted to guess.

As Randy and I left with my aunt for the airport, I dared to hope that Ron and I had made some genuine progress. He was not threatening to kill me or my family. He actually said he'd try to accept being apart.

January 1972

Back in Massachusetts, Randy and I built block roads for his new little cars. We played hide and seek with Brenda and Daniel. I read Randy stories. He pulled Dr. Seuss from my hands and pretended to read, then took off with his John Deere tractor in hand. Like his mommy, he treasured any semblance of the farm.

Like a mother hen, I clucked around preparing for my second semester at Boston College. Returning to Boston meant returning to school. This miraculous opportunity I struggled to achieve felt like a mountain to climb. I rearranged piles on my desk, gathered notebooks, filed papers, and studied my class schedule.

Brenda and I buzzed through our Darby Street apartment, singing harmony for the hundredth time with Rod Stewart's "Reason to Believe." Her old stereo, my record. We discussed our dislike of welfare—how we stretched the pennies, how few people understood what it meant to raise a child like Brenda's, often sick with asthma and colds. How could she keep a job? Why should she—or I—be stigmatized when we were caring for our sons the same way as when we were married? It was even harder now for Brenda, as her ex didn't watch the baby as often and didn't pay as much as when they were married. Why were mothers blamed and penalized?

"Brenda, I think it's past my turn to cook supper. I'll make pork gravy over rice. We've got rice, don't we?"

"I think so. I'll check the cupboard."

"Poor little Daniel. I can tell by looking at him that he doesn't feel well. His eyes are bleary," I said.

Hearing a knock at the door, I said, "I'll get it. Did you invite your sister?"

"No."

As I opened the door, a silver handgun pointed at my heart. Ron pushed in.

"Brenda, get the boys and leave!" Fortunately both boys were with her in the kitchen. She saw what was happening and raced with them out the back door.

Frightened, I asked Ron to put the gun down. "Please."

"No, I won't. I'm bringing this to an end. You shouldn't be breaking up a marriage, you fucking bitch."

"I can't talk with a gun pointed at me. My knees are weak. I might pass out."

"Sit down!" he said, waving the gun toward a hardwood chair.

I did. Black closed in and my vision faded. I lowered my head to my knees. I shook my head and clung to coherence. "If you want to talk, Ron, you have to put that gun down. I can't think with a gun pointed at me."

"Fine. I'll point it at me." He pointed the gun at his right temple. "Does that make you happy? I'll just blow my head off right here, right now."

Desperate ideas for escape whirled through my mind like a cyclone. "No, Ron. I told you. Put the gun down!"

"You're leaving with me right now or I'll pull the trigger."

"Ron, let's talk. I know you're upset. I know you've tried hard to be alone. It's really difficult for you. Please put the gun down so we can talk."

"I'm not a fool, Leona. I got this gun to use it here. Now! I'm telling you one last time. Get out that door!"

Panic sweated my palms and screeched warnings from synapse to synapse. "Go with you where? Where do you want us to go?"

"Where is not important. We've got to go now!"

I had little idea if he intended to kill himself, me, or both of us. I spoke softly, cajoled, and bargained for time.

"I said, march out that--"

He noticed first, and then I did, that we were not alone. We were surrounded by guns. Outside every window, police pointed their weapons directly at us.

"Ron, don't move or we'll both be dead."

The police yelled at him to put down the gun. He refused.

It was a bitter four degrees outdoors. The police wouldn't stand there long, waiting for Ron to make up his mind. Their guns terrified me almost as much as his did. When would the shooting frenzy start?

They yelled negotiations. He refused.

"Ron, please! There's no way out of this. Let the police come in!"

"Shut up!" he yelled at me.

The police shouted that they wouldn't come in if he'd let a priest enter and talk to both of us.

Ron asked for a little time to think about that.

I wished to hell I could pray. I hoped he wouldn't kill himself but I didn't know why, because another part of me hoped he would. My mind darted from one hideous scenario to the next. Would Ron point the gun at me again and pull the trigger? Would the police start shooting wildly? Would he or they kill us both?

A man in robes knocked. With his gun still pointed at his own head, Ron nodded approval. The priest told Ron that things would be OK if Ron would just hand him the gun. He meant him no harm. God understood his distress.

Ron eventually acquiesced, and police suddenly crowded the room. I thanked Ron for listening. A cop told me to get in his car. I supposed he needed to ask questions and write a report. I obliged.

Another cop directed Ron into the car seat next to me. I was stunned. How did this happen so fast that I couldn't utter a word? I felt Ron's breath on my neck. They carted us away to an emergency room with a psychiatrist on duty. They asked Ron if he'd talk to a psychiatrist. He agreed. They guided us to the waiting room. While Ron checked in, I turned to ask the police what they needed from me. They were gone. Not a single cop was in the room!

My stomach clutched. I was freezing cold and sweating profusely. Fear clogged my throat. I didn't have a dime. I didn't have my purse with me. The goddamned police actions were incomprehensible. Brenda must have told them I was being held hostage, that Ron entered our apartment with a gun in his hand, that I was Ron's victim. How could they leave me with him, unprotected?

We waited, sitting side by side, too exhausted to speak. I watched the clock. When would the psychiatrist call for him? What the hell did the cops think? That I was just another welfare bitch and they'd be glad if he took me out?

When the psychiatrist finally called Ron into his office, I hitchhiked home. Brenda hugged me and confirmed that she had described the events as they had occurred. Neither of us could fathom why the police hadn't protected me.

The only further information I got came the next day from the Charlestown paper: the priest was actually a policeman dressed in a borrowed robe. He had a gun under his black garment. And he had forgotten to take off his wedding ring—neither Ron nor I had noticed.

Chapter 27 - THE ASSISTANT DA

"What do you mean you can't do anything?" I asked incredulously.

Mr. Bellington, an assistant district attorney for Charlestown, leaned back in his chair, hands clasped behind his neck with his arms bent forward, covering his ears. Resting, with one foot on his massive desk in front of him, he seemed unruffled. He was in his mid-thirties, had that many extra pounds around his middle, and was bored.

"Look, I'd like to help you, but from what you told me, no crime was committed."

"He came into my house with a gun pointed at me. That's not a crime?"

"No. You opened the door and let him in."

"Of course I let him in! I was terrified. What am I going to do, slam the door in his face? How would that keep us safe? He could easily have smashed the glass window in that door or just shot through it."

"Take it easy here. I'm not trying to upset you. I'd help you if I could. The problem is, you're married to him."

"I'm only married to him on paper because this damned Catholic state has a two-year residency requirement and because there was no way I could divorce him as long as that meant I had to give him my address."

"You said he didn't threaten to kill you, he threatened to kill himself. He didn't hit you or anyone else in the house. He wanted to commit suicide in front of you. That might be unpleasant, but it isn't a crime."

"He pointed a gun at me! Isn't that a threat to kill me? You're acting like the damn policemen. They stuck him in their car next to me. They hauled us both to the hospital and dumped us off. What's the matter with you people?"

"This isn't getting us anywhere. I have work to do."

"What? This is just normal everyday stuff to you? I'm making a big deal out of nothing? If I was stupid enough to marry a man who would be violent, well, that's my problem?"

"If you had a case, I would help you. I can't do anything unless a crime has been committed."

"If you don't help me, who will? I'm pretty certain that when I walk out that door, I'm going to die a violent death. Maybe not today, but sometime soon. You said they released him. He's on the loose. He's looking for me right this minute."

Mr. Bellington looked up to the ceiling and sighed. "Let me ask you a couple of other questions," he said wearily. "You said he came in the front door, with the gun pointing at you, but he didn't verbally threaten you."

"He didn't have to verbally threaten! I know when to feel threatened by him. I've known him for six years. He's beaten me and come damned close to killing me. I'd be a complete fool not to know. I don't believe that he knew whether he would commit suicide or homicide or both when he walked in the door. His gun was pointed at me. What might that lead you to believe?"

"Why didn't you pick up your son and run out the back door with your roommate?"

"He had a loaded gun pointed at me. He would have shot me in the back if I had made the least bit of a gesture of leaving him. That's why he came to my apartment. He wanted to force me to come back to him. The reason he tried to kill me the first time was because he thought I wanted to leave him! When someone has a loaded gun pointed at you, someone you know is capable of murdering you, would you do the very thing he most wants you *not* to do?"

"How did you know he wouldn't kill you when you yelled at your roommate to take the kids and leave?"

"I didn't."

"It's OK," Brenda assured me, "my sister will let me stay for a while."

"Thank goodness, because I know we can't be here. After I begged him, Mr. Bellington said he'd have the cops pick Ron up, but he said they wouldn't have enough to keep him. He'll be turned loose again soon."

"Jesus," Brenda said, rolling her eyes.

"That was such an intense experience. First Mr. Bellington wanted to run me out of his office. Then he wanted me to tell him the whole story, start to finish. I thought I'd never get out of there."

"I hope he'll help you, Leona. When will it be safe for us to come back?"

"I don't have any idea. Let's stay in touch. God, Brenda, I feel terrible about this. You're being run out of your apartment because of my problem."

Pulling back the curtains and looking out to the street, Brenda said "Come on. Let's get out of here! My sister just drove up."

"Randy, you can bring your tractor and that little truck. I put *Make Way for Ducklings* and Teddy in our bag."

We quickly locked the front door and hugged Brenda's sister, Sally, for taking us in her car. Friends of Dean, a young man I'd been casually dating, had offered Randy and me temporary shelter. Thankful for the makeshift mattress in the utility room, Randy and I found a special place for his toys next to the washer. "This can be your field," I said, pointing to the spot of floor that wasn't covered with the mattress.

Jake and Russell showed us around their apartment. With the gratitude of a refugee, I told them a brief version of our dilemma. I was sorry I didn't have money to pay them. I still had to pay rent on the place I shared with Brenda. I also didn't know how long I would have to stay. I'd make it as short as possible. I didn't like being a burden. I was deeply grateful for their friendship with Dean and their willingness to help.

When Dean arrived later that evening, I thanked him, too. I wondered what I owed him for this favor. Why did I feel obligated? Was he projecting that expectation? After all, we'd had sex when he hadn't done anything for me. I didn't feel manipulated then. Why couldn't I figure this out?

The police offered little information about Ron. They picked him up and released him, they said, with "charges pending." They would do nothing else. I'd like to think he went back to Kansas, but illusions wouldn't suffice when reality could destroy. Like a wide-eyed owl scans the night, he would hunt. He would hunt until he found me.

I was afraid to leave the apartment, but I couldn't stay long. I was imposing. These guys knew little about almost-three-year-old children; their apartment held expensive stereo equipment and other treasures Randy could ruin, and I was not focused enough to keep him away from every gadget. They thought I was too lenient, that I should spank or punish, but I preferred correction and redirection.

As I spent my days at "home," I was losing out on my college education. It was time to face facts: no one was going to save me from Ron. The court date would not be scheduled for months. Even if they convicted him, they most likely wouldn't jail him. If they didn't incarcerate him, I'd remain his prey—he would be free to follow me right out of the courtroom.

I realized I must handle my life the same way the assistant DA wanted to treat me—I would send myself out into the world with few defenses. I couldn't afford to care if I died a violent death. I had to take my chances. Staying locked up in someone else's apartment was a dead end. I told Russell and Jake, with gratitude for their hospitality, that we'd return to my apartment. Could one of them please drive us there?

To my surprise and relief, Brenda, Sally, and Daniel were home.

"I couldn't keep Daniel out of Sally's stuff. He was so unhappy, and her apartment was way too tiny for the three of us. We didn't think Ron would be focused on us."

"You're right. I don't think he would harm you. I probably overreacted. Anyway, I'm glad you're back." I thought for a moment. "You're probably not so glad I'm back."

"It's not that. We just don't know what to expect. We want you and Randy to be safe, too."

I understood this lukewarm welcome was the best she could do. Neither of us had alternatives—poverty closed off ninety percent of our options. We took what was left.

Chapter 28 – BELIEVING THE BIGGEST LIE

The next morning I sent Randy to daycare. He was clad in two mismatched mittens and a coat with several folded and colored paper airplanes in his pockets. I picked up my books and a warm coat and headed to Sullivan Station. I was tense and grinding my teeth.

I was aware of everything, as if my pores were equipped with radar. With eyes opened wide, I steeled myself to round each corner, pass an alley, or cross a gap between buildings. Menace lurked in every space that might conceal Ron. I circled as far as I could to the other side of an industrial trash bin. The slightest move would trigger me to kick or run.

As alert as I was, I didn't see him. Suddenly I felt his hands twisting my arm behind me and then the knife at my back, just like it had been at my neck a few years earlier.

"You walk the way I tell you to walk," he said through his teeth. "If you make any wrong move, you're dead. Don't even think about yelling or trying to run." He twisted tighter, wedging my shoulder to pop out of its socket. The searing pain didn't stop the words *you're dead* from puncturing my thoughts like a nail in a tire, going around and around until the air runs out. How soon would my air run out? Would it be a blowout or a slow leak? Dead. How soon was dead?

"Please, Ron," I pleaded quietly, hating the sound of my voice. "You're going to make me scream because of the pain. Please don't twist my arm so tight."

He relaxed it a bit and pushed me forward. "Keep walking!"

"I am. Just don't hurt me."

"You'll have a reason to think 'don't hurt me' when I'm done with you! Do you feel the knife at your back?"

"Yes, I feel it. Very much."

"Quit putting your head down! Look straight ahead."

"Ron, if I can't see where I'm walking, I might stumble. You'll think I'm trying to escape."

"Just keep walking!"

"I am! I am! But if I fall, please don't stab me. I'm not trying to get away."

"Shut up and walk."

His threats wrapped around me like a chain. With adrenalin pounding, I wanted to kick him in the balls and run. I've walked miles to and from subways, hiked around school, and carried Randy, too. Yet I knew he was stronger and faster. Even if I wrenched myself so my shoulder popped out, it didn't necessarily mean he'd lose his grip on my wrist. How many seconds would I have before he stabbed me or slit my throat? What were the odds? I didn't care about the knife at my flesh or my shoulder popping out, even though it hurt. *Come on, Leona, calculate the odds! What is my best chance to survive?* Maybe I'd wait for just the right moment to strike, just the right distraction to tip the odds. I didn't care about pain. I was in it already. I *did* care about death.

He pushed me down more streets, zigzagging to confuse me or to avoid trafficked places. Fortunately, we had quite a distance to walk. I hoped that his rage would subside. Suddenly I saw a police station ahead. Could I wrest myself free, run up the steps, pull open the door, and get inside the station?

Could I? Would he stab me to death long before anyone would notice?

"Don't get any ideas just because we're going past a police station. You'll be dead if you try anything."

If only a policeman were standing outside!

We walked for perhaps another mile in vehement silence. I searched for any possible diversion or assistance. At the same time, I was strategizing how to survive once we arrived at his destination. My mind was splayed open with impossible possibilities. How could I? Where? What would happen? Every option had the same fatal ending.

I felt heavy, like a stone-filled sack sinking to the bottom of the sea.

His tiny rental was a one-room furnished apartment—kitchen, bed, and sofa all in the same area. As I stepped into the room, he shoved me to the floor. I wondered if any of what was happening now would actually count as a crime, should I live to tell the story.

"Get in bed, before I kick you over there!" He kicked me in the butt to show me he meant it. I crawled to the bed. He jerked me up. Buttons flied as he ripped my blouse off. He yanked at my jeans. As instantly as he undressed me, I was clothed in humiliation.

"Now you take my jeans off. I want you to see what's coming to you."

I hated him and in the same moment felt sorry for him. He was actually proud of his hard-on, proud of its size. He wanted to be admired while he raped me.

As he pumped and pounded my body, I searched frantically for the thread of a story he might believe. My body was naked and drenched under his sweaty control. Once he met his own exhaustion, words would be my only hope. How could I convince him to let me go?

Leona Stucky

Think, Leona! Whatever story I chose, I must introduce it gently, massage it with accurate characterizations and add enough substance to carry him along. One wrong word could have awful consequences. I must convince him that he needed me alive. And that I needed him, too. That I would not leave him again. But how? How? How could I give him a reason to believe?

I caressed and soothed. I feigned a sense of sexual hunger for him, a mutuality in this endeavor, and a lighter feeling that allowed us to engage in conversation. After considerable exertion, he relaxed a bit. His muscles lost their taut edge. I was wound tight and couldn't imagine relaxing, but I rested beside him as casually as I could muster.

I confessed that I was realizing I was not college material. I was disappointed in myself. I couldn't concentrate when I read. I told him that Randy always needed something. It felt right to admit that to him, I said, and I hoped he wouldn't think less of me. I paused, adding softly, "I keep dreaming about a log cabin in some woods, near a crystal-clear mountain stream, like some I've seen in Vermont."

He breathed heavily, his hand not far from the knife. He pushed up to look into my eyes and squinted. Perhaps I'd said too much too fast. Would he start now? I opened my eyes wide to show trust and hopefulness. I pulled him closer to me in a gesture of good faith, indicating for him to snuggle up a bit.

I strung along lengthy descriptions of the cabin, the garden of corn, peas, radishes, lettuce, and beans. What did he think about carrots and potatoes? The soil was so rich there. It wouldn't be hard to clear a plot and create abundance. I'd heard that blueberries and blackberries grew wild in those woods. Apple trees abounded. With a little hunting, whole meals could be taken care of. Deer and rabbits were plentiful.

I dared not say "we" too quickly in my story. He had to put himself there, or he'd know I was stringing him along.

- 186 -

"I think it would be a good life for Randy." It felt like I was making little Randy into a need-satisfying object, the same way I was being treated. But I knew Randy reminded Ron of our connectedness, and that link grounded his trust in me. "He loves nature. He can play outside for hours. He's happier with trees, grass, and streams than with all the toys in the world. I used to be that way, too." I droned on, describing endless farm entertainments.

"I don't really know much about hunting, but I used to set traps when I was on the farm, and I caught more than my cousins did." I told ancillary stories, like the time I trapped a skunk and Dad made me turn him loose—a virtual impossibility without getting sprayed. I circled back to the dream of a log cabin and my adeptness at making this dream a reality.

My words trailed away as he returned to his own desires. In a haze of sexual exertion, fear, and pretense, I held my breath when he pushed his head and torso up and stared blankly at the flaking paint on a baseboard. Perhaps he understood that his efforts to make contact, though strong and passionate, couldn't penetrate beyond the cruelty he inflicted. Though he forced sex, he couldn't force me to love him. Sex was a poor substitute for the lonely longing of his heart. Was he pondering his next move? Was he teasing dead-end notions through the paint curls and savoring each one? The neck. The knife. Breasts and vagina. He could opt for his truth.

When he bent his elbows and rested on my chest, I soothed him with comforting sounds and words. For the time being, he settled for immediate attunement and gratification, for illusions and deceit. When his breathing slowed, I continued to present my option. I was talking more with him today than I had ever talked before. I subtly dissembled differences for hours, telling one unifying story between reassuring physical entanglements. I *must* offer him a reason to believe me—silence wasn't going to produce any escape prospects. Without a different plan, he'd return to his own thoughts.

Actually, the story held appeal for me, too. It wasn't what I desired, but it presented a retreat from daily pressures. "I reckon I could learn whatever is necessary. I'm no stranger to hard work. Everything I learned on the farm would come in handy in this new life. If I could manage to get a cow, I'd know how to milk her, how to separate the cream off and make butter, how to make cottage cheese. Fences and a lean-to for the cow would be a snap. Randy would love it. We'd be singing Old McDonald a thousand times. He'd look right into those big, sad Holstein eyes. Whenever we're around cows, he loves me to hold him up high so he can run his fingers over the ridges on their backs. I think he'd rather ride a cow than a horse."

I ran my fingers over his lips and caressed his cheeks as I invented the vision and invited his input. His forehead and eyes softened.

"There'd be fish in the stream, probably trout. Have you ever cleaned and cooked trout?" I spun yarns about hand-fishing in the Smoky River. After stopping periodically to catch my breath and ask him neutral questions, I held his hands and reassured him. I talked on and on, always weaving back to the main theme of a cabin in the woods, a new life for me and Randy, with the slightest hint that this new life might be for him, too.

Finally, after hours of build-up, I presented a problem I might not be able to solve on my own. What about nights? Would I be scared or lonely? "I sometimes am scared at night. I hear noises and I don't know what to do. It might be scary to be in the woods, so far away from everyone."

Now he found his place to enter as the hero.

"You wouldn't be afraid if I was there."

"You're right," I said "I wouldn't." I snuggled closer and stroked the muscles on his upper arms. "I wouldn't have to face the dark alone. You'd protect me. Do you think you'd want to be there with Randy and me?"

We proceeded to plan the practical things. Would Vermont welfare add up to about the same as Massachusetts? If we had a big-enough garden, could we live on that amount? His ability to hunt could help our situation. We could see how it might work.

More "love-making" removed anxious doubts. I watched him closely and noticed the vulnerable flicker in his eyes just after he ejaculated. In a flash of insight I sensed that flicker represented his dim apprehension of his own finitude, of a life force known and lost. Perhaps it was a moment when he couldn't reconcile his need to kill me, given that the incessant yearning of his deranged love was for me—or, more accurately, for the "home" I provided.

His labored breathing returned and, like the flutter of butterfly wings on the outer edge of vision, my insight vanished. Though I had known him for more than six years, I didn't know him; nor could I, because he refused to know himself. His actions constituted his only true communication, and they spoke of meeting his own desires no matter what cruelty was required.

By 6:00 a.m. he was pretty convinced that I'd mended my ways and seen the light, his light. I hoped he was as faith-filled with me as I used to be with God.

Now I attempted the plan I had reworked in my mind a thousand times in the last twenty hours. "You know, Ron, I've been thinking about something I need to talk with you about," I said. "I've been thinking about little Randy. I know how much he is missing me and wondering what happened to me. He needs to be a real part of our new future. He will be so glad to see his daddy again."

I took a breath and studied his face. I looked in his eyes so that he could judge my sincerity and trust me. If I saw any sign of disbelief, I would back up and cover my tracks, reassuring him that we could find another way to solve the problem I was presenting.

"I'm also thinking that when Brenda wakes up and finds that I'm not home, she's going to call the police. I know we don't want the police involved in our lives right now. So I think I should get home before she gets up." I promised to smooth things over with Brenda and bring Randy back with me. I took another deep breath, waiting to see if he would believe me or strike out at me. At least he didn't have the knife in his hand.

"I think I'd better go now, because she'll be getting up soon. I should get back here within an hour. It won't take me long. You can rest a bit. You're exhausted."

I started to move away from him slowly, so I didn't alarm him or appear to be running away. With difficulty keeping his eyes open, he laid his head back on the pillow. "What time will you be back?" he asked.

"Well, it's about six now, so I should be able to be back by seven. It won't take me long. I'm sure Randy will be happy to see me and then happy to see you!"

"Hurry back!"

"I will."

"Just hurry back!"

"All right, I'll see you in a bit." I was mostly dressed. I grabbed my coat using it to cover my ripped blouse with missing buttons. I stepped through the door, closing it gently behind me. I walked briskly, but didn't run, for fear he would look out the window and think I was running away. I turned at the first block, to remove myself from his view, and started running. Confused about my current location, I looked for any street I might recognize so I could find my way home.

CHAPTER 29 - POLICE AGAIN

Breathless, I knocked loudly on our door. "It's just me!" I yelled. Brenda opened it with fear in her eyes. "It's OK, but lock all the doors and windows. Pull the curtains closed tight."

"What happened?" she asked.

"I'll tell you in a minute. I've got to call the police first."

I spat out informative bits with Brenda while the police sifted me through several people until they connected to the right department. The detective asked a few questions. I struggled to be precise, to give them an overview and the location of Ron's furnished apartment. Would they pick him up? They probably would but needed more information first. If I didn't mind, they'd come to my apartment to talk.

I told Brenda and Sally that the police would arrive soon. They quickly threw on jeans and shirts. We synchronized in a cyclonic cleanup. I took a few minutes to snuggle with Randy, who was, thankfully, still asleep. I was careful to not fall asleep, too, which I could do in a heartbeat if I closed my eyes. I'd been awake for more than twenty-four hours.

Two detectives knocked on our door. I welcomed them in. They, however, did not sit down to talk. One walked to the fireplace mantle. He stirred the ashes in the ashtray. The other walked through the house, checking other ashtrays and snooping. Oh my God! My heart stopped. They didn't give a shit about the crime just committed. They were probably pissed because this welfare bitch was a nuisance. They wanted to punish me for the trouble. I sat down, put my hands over my eyes and shook my head. My mind stumbled through recent social events. I didn't remember if we'd had company or who might have brought pot. I didn't remember when we last emptied the ashtrays.

Apparently they didn't find evidence because they didn't mention it when they finally joined me in the living room. I started explaining the events of yesterday morning. They wanted to know the route we took. I didn't know exactly. I couldn't concentrate on streets. I was formulating escape plans—looking for any plausible openings. But I knew we walked down Taylor Street.

"You walked down the street where the police station is?" They were incredulous.

"You don't understand," I said, as calmly as I could. "This man had a knife in his hand. And I know he is capable of murder. If I made a false move, he would stab me a hundred times before any police person would even notice, much less be there to stop the attack. There was no policeman visible out in the street. I was alone with a man holding a knife to my back!"

They looked at each other and shrugged. What happened after that, and after that? With clutched hands and arms pressed across my chest, I respectfully repeated the humiliating charade for these apathetic bastards, expletives deleted. They said I could call in a few hours to hear what they would do.

After they left, I placed a call to the DA's office and left a message. Now I was exhausted beyond the breaking point. Randy was awake. After bringing chaos and fear into Brenda's world, after leaving Randy with her unannounced all evening and night, I had to ask her to help me again by watching Randy. My throat was on fire. I could barely swallow. I couldn't even take the shower I craved. I passed out on Randy's bed.

In the afternoon I woke up just in time to run to the bathroom and throw up. Heat radiated from my face and cold snuck up my spine. The thermometer showed 102. My throat raged. Guessing it was strep or tonsillitis, I took some aspirin and sank back into sleep.

That evening I woke up feeling grotesque, filthy, greasy, hideous, and hopeless. I took a shower and put on pajamas. Lying back down on the bottom bunk, I invited Randy to snuggle with me so I could read to him. He was not three years old yet, but he knew already not to ask too many questions, not to seek to know more than he needed to. He accepted what was, like any child who could do little to change his circumstances. Every difficulty that I couldn't bear necessarily affected him. I read, and then I cried quietly, for him and for me.

Chapter 30 - A Crime?

Once again the assistant DA sifted through papers on his desk when I sat down in the wing-backed chair closest to him. He took several moments before looking at me. I assumed he had the police report saying that they picked up Ron and put him in jail. "I need to hear your version of events. From the looks of it, you've had a rough time."

"You could say that, Mr. Bellington. I want to thank you for meeting me first thing. I really need to make as many classes as I can. I've already missed so much that I don't see how I can catch up."

"What happened, Leona?"

I began relating the miserable story and, as with the police, he interrupted when I said we walked past a police station. I repeated what I told the police. I reminded him that Ron becomes murderous when I leave him. The most dangerous thing I could have done was to attempt escape and not accomplish it. I thought and thought about fighting and running, but I knew I didn't have a prayer.

I wondered why it was so hard for people to grasp helplessness. Couldn't they understand I was overpowered by size, muscle, and the real threat of immediate death? Why blame someone for being unable to win against superior strength? I stared at the shiny squares on the floor as I spoke. Several times he asked me to speak up.

"We're not going to be able to do a whole lot more with this one than the first one," he said.

I looked straight at him. "Don't tell me no crime was committed!"

"We can use the fact that he had a knife and threatened you and forced you to move from one location to the next. We can try assault and battery, and kidnapping.

"What about rape?"

"Not much we can do there. You're married."

"He can kidnap me if we are married, but he can't rape me? That doesn't make sense."

"It's how the law works."

"It still doesn't make sense. You mean he doesn't have the right to move me from one place to another, but he does have the right to fuck me any time he wants to? A piece of paper, a marriage license, gives a man the right to force a woman to have sex with him anywhere, however he wants, as long as it is not in public? That's the law?"

"Look, I'm on your side. I can see you've been through hell."

"Goddamn it! This is crazy. This is almost as crazy as he is. I know it's not your fault. It just burns me up."

"How did you escape?"

"Oh, brother! This isn't going to make the cut. You won't believe me."

"There's not much I haven't heard in my line of work."

"I told him a story, and I endured longer than he could. I had to. My life depended on it."

"You told him a story?"

"I soothed him. I had to. I did everything he wanted. I had to make him believe I'd come back to him, live with him, love him forever."

"I can't even write this shit down. If this is what we have--"

"I'm telling you the truth. I couldn't fabricate this, though I did make up a whopper for him."

"You told him a story?"

"I told him about a log cabin in the woods near a mountain stream, where we could go and live together with Randy. Only I couldn't say 'we' because he had to add himself into the story or he wouldn't have believed me. I had to make him believe the sex was mutual. I had to make him think that when I left him to go pick up Randy, I would come back to him—that the three of us would live together happily ever after. That was my only ticket out of his clutches."

"You made him think you were happy to have sex with him? And yet you want me to charge him with rape?"

"I know it sounds stupid, but it's what I had to do. I sure as hell wish someone would call that rape. That's what it felt like to me. How else could I have left?"

"I don't know what to say. This won't fly."

"We have kidnapping, don't we? Can you keep him locked up with that?"

"I'll do what I can. I don't know for how long."

"I guess that's as good as I'm going to get, huh?"

Mr. Bellington stared at me, shaking his head.

"I'm sorry," I told him with clenched teeth. "I didn't mean that the way it sounded. I appreciate your help. I really do."

"Look, Leona, I like you. I think you are an exceptional person. You're intelligent, motivated, thoughtful, and beautiful. I respect you. You can count on me doing what I can to keep him behind bars. I know what it's like to have a sense of impending dread and fear." Mr. Bellington pushed away from his desk, moving his chair a bit closer to me. "I'll tell you something: I haven't seen my brother in three years."

"Why not?"

"He came back from Vietnam and couldn't make it in his old life. Whatever my parents did for him set him off." Mr. Bellington took a deep breath and looked down at his hands. "He wouldn't accept my help. He just left. He left the family.

He's been wandering around for three years. We think he's in Mexico. Sometimes I'd like to chuck this job and go look for him. It might take months, but I think I'd eventually find him."

"I can see how that would be a real bind for you. You must think about that a lot. It would be a tough decision to make."

"I go around and around. If I knew for sure I could find him and help him, I'd do it."

"Do your parents think you should?"

"They don't want to force it on me. But they can't do it, and they're desperate to know he's OK."

"It's a heartache for all of you. Maybe there isn't a right answer."

"You do understand, don't you?"

I nodded my head.

"Most people don't really care about other people's difficulties."

I considered telling him he didn't really care about mine the first time I met him.

"I've got to get to work, and I know you need to catch your classes. Is it OK if I call you in the evening if I have something to report?"

"That's about the only time to catch me at home. Please do let me know if you find out they're releasing him. I need a warning."

I dumped my schoolbooks on the small table that served as a desk in Randy's and my room. Brenda relayed that the DA called.

"Did he leave a message?"

"No. Just that he might call later."

"I sure as hell hope they didn't release Ron." I caught Randy as he ran past, taking a clothespin out of his mouth and giving him a hug.

"He didn't say. And, yes, I've made certain that everything is locked. The curtains are closed."

"Aren't you sick of this?" I asked.

"I can't stand it! I don't know how you're surviving."

"Do you think we should put a knife close to each door, hidden somewhere that the kids couldn't reach them?" I asked.

"Would we use it before it got used on us?"

"I have one under my pillow, but I don't know if I could use it," I said.

"Why don't we put one on the fireplace mantle? The kids couldn't reach it. That's not too far from the front door. We could hide it under a cloth or something."

"That's a good idea."

Nonviolent principles still appealed to me, but if violent actions would stop an immediate attack, I knew I would fight, though a knife seemed like a dangerous gamble. It sank in now that I'd left my dad and my Mennonite roots in another way. I could no longer claim to be a pacifist. It took several years before I realized that my disdain for the police was akin to BC students who berated butchering farmers while stuffing their faces with cheeseburgers.

Mr. Bellington called, solicitous of my well-being. Could I catch up in my classes? "We've had to move your man from the jail into a locked ward at Westborough Hospital. Seems he was not willing to conform. He got himself in trouble with the other prisoners."

"First of all, he's not 'my man,' and--"

"I didn't mean it that way. Just that he's the one we are dealing with on your behalf."

"Thank you."

"He refused to cooperate with the other prisoners on a hunger strike. He sat down right in front of them and ate. That didn't set well with the others. They took it out on him later."

I imagined him sitting and eating in front of the others, thinking there was no need to collude with hardened criminals when his only crime was needing one woman too much. "You mean they beat him up?"

"They worked him over pretty good."

"Can't they put him in an isolated cell so he isn't hurt?" As soon as those words tumbled out of my mouth, I regretted them. I didn't know why I cared.

"They called in a psychiatrist and evaluated him. The psychiatrist said he's not competent."

"What does that mean?"

"He's not competent to stand trial. It means we can't proceed with your charges against him."

"You mean everything we talked about is completely useless?"

"Basically, that's right. We can't proceed with a case against him if he's not competent to be on trial."

"What will happen?"

"They moved him to Westborough, inpatient, in a locked ward."

"Are you sure he can't escape the locked ward?"

"That's why they are locked, so people won't escape."

"They need to know they've got to be extra careful not to let him out. How long will he be there?"

"He's in for a thirty-day evaluation. Depending on their assessment, they might renew his stay for another thirty days. We won't know until then. I'll keep you posted if I hear more."

"Thanks for letting me know. Brenda said you called, and I was afraid they let him go."

"I've made everyone abundantly aware that you need to be notified before he is released from anywhere."

"I really appreciate that. Thanks so much for all you've done to help. I hope your situation with your brother finds some positive resolution."

"Maybe someday. I'll check in with you later."

With a pounding heart I hung up the phone. "Guess what, Brenda." I called to her in the next room. "He gets out of it again!" She changed Daniel's diaper and returned to the kitchen. I gave her the full update.

"God, Leona. How can this be so messed up?"

"It pisses me off. When he gets a taste of what he has dished out to me for six years, he just flips out. They give *him* protection. What about protecting me?"

CHAPTER 31 - STOPPING RON

I realized, heading on the Green Line toward Haymarket Square, that just as I comforted Ron in those desperate hours, I needed the same treatment. In my busy routine, however, there was little room for solace. Spending time with Randy and keeping up with my classes were my top priorities, but then there were also dishes, cleaning, and cooking. I was too busy to be much company with Brenda. Dating went from infrequent to none. Too many different, isolated, and demanding worlds drained my energy.

Ron remained on my radar, but dealing with him—and the threat of him—took everything I had and more, like dealing with a tornado that sucked up my volition and sent it flying in a thousand directions. Riding the subway, I puzzled over why he believed the story I told him. Perhaps we were all suckers for what we'd most love to believe. Capitalism? Communism? God? Love forever? War will create peace?

Ron didn't fully buy into my story until he added the most fantastic lie of all—that I would be safe if he were around, that I would not be afraid if he were in my cabin to protect me, that he could be my hero. Was that how belief works? If we embrace the most fantastic lie, then the rest of the details must be true? And if I believe that Jesus personally loves me and will help me, if I accede to that phantasm, will I then accept Scripture and dogma, including aspects that contradict reality?

The subway screeched to a stop. I joined the exiting throngs. Heading home, my thoughts turned to Randy. He and I were in a power struggle. I needed to potty train him but he was uncooperative. His daycare center said they don't do diapers, and they were tired of changing his underwear. Because the daycare said he should be potty trained, I thought his behavior unreasonable. Why was it so hard to teach him to conform to cultural norms? He didn't usually wet the bed, but going to the bathroom during the day was a challenge that baffled and frustrated both of us. I talked with him till I was disgusted by my own repetitions. Nothing changed his behavior.

To ameliorate this tension, I threw a small party for Randy's birthday. I invited his neighborhood friends. When I told him about the party, he said incredulously, "You mean for me?" I hugged him and said I meant exactly for *him*, but his innocent question pierced my heart.

Thrilled to get presents and special attention, to share cake and ice cream with his friends, Randy practically danced through his party. I smiled at the pleasure of doing something special for him, loving the excitement in his eyes.

February 1972

One Saturday morning it fell apart again. Seeing movement in the hallway, I panicked and screamed. Brenda came running.

"Call the police!" I screeched. I picked up a rolling pin.

"It's Ron," I yelled. He was on all fours, crawling through a back window, low to the floor. "If you move one muscle, I'll clobber you with this rolling pin."

Brenda ran back, a cast-iron pan in her hand.

Ron asked us not to hurt him. He was heartsick. He needed *home* and wanted to be with me again. He had no weapons and meant no harm.

"Why aren't you at Westborough?"

"I walked all way here. I'm freezing."

I was letting a pivotal moment pass. I could smash his head right now. Possibly not too many questions would be asked: he was breaking and entering; he had a history of violence. And yet he was pitiful, lying on the floor with his head in his hands and unremitting desire clouding his thoughts.

He was still like that when the police arrived and hand-cuffed him.

"Are you going to lock him up so he doesn't come back here?" I asked.

"We don't know yet what we'll do with him. You'll have to call our station in a few hours."

"He was in a locked ward at Westborough State Hospital. He escaped. He definitely needs to be locked up."

"You can call the station. We'll check his record and decide what to do."

"The four of us are in danger if he's not locked up."

"We'll take care of it."

"I want you to know that he kidnapped me from Sullivan Station a few weeks ago. He held a knife to my back and forced me to do unspeakable things."

"I'm sure we'll have that on our records."

The police pushed Ron out through the front door. I called the assistant DA. No answer.

Though Ron remained a threat and the police remained uncaring and the DA remained useless, it felt that things had changed. Brenda and I both swore we'd have knocked Ron for a loop if he had moved a muscle! We held Randy's and Daniel's hands and danced around the living room. "We did it, we did it! We stopped him!"

Finally the adrenalin rush didn't feel so awful.

Chapter 32 - MR. BELLINGTON'S CALL

The assistant DA called on Monday morning, but I was already gone. Using a stream of dimes, I called him several times from school but couldn't connect. He telephoned again in the evening and told me they would send Ron to Bridgewater Institute for the Criminally Insane for a six-month evaluation. Yes! We had six months before we had to worry again. I thanked him profusely.

He told me that he hadn't been able to get my case out of his mind. In fact, he thought about me a lot. I'd made quite an impression on him, he said, and he wished he could help more. Tongue-tied and astonished, I thanked him again.

Gradually over the weeks his calls became less about business and more about him. Would I like to chuck this mess and move to Mexico with him? While anything that would take me away from the realities I faced sounded appealing, I wouldn't throw away my scholarship. I had too much invested to walk away from college. I kept the line in the sand clear.

I told Dr. Shepherd the developments with Mr. Bellington— one more crazy detail in an unbelievable chain of events. He wore a poker face.

The next time I heard Mr. Bellington's voice, he was yelling. "Goddamn you!" he said when I picked up the ringing phone. Who was this, I wondered at first. What was happening?

"Why did you tell? You've ruined my whole career!" he said.

"What are you talking about?" I paused for a moment to determine if it was Mr. Bellington on the line. "I didn't tell anyone."

"You sure as hell did!"

"No. I didn't tell anyone!" I insisted.

"You got me fired! I'm fired from my job! I had to clear out my office this morning. You've ruined my life!"

I could hardly breathe. What had I done?

"This is the thanks I get for doing all I could to help you."

"Mr. Bellington, I'm horrified. I'm sorry. I don't know what happened. I didn't tell anyone."

"Don't lie to me! You had to tell *someone*. Just admit it. You ruin my life and now you want to lie about it? You talked to the attorney at BC, didn't you?"

"No, I didn't. I don't even know an attorney at BC!" What could he be talking about? My thoughts ran through a sieve and one little shred remained. "Oh my God. I might know what happened. I talked to my counselor. That's the only person I talked to at college."

"I told you you talked to someone! You little bitch!"

"I had no idea my counselor would do anything. He's sworn to confidentiality. Honestly, I didn't think I was hurting you!"

"No one asked me questions. They just said 'get out!'"

"Oh my God! I'm so sorry. I didn't mean to harm you. Honest, I didn't."

"It doesn't matter what you meant. You got me fired! I'm sick of your goddamned excuses. 'I didn't mean to,'" he said, mocking me. "The point is you *did*! You'll never hear from me again!" He slammed the phone down.

I sank to the floor and rocked back and forth. What had I done? I hurt someone who trusted and tried to help me. What the hell was Dr. Shepherd thinking? Why did he go behind my back? Did he think I would eventually throw away my scholarship? Did he think Mr. Bellington didn't care about me and just wanted a piece of ass? Why did he do it? Now I'd destroyed Mr. Bellington's life. I hated myself. Everything I touched turned into a disaster!

Immediately Dennis, the young man who five months ago raped me in this apartment, popped in my mind. How could things that seemed relatively innocent turn so quickly into nightmares? How could I, despite my best efforts, become the bad guy?

The next morning on the subway I tried to shed my despair. I felt sad for Mr. Bellington and for the way life seemed to strangle the budding good in situations before they could flower into whatever fleeting beauty one might behold. I imagined that many people, among the hordes crowding the Orange Line, had experienced ruin before hope matured. They were breathing in and out right now, just like me, hanging onto the poles or the looped belts, just like me, gathering courage and fortitude to face their days, just like me. When their eyes met mine, I sensed a shared knowing. We were facing another day.

CHAPTER 33 - A REASON TO BELIEVE

In the spring, Brenda and I decided we'd better not renew our lease. Ron knew our address—which meant we also had to avoid Charlestown and the Sullivan Station neighborhood. When Brenda decided she'd rent a place with her sister, I felt shattered. I'd failed a friend. I lost touch with our shared world. The periphery was no place for a good friend. I'd given up on men, and I hadn't had time for our once joyful paint-the-town adventures. The studies that captivated me bored her. I'd brought chaos and fear to her relatively sane existence. Too much of our lives had been about my needs and traumas.

I kept hurting people, especially Randy, and I hated it. He would love to play with me, but I was too often too busy. Why did I labor so hard to be something I was not? I studied and studied. Who did it help? I thought I could finish college in three and a half years instead of four by taking twenty-one hours each semester and attending summer school. I'd get off welfare quicker. Some part of my brain kept chanting, *Do, Do, Do—and don't stop*. I pushed and pushed, trying to keep going against the pressing need to stop, just stop, and feel the devastation piling up in my heart.

But the world didn't stop. Mid-term exams were pressuring as I was looking for a new place to live. "Thanks very much," I said on the pay phone at BC, feeling in my pocket for more change. "That wouldn't work for me." I looked at the not-cheap-enough ads I'd circled in the *Globe*. Some were in outer Slobbovia.

The student at the next phone hung up when I did. I apologized if I was too loud. I was not usually that way, but finding a place to live was frustrating. We talked for a few minutes, and then Sam offered an option.

"Ours isn't really a commune. Just a bunch of guys living together, splitting the rent. Anyway, if you want to come, it would be fine. One of the guys moved out a month ago, so we have a space. You'd be farther from public transportation but closer to the college. You could get rides often, we're always coming and going."

"Are you sure it will be OK to have a kid?"

"I don't think that would be a problem, as long as we don't have to do anything different. We're a little noisy. Some of the guys are in a rock band. They practice several nights a week."

"You wouldn't have to change anything for us. We are highly adaptable," I wondered where this nice guy appeared from. How lucky could I get? And it was a place I could afford!

Randy and I gathered up his toys and packed our bags, then dismantled our metal bunk bed. Sam helped load our two twin mattresses on his VW Bug roof. With his Bug packed to the gills and Randy on my lap, we arrived at our new home. Unfortunately, Sam the friendly guy had a different outlook than his housemates. They weren't favorably disposed to sharing their space with a mom and kid. They vetoed the plan and wanted Randy and me to leave. Only when they realized that we had nowhere to go and all our earthly belongings were in Sam's Bug did they relent.

This situation wouldn't last forever, I told myself. Some months ago I had found out about government-subsidized housing, and I added my name to a long waiting list. I was told that when my name came to the top, Randy and I would probably be able to have a small apartment on our own; no more single rooms and shared bathrooms and kitchens. We would celebrate big when that happened!

Meanwhile we were given some shelf space in the small refrigerator and a room to ourselves. The house was a large, two-story New England home with a basement. It reminded me of our old family farmhouse: spacious and, in a former life, quite elegant.

We reassembled our metal bunk beds and several of the guys gave us their reject chairs and a small table. The guys seemed nice enough, like they cared naturally, without an effort. We checked schedules and agreed that I'd get the bathroom first. Randy and I would be out of it by 7:00 a.m.

Since our new home was out of range for Randy's daycare, we had to make a change. With some struggle and finesse we switched to Newton Corner Daycare and Preschool. Our housemates seemed nice enough and content to ignore us. We played in the yard, walked to the store, and negotiated bedtimes while they pounded drums and rocked the house. I learned to block out the pulsating walls to read textbooks and write papers. Randy ignored us all, created miniature mud forts in the yard, and emulated Speed Racer.

A few weeks later, I was proud to welcome my hitchhiking cousin, Steven Stucky, to our household for an evening. With his guitar, harmonica, and enigmatic smile, he rolled out sixties peace music. Randy and I and the hard rockers in our household swayed to his tunes and savored the magic of this togetherness.

At the end of that second semester, in May 1972, my literature professor asked us to write the names of students who had made a positive difference to their class experience. I received the largest number of positive comments for understanding the characters we discussed. When Dr. Teasdale congratulated me, I was awestruck. This was the first contest I had won, the first time I'd been recognized for having a mind, the first time I felt appreciated by my peers. I had thought maybe I was too assertive when I made an issue out of the treatment of women in Jack Kerouac's *On the Road*, but I guess my classmates didn't mind.

When the welfare taxi brought Randy home, I whirled him through the air like he was riding a horse on a merry-go-round. To celebrate, we went out for an ice-cream cone. Later I listened to Rod Stewart's "Reason to Believe." I didn't know why that song haunted me. I could hear it a thousand times and not tire of it. Funny thing is, I couldn't think of a single guy, except for God, who fit the lyrics: "If I listen long enough to you, I'd find a way to believe that it's all true . . ." Only with God — and perhaps myself, too — was I perpetually searching for a reason to believe.

Chapter 34 - SUMMER AT HOME

At the end of the spring semester I sweated bullets over tests, papers, and grades. Yet I was generally not a slacker in school, receiving mostly As and a few Bs. Not too bad for a state-assisted, overwhelmed mom. As summer approached, I hunted for odd jobs like cleaning and babysitting to earn enough money under the table to travel to Kansas. Another chance might not come for a long time. With Ron in Bridgewater, I'd be safe. Who knew where he would be by next winter or the summer after that? All the pieces came together when I answered an ad from a woman traveling to Kansas City. She was driving. We could travel with her and share the cost of gas. How perfect. Randy anticipated the family reunion by riding his pretend pony constantly, as if it would get us there sooner.

He thought of the farm as the best playground. New adventures awaited, with animals and buildings, bales, creeks, woodpiles, and pastures. "Oh, goodie," Randy yelled, when we finally arrived. He squirmed out of my lap, and his eyes lit up when he saw Lynnie and Carla. Dot, Butch, and Dad left their work stations at the barn or shed and greeted us with warm hugs. I was impressed with their sense of purpose and direction. Like pioneers on the plains, they knew the tasks they must accomplish, and they were rough and ready to face challenges. I relished their energy and know-how.

Randy felt at home, and so did I. Perhaps we could both relax into a nurturing equilibrium. Odors of Dad's pot roast wafted through the kitchen. I tore Randy away from the girls long enough to say hi to Mom. She looked about the same as she had at Christmas. I couldn't understand what she said, but I nodded to affirm I was listening. Here and there I caught a few words, and I swallowed my profound sadness. I fought back tears and felt a wave of heat splashing from my chest to my face. If I could let myself, I would lie next to her and sob. I recognized my own exhaustion in her.

Yet I, like Dad, must keep going, must strive against the odds. I had a future ahead of me, and I could fancy that someday I'd achieve it. I didn't imagine Dad retained that same vision.

How had we come to this place of devastation? I remembered in this room, where Mom now lay slowly dying, the bliss of family, the crackle of laughter, the sheer delight of Mom and Dad playing with us kids. Mundane days at home had thrilling moments.

An inert depression hijacked my energy, and only raw anger could wake me and drag me out of bed. I wanted to collapse under the strain of being me. I was drained of innocence and blind trust. I was tired of making dumb mistakes and hurting people. Not only had I hurt Mr. Bellington, I no longer had his help. Ron's days in Bridgewater were numbered. As soon as I returned to Boston, I'd have to confront that disaster. I was tired of being an outcast no matter how hard I strained to accommodate, tired of having no money and facing the pressures of college, and tired of being a go-it-alone mom.

I felt more distant from Dad, though he applied no restrictions and asked nothing of me. I was no longer a Republican. I hated Nixon. I no longer believed I merited the title of Daddy's good girl. Somehow, I'd become bad. I was angry to the core.

It happened so slowly I didn't notice it. But I was not the same girl who had been here at Christmas. I felt hardened and rotten.

Several kind women from Hopefield helped Mom each week. A home health aide bathed her weekly. They did more for her than I did. I picked up cooking and cleaning tasks, but my heart wasn't in it. I played hide and seek and read stories to Carla and Randy. When Dad wasn't in the house we changed the radio from KFH to KOMA, and I taught the kids the little I had learned about dancing. I told them about college, riding the subway, and living in one room of a shared house.

I pretended that Randy was fine playing with the girls, and paid little attention. I degenerated into the worst kind of teenager, angry and hungry for action.

One evening at twilight Dad and I leaned against the propane tank and talked about my welfare experience.

"What's it like?"

"It's not so terrible. I keep Randy and me on an extremely tight budget. We don't eat out or go to movies or buy more than minimal groceries. I only need two pairs of jeans for college, a few shirts, and a nice blouse I made. Randy doesn't need much either. I keep back money for the subway and emergencies. If I can earn even a few dollars under the table, I put that away to come home. We live as cheaply as anyone could and barely make it, but it's OK."

Dad nodded. His lowered eyelids formed shades for his thoughts.

"Why do you ask, Dad? What are you thinking?"

"Does your welfare insurance cover things?" he asked.

"It's pretty good. Sometimes it's hard to find doctors or pharmacies that will take my welfare card, but I haven't needed it much. I think the worst part is the way people look at you when you use your card. They judge whether I've spent money on frivolous things. It's like I owe every person who is not on assistance an explanation for how I live."

"I imagine it helps that you are living among people you don't know."

"God, yes. I've had enough shame for one lifetime. Anonymity is crucial. Boston provides that."

"Sometimes I think about it," he said.

"About what?"

"About giving the farm to the creditors. I'd get a trailer-house somewhere in Arkansas."

"Dad, that's a great idea!"

"We'd probably all get better medical care. I can't keep up with bills."

"Dad, I think you should do it. I really do! You could be with Mom more, and the kids wouldn't have to take care of her so much. They'd get more of you, too. You shouldn't keep carrying the load. I don't know how you bear up under it!"

"We could have a big garden and grow a lot of our food."

"I think it would do you all some good to get away from this area. See some of the rest of the world. Not every place is this judgmental. I'm serious. You should do it!"

We leaned into silence for a while, both knowing he was not yet willing to take the plunge. It would mean admitting defeat, foregoing everything he knew, and losing his last wrinkle of pride. The loss of respect would be partially abated by not looking into knowing eyes. He would plummet and then perhaps adjust and accept the financial assistance he needed.

"Dad," I said, breaking our silence, "I think you'd be happier on the other side of this disaster. And if you are happier, Mom and the kids will be happier, too."

Dorthy and I went out together some evenings. We were determined to be part of the action—to find a group of hippie rebels who, like us, cursed our hypocritical, warmongering culture.

We sang *The Eve of Destruction* and listened to Mick Jagger and
Bob Dylan. I smoked a few joints with the others. We communicated through grunts of *grody this* and *goddamned that* until
giggles set in and we realized we were starving. We knew in
common that something was essentially screwed about the
world. Life delivered a losing hand. We played heartily and
well, but earned few concessions. Revelry belied the torment
of our defeat, which was entirely predictable. We knew the
edges of covert, controlled, rank malevolence, and surmised
how it was unleashed against unsuspecting and weaker souls,
like those in Southeast Asia. Cognizance of human depravity
bound us. I thought I'd learned those pulverizing lessons better
than most.

One evening when Dot and I came home, we found Dad
sitting in a kitchen chair, waiting for us. He'd fallen asleep. His
chair leaned back on its two hind legs. As usual, the back of his
head bobbed against the freezer and he snored like a tractor
pulling an oversized load. We tiptoed around him. Laughing,
we fell on dirty clothes piled high in the bathroom closet. The
commotion woke Dad and he trudged to bed. The next day we
smiled because we had laughed hard the night before, but we
couldn't remember why.

Though my spirits careened and stumbled, I sensed a vague,
simmering recollecting. Our farm reminded me how capable I
was as a child. In spare minutes during the summer of my elev-
enth year, I had trained Kokomo, the Shetland pony Dad gave
us one Christmas morning. Finally Kokomo allowed mounting
by running up behind him, placing hands on his rump, and
leap-frogging onto his back. I practiced tricks with him: standing on his back and sliding my shoes slowly down his tummy,
turning around and around on his back like a spinning top,
and leaning to one side at a run, as if to pick up another rider.
With Kokomo I experienced the magic of mastery, the joy of
making a horse my own.

Chocolady, a full-sized quarter horse, was large for a nine-year-old. Already broken when Dad bought her, she cut cattle so well *she* trained *me*. Grateful I could ride her, Dad gave her to me. He rode a cantankerous palomino blend. Riding together, we felt like we owned the breeze, like the road was not too long and the hours of work not too tiring. We borrowed the horses' sweat and spared our own. I loosened the reins and leaned my body into Chocolady's movement, like a pianist led by a song.

If I could master breaking and riding horses as a child, perhaps I could face summer's end, try to be the best mother I could be, tackle Ron's release, and meet the next school year. Perhaps I could believe in myself again.

On one of our adventures, Dorthy and I drove Dad's Plymouth to Newton. We checked if Ron's old pieced-together Saab still rested in his parents' yard. It did. I could go back to Boston in that car. Legally it was mine because I was still legally married to Ron. Wrenching it from Bill and Judy took the rest of the summer, but I prevailed.

Ron had not allowed me to drive after we married. Before that, I had driven only in local towns and rural areas. I had not driven long distances or in big cities. Not deterred by inexperience, Dorthy and I pleaded with Dad to let her come with me. She could fly home. I needed her help reading the maps and taking care of Randy in the car. Dad agreed. He sprang for Dorthy's ticket home.

We hit Kansas City during rush-hour traffic. Our adrenalin ran as fast as the cars on each side of us. We landed behind a large semi. Unable to see road signs, we screeched to a halt in the median where two highways split and stayed put until we figured out which road to take. After splashing into traffic again, both Dot and I gasped and laughed.

We slept in the car, windows down for a breeze, under a motel streetlight for safety. Bugs feasted on us. The next night we stayed in a cheap motel. Dad had given us two hundred dollars to make it to Boston. We lost one hundred and sixty when a cop pulled us over for speeding and made us pay cash. Sometimes Randy rode up front with us, sometimes Dot sat in the backseat and read stories or played with him. We all sang *Old McDonald Had a Farm, Row, Row, Row Your Boat, The Little White Duck*, and every other non-religious child's song we knew. We nearly hyperventilated each time we approached a big city. We both considered it a miracle when we found Newton, Massachusetts, and located my house. How cool—our Saab left Newton, Kansas, and arrived in Newton, Massachusetts.

I walked Dot and Randy around Boston College. Randy hailed his favorite ducks at the commons. I scheduled a doctor's appointment so I could get birth control pills for Dot, to spare her the anguish of sending prayers into ether, the way I once did.

Dot's return home depressed me. Without words on my lips or songs in my heart, I sucked on Necco wafers and felt sorry for myself. Where was my horse-riding spirit? Soon I'd have to worry about Ron unless I could convince Bridgewater to keep him longer. I couldn't go back to the assistant DA's office. I asked advice from several friends. Maggie told me to call a college friend of hers who worked in the offices of a famous attorney.

"Mr. Lanheim makes so much money, I'm sure he could see you pro bono," she said.

"What's pro bono?"

Chapter 35 - DILEMMA

August 1972

The sleek waiting area featured yacht models. Mr. Lanheim, the attorney, invited me into his office. I sat in a swallowing leather chair close to his desk. Even dressed up, I didn't belong here. Sparing unnecessary detail, I calmly portrayed my problem: could he pressure Bridgewater to keep Ron longer?

Mr. Lanheim affirmed the job could be done. Perhaps it would only take a phone call from the right person, an attorney with clout. He would be willing to take my case if I would be willing to spend some weekends on the company yacht. It would be a lot of fun. There'd be plenty to drink, smoke, or snort, and a cadre of high-powered people partying. He was quite certain I'd enjoy it. With eyes wide open, I shook his hand and told him I'd call him in a few days, if that was OK. How many men wanted women as indebted sex toys? How did this keep happening? Are these guys for real?

What was sex worth—what *should* it be worth—to a person like me? After I used sex to save my life, after I gave it away for the most important and loveless reasons? Should I object now, when the rewards might save my life? I'd enter a whole new world for which I had no frame of reference, but one that would probably be safer than the world in which I now lived.

If I became involved with rich people like Mr. Lanheim, surely I'd get beautiful Oriental rugs like those in the law office. Maybe a house, too, eventually. I'd start as a lowly piece of ass, but maybe someone would recognize I was a real person.

After all, if Ron was released, I'd probably at some point have to use my body just to stay alive. Even then, *would* I stay alive? I couldn't imagine conning him a second time. He'd most likely rather kill me than let me go. If I used my body to keep Ron in Bridgewater, I'd at least survive. I was already a wanton woman. A classy wanton woman was more respected than a wanton welfare mom.

On the other hand, I'd not been away from Randy for a weekend, hardly ever for a night. If I worked on the weekends and went to school during the week, when would I have time with my boy? How many weekends would I have to work? And in six more months, at Ron's next evaluation—how many more weekends for another legal favor? What about all those highbrow manners? I was an unsophisticated farm girl.

Clearly this venture was contrary to the four hundred years of Mennonite blood coursing through my veins. Dad would be appalled, as would anyone who knew me. But did they know what I was up against?

What if Ron hurt my family? What if he killed one or all of them? Then I would regret forever that I didn't take Mr. Lanheim's offer. If Ron trapped me again, would it matter if I escaped? How much more damage could my psyche take? And if he murdered me? What would happen to Randy? I might not be the best mother, but I was all he had.

Was I willing to trade my life or the life of anyone in my family for the sake of hanging on to some last shred of morality? How much of life was a game? How ready should one be to play? In the end, I didn't know an answer to any of these questions, but I knew I wouldn't be away from Randy for a weekend.

Sam broke the news to me: the lease on our shared house wouldn't be renewed. But the silver lining was that Legal Aid could proceed with the divorce using that address, no problem—by the time Ron got out of Bridgewater, it would no longer be valid, and he wouldn't know how to find me. I'd met the two-year residency requirements. I signed papers, taking their word for their legalese. I didn't really expect it, but I was still disappointed that Legal Aid wouldn't help me with Bridgewater negotiations.

I called my caseworker and told her I had a car, a Saab. Astonished, she wondered how I could legitimately come into possession of a Saab. Had I broken some welfare regulations? I carefully explained the circumstance, several times.

Randy and I ran to the store for cereal, milk, lunchmeat, and candy. We munched while the practicing band rocked the house. We played catch outside. Then I sat down to implore Dorthy to write. I didn't have much to say. I wouldn't write about the grimy decisions that hounded my days and induced nightmares. I wanted to feel her presence, to know our family was surviving. She said my letters gave her a sense that life existed beyond the farm. Reading her letters dipped me back into the sweet redemption of familial love and hard work.

School would start soon, but not soon enough for Dr. Shepherd's help with my dilemma. I couldn't imagine he would be any more kindly disposed to my starting a sexual encounter with Mr. Lanheim than Dad would be. I began to realize that though they listened, though they commiserated, they didn't experience the danger viscerally. They didn't "get" the real threat I lived with.

I called Mr. Lanheim and left a rehearsed message. "Hi, Mr. Lanheim. This is Leona O'Brien. Thank you for meeting with me. I would very much like your professional help. However, I'm not comfortable with your proposed yacht experiences. If you would be willing to help me without that agreement, please call me. I would appreciate hearing from you. Please call." I repeated my phone number twice and said, "Thanks. Bye."

Chapter 36 - BRIDGEWATER

Mr. Lanheim didn't call back. I was alone. No father, no sister, no friend, no lawyer, no counselor, no caseworker could help me.

Resigned, I made an appointment to speak to Bridgewater myself. They promised that Ron would not be present. I practiced different approaches to best present my case, to make them understand the danger to me and my family. Why did Mrs. Mitchell, my first caseworker, understand so quickly, yet no one else got it? Was I crazy? Overreacting?

In addition to preparing a statement, I needed to learn how to drive to Bridgewater. My sense of direction was about as trustworthy as Scripture. I left early, granting time for wrong turns and straying down erroneous roads.

Sitting in front of four professionals, I tried to impress upon them the dangers of releasing Ron from secure treatment. Even if he seemed OK in their contained environment, he was still obsessed with finding me. He would continue to hound and harm me, my son, or my family. He had threatened to kill me and my family if I ever left him. The time he thought I *was* attempting to leave him, he nearly did. When I was with him, he was violently abusive. With his one-track mind, he searched until he found me and then forced me to stay with him. He had followed this pattern for six years. It would be impossible to calculate the damage he had caused. My family and I would be in danger if he was released.

Nothing I said articulated the perfect storm I faced. My words sounded overblown, even when I related the instances of knives and guns, kidnapping, rape, and terror. *If he had been a stranger and had done those things, it would seem hideous. But since I had known him intimately, it somehow didn't seem so bad to other people.* Somehow they excused and accepted it.

As I revealed all these vulnerabilities and fears, emotions ripped through me like electrical shock waves, as if I were accused, convicted, and sitting in the electric chair. I felt like the guilty one who was pointing a finger at someone else. I broke down. I caught my breath and continued. My voice was tense and shrill as I eked out words and stifled sobs. They interrupted to ask a few questions, revealing their regal indifference. Finally they dismissed me, saying they couldn't discuss the issues with someone who was so emotional.

I drove home, caught in the spinning force of my fury. These were mental health professionals, and they couldn't deal with emotion? I was soon lost in a maze of Massachusetts roundabouts. Where was home anyway? Who the hell was I, and where did I belong?

I longed for simpler times. I yearned for the long winter hours Dad and I spent together in the shed while he overhauled his tractors. To remove an engine part, he called for a nine-sixteenth wrench. I fetched it. He gave me a cap, gasket, or bolt to wash. I dumped it into our five-gallon bucket of gasoline, swished it around, rubbed it with a dirty rag, and placed it on the workbench to dry. After a spell of undisturbed quiet, which made the sounds of birds, mice, and horseflies louder, he wanted a pair of pliers, a monkey wrench, or a hammer. Those were the hours I longed for—in those peaceful times while we worked, Dad's unspoken thoughts filled the massive corrugated metal shed. Like smoke, Dad's encompassing being permeated voids as well as surfaces. His thoughts became a buffer against the outside world, the container that held weakened and infirm inhabitants of the shed, like the old Ford truck with rotted seats. Or the yellow Z tractor with its flat tires and a crank stuck in the front. Or the pile of wood that might someday be recycled into a gate or ladder or barn patch. If only I could be one of those inhabitants now.

On those days, I knew exactly where I belonged. I had no doubt I was held in his thoughts, along with Mom and the other kids. Somehow, in his six-foot bulk there was room for all of us, crippled and impure though we were, even as he was, too.

Later I learned they had released Ron to the care of his parents, who promised to be responsible for him and to return him to Kansas. I seethed with disgust. I'd lost again. Somebody would pay. Hopefully it wouldn't be my family.

Ron's release might be a good reason to leave Massachusetts, go deep into hiding so he wouldn't be able to find me. I could forget my dream of college, play with Randy, live on welfare crumbs, and relax. I'd be hopeless and depressed—but safe, for a while. But how could I get money to relocate? Was it worth risking my scholarship?

I took a deep breath, realizing that I wouldn't—couldn't—let anything stop me, not life nor death, not fear nor loneliness, not dread nor exhaustion. I pestered the state for immediate housing assistance and went to my classes.

A few days after Ron arrived in Kansas, Dad called. Instantly I knew something was wrong. They no longer had a telephone at the house, so if he called, he had a serious reason. In a deep, sad voice he said that in the wee hours of the morning Ron snuck into the house, went upstairs, and found Dorthy asleep. Terror ricocheted through me while I listened to Dad's brief outline of the dangerous kidnapping, and I breathed again when I learned she had been found. Dad thought she'd be all right, but he had to hurry back to the farm. Dorthy would call in a few days to give the full report.

Pacing back and forth, I resisted a powerful urge to hop in my Saab, drive to Kansas, and kill Ron with my bare hands. I was so sick of this miserable mess. If no one else would handle this, I would.

Chapter 37 - DORTHY'S TRAUMA

September 1972

During the weeks I waited for Dorthy's call, the time felt so long I could have graduated from college, earned a PhD, and finished a lifetime career. Finally hearing her voice, I was shocked. As I suspected, Dad's brief description merely scratched the surface. In her accounting, the terror was familiar to me. I could see it happening. She described the Ron I knew and the inevitable reactions one had to his aggression: the unforgettable traps, the fear, the hopelessness, the racing mind to catch any possible out, the desperate need to use one's wits and ability to soothe, the crushing weight of the trauma that ballooned into enduring anguish just when you thought it would be over.

"I was sleeping in my upstairs room," Dorthy said. "It was a hot September night. Leona, you know how it is here—not even a fan. I was just in my underwear. I woke to the pressure of a twelve-gauge shotgun barrel on my forehead. Ron was straddling me, one knee on each side of my legs."

He told her that if she made noise, he would kill her right then. Startled and terrified, she assured him she wouldn't. When he trusted her, he slid off to the side and talked about his plan to just kill himself, but then he thought he might as well get a good piece of ass first.

Sick with fury I said, "He always says that, Dorthy. He acts like he might kill himself but what he really wants is to terrorize other people and take advantage of them! He *could* kill himself if that's what he wanted to do."

"He wanted you, Leona. He said he wouldn't force me to have sex with him, but he demanded information. He knew that I was the one person who would be able to contact you. He said he had to find a way to see you, and then he could kill himself. I think he was unsure of what he'd do. The longer we talked the more I realized his crazed need for something really bold, like slaughtering the whole family. He told me to get up but not get dressed. I grabbed the bedspread and wrapped it around me. He wanted me to walk him to the door."

As quickly as I replied that he wouldn't let her go at the door, Dorthy confirmed it. But that wasn't the worst part, not even close.

Right before he forced her down the stairs he told her that if she made any sound that woke up Dad, he would kill the entire family. If Dad woke up, she better say she was just going to the bathroom. He would be right behind her with the gun pointed at her.

Dorthy told him that she knew he meant it. She promised everything and tiptoed to not squeak any steps.

"I'm telling you, Leona, I knew at that moment that I would do anything he said, no matter what it was. I was terrified that he'd kill all of us."

What could I say to that? I carried that fear with me for so many years, along with the knowledge that the lives of my whole family rested on obedience to a crazed man, primed to kill. But I had failed, and now Dorthy was in this hell, too.

When they made it to the outside door in the chore room, he told Dorthy she had to go with him. Her complaint that she wasn't dressed and had no shoes didn't matter. He picked her up like a sack of potatoes. He tried to close the door behind him.

She pushed it back open with her foot, hoping that Dad would know something was wrong when he saw the open door.

When he tired of carrying her, he made her walk barefoot across the fields. She stepped in stickers and was injured as she climbed over barbed-wire fences with her white bedspread, a feat that could only be accomplished out of sheer desperation to keep him calm. When they got into his car, parked at Hopefield Church, Ron said they were going to his dad's car lot. Dorthy told me, between clenched teeth, "Ron planned to have me call you and tell you I would be dead if you didn't come take my place."

With her mind on terror's high alert, Dorthy had to decide what to do when he stopped the car to relieve himself a few feet away. Though he left the gun in the backseat, Dorthy knew that if she grabbed it, he would make her use it. She didn't know how to shoot a gun and might fumble the attempt. Plus, she didn't know if she could actually shoot a human being–even a homicidal one.

He came back into the car, joking about giving her a chance, saying he knew she wouldn't do it. Dorthy told him that she didn't use the gun, but she also wouldn't call me, no matter what he tried to do to her. Ron stayed quiet for a while and kept driving, not going straight to their garage in Newton. Dorthy wondered if he had given up on his original plan, was just delaying, or was cooking up a new one. Then his car ran out of gas on a country road just past a farmhouse.

He told her to not even think about leaving the car. He would siphon gas from the farm and would shoot her if she opened the car door. It was dark but she could see the farm and realized he would be able to see her. He also knew she couldn't get far without clothes, shoes, or light.

Dorthy described her frantic review of her options. Where would she hide if she ran? A single row of trees across the road was far too obvious. Just then she saw headlights coming.

Knowing this was likely her only chance, she jumped out of the car and stood in the road, flagging down the vehicle. To her amazement, the driver stopped. Fearful that a bullet would pierce through her any second, she told the driver she was Carl J. Stucky's daughter and needed a ride home.

"God, Leona, when he paused and looked at me skeptically, I thought I was not going to live. But then he told me to get in and I jumped as fast as I could."

The man asked her where she lived, and she started crying hysterically. She couldn't think of where home was. She couldn't tell him how to drive there!

I tried to comfort her, explaining that trauma and terror scramble your brain. Her tears and inability to think was a normal, often a necessary release at that first recognition of help. Even now I could hear the tears choking her as she reported the next scene, pieced together from accounts Dad and Butch told.

Dad had risen before dawn, as usual. He called from the bottom of the stairs for the kids to come down. Butch, Lynnett, and Carla showed up, but not Dorthy. Finally Dad sent Butch to get her. When Butch couldn't find her, Dad immediately seemed to know what happened. He found the open outside chore room door, and that made him more certain. Dad told Butch to keep watch while he drove to Hopefield Church to make calls. Thinking there might be a chance Dorthy had gone to her boyfriend's house, Dad called Grant first. Then he called the sheriff.

I could picture Dad putting the pieces together. When he returned to the house, he told Butch to get the hunting rifle from the back of the pickup. Butch said he would get his, too. But Dad said, "There will not be two people in this family who have to use guns." Butch couldn't believe Dad would hold a gun against a person, and he feared Dad wouldn't use it, no matter what the consequences. But he took everyone else upstairs, as instructed. Butch blocked the other doors with heavy furniture. He kept a lookout from upstairs. Dorthy and I both could picture everyone, huddled together, the older ones trying to comfort the younger ones, and each of them facing an unimaginable threat.

Dad saw the pickup that brought Dorthy home pull into the driveway. He ran out and hugged her. Dorthy briefed him on her experience and said that Ron had threatened to kill the whole family. Grant arrived soon, and Dad asked him to keep watch while he took Dorthy to a neighbor's house. Ron could still show up at any moment.

"It was surreal, Leona, seeing Dad armed with a gun. I felt so guilty that he had to abandon his principles to do something for me and for the family that he wouldn't do for himself, something that he went to jail over."

Ron did appear, but he drove his damn car into the cornfield. From upstairs, Butch could see where he stopped and that he just sat there behind the wheel. They all had to wait more than two hours for the sheriff to arrive with his men. Grant, with his Vietnam training, helped them go after Ron. Ron had a gun pointed at his head as they approached. It took some time for the sheriff to talk him down.

"I'm sorry the sheriff succeeded, Dot," I said. "Ron always seems to wreak havoc on us and then he gets away with it."

"You're absolutely right, and the story only gets worse."

My sweaty palms almost let the receiver slip through, but I had to hold on. I had to hear the rest.

After the deputies took Ron away, the sheriff told Dad they'd put Ron in jail. They wouldn't let him out for at least forty-eight hours. He wouldn't be able to post bond before then. They'd let Dad know before they let him go.

I knew that pack of lies, and rage started pumping through my heart—and I could hear it creeping into Dorthy's voice. "We didn't hear a word. Ron's mom went up. We later found out those jerks released him to her right away! I don't think he spent a minute in jail. But at first we didn't know that. We thought he was locked up. Grant kept regretting that he didn't shoot him in the cornfield. I can't imagine how we would have dealt with that. Anyway, I was still in shock. I felt shaky. Everything seemed unreal."

Even though they thought Ron was in jail, that night Lynnie slept with Dorthy in her room. They pushed heavy furniture in front of all the doors. Fear rattled through them. Lynnie finally fell asleep, but Dorthy couldn't. When she heard scratching under her bed, she thought Ron was under there; that he was just toying with her. She told herself it couldn't be true, but the noises continued. She felt paralyzed and at the same time compelled to act. Finally she jumped out of bed, turned on the light, and looked under the bed. There was the culprit: a tiny mouse eating crumbs.

Dorthy wouldn't be able to sleep in her bed or even at home for a long time. She started staying at a friend's house at night. When she found out they had not kept Ron in jail, she had been furious. They had to go to McPherson to see the district attorney, Mr. Harvey. Dad told her that he was a professional and a busy man. He wouldn't want to hear a lot of crying or emotion. It would be her job to explain the situation as calmly as possible.

"Dad probably said that because he knows that I blew it with Bridgewater when I became too emotional."

"Well, Mr. Harvey talked to Dad for a while—about the price of wheat! I waited and waited. He finally said he heard there was a family problem. So I told him the whole story, calmly, just like Dad instructed."

My heart ached for her as she described Mr. Harvey leaning back in his chair and rubbing his thumb over his chin. Looking Dorthy in the eyes he proclaimed, "You're too calm. Something about this isn't real."

Dorthy was flabbergasted and then infuriated when he asked if she had invited Ron into her bedroom. She told him in no uncertain terms that she didn't, and next he wanted to know who opened the door of the house. Dorthy explained why the doors were always unlocked.

Finally Mr. Harvey called the sheriff, and Dorthy surmised from his side of the conversation that the sheriff was confirming her story. But Mr. Harvey didn't apologize.

"I felt so desperate, Leona, to make him understand. He was so callous. Finally I said that even though the details sounded bizarre, I experienced the trauma with Ron exactly like I told him. And then Mr. Harvey said the impossible. He said the situation wasn't bizarre at all—that he heard this kind of thing all the time!"

"No!"

"Yeah, like young women are abducted from their homes at gunpoint in McPherson County all the time. He couldn't be right about that!"

Mr. Harvey presented Dorthy two options: send Ron to jail or make him get counseling. With jail, he'd get out sooner or later and likely be more dangerous. With counseling, maybe they could convince Ron to abandon his obsession. Dorthy and Dad opted for counseling.

I told Dorthy that was probably a mistake.

"It sure was. A couple of weeks later I called the DA to get the counselor's name. I wanted to be sure they knew the whole story and that Ron was following through with sessions. That's when I learned Ron had been ordered to only one session!"

"Oh, Dorthy, that's horrifying."

"I felt ill. Betrayed. And now the family will be in danger for a long, long time."

"No one in the system gives a shit about attacks on women in their homes. That's the ugly truth of it." I was ready to smash my phone receiver into the doorframe until it broke into smithereens. "Dorthy, I'd do anything that would help. I feel bad I haven't done more to protect you. I want to kill Ron with my bare hands!"

Somewhere, somehow, within our whirling rage we found the peaceful eye of our storm and managed loving goodbyes to each other.

I punched my fist into my hand. My heart pounded and I broke into a cold sweat. If I could get hold of him right now, he'd be toast. I'd pound his face. I'd kick his dick so hard he wouldn't have one. I'd rip his eyes out of his head. I should have bashed his head in when I had the chance. I should have taken Lanheim's offer!

I raved on, shouting my impotent rage, condemning myself for stupid decisions. It seemed I was always a little late grasping how rotten the world really is—always a little naïve. I or my family paid the price. I should learn this lesson once and for all: there is no way to be too cynical.

My body felt like a steel beam: heavy, hard, unyielding. God's little sunbeam was now ready to be a shiny bullet, shattering the politeness, the unspoken lies, the easy beliefs, the suppositions that this world works pretty much the way it should. I hardened my heart until it was as cold and merciless as the windiest icy day in a Kansas winter.

PART V – LOVE TENDERED
WITH FAITH

FATHER SEVERINUS

1. JACKDAWS ON THE TOWER

Jackdaws are perched on the tower outside my window.
Another year gone and nothing has come of my resolutions.
The cities, more and more populous, in an opulent sunset.
Awaiting the end, as then, in Antioch, Rome, and Alexandria.
A promise was given us, though it was two thousand years ago.
And you did not return, O Savior and Teacher.
They marked me with your sign and sent me out to serve.
I put on the burden of ecclesiastical robes
And the mask of a benevolent smile.
People come to me and force me to touch their wounds,
Their fear of death, and the misery of passing time.
Could I dare to confess to them that I am a priest without faith,
That I pray every day for the grace of understanding,
Though there is in me only a hope of hope?

> – excerpt from *Second Space*, Czeslaw Milosz

Tell us, they'll say to me. So we will understand and be able
to resolve things. They'll be mistaken. It's only the things
you don't understand that you can resolve. There will be no
resolution.

> – *Smilla's Sense of Snow*, Peter Hoeg

CHAPTER 38 - ON BEING A WOMAN

Now that I connected to the intense anger in myself, I noticed that Randy was becoming more angry and willful. I had to drag him out of bed and pull him away from distractions to get him dressed. He dawdled with his toothbrush or put toothpaste in the sink holes to make the water overflow. I was forever reminding him to grab his jacket and close the door. He resisted going to daycare, he struggled and cried, and then he ran in the opposite direction when I tried to pick him up. He had a jar of coins that he poured onto the floor of our room. He turned away from me when I tried to talk with him.

We enjoyed occasional moments of harmony: when I laid down with him to read a story at bed time, we snuggled, I tucked him into bed, then shook myself awake again to study. And at the Laundromat—now that we had a car to go there—Randy typically drove his little cars along the long Formica table for folding clothes. He created a make-believe speedway on the floor. Then he would run, drop to his knees, and slide along the dusty floor. I'd start the loads, play ring-around-the-rosie with him, read, and feel sleepy. I chewed gum and bit my lip to keep one eye open for Randy, feeling frustration and deep sadness that he wasn't always carefree.

Feminism smacked me right between the eyes in several classes. For the first time in my life, I was hearing hints that women matter. They might even be equal to men—a revolutionary idea! I liked the sound of it. Some women thought that females were as valuable as males and therefore should have as much respect, power, and pay, along with the equal right to make decisions. If they were correct about all this, maybe I could have hope. Maybe I didn't have to sink into the abyss that was my mother's world.

I really wanted to believe these women, but I was worried that the theory could be ripped apart. In spite of my stunts to prove I was equal to my male cousins, I'd known from childhood that I was not as important. Ubiquitous men around the world appeared on TV, making key decisions for our or other nations, reporting the news, playing the leads in sitcoms. The Boston Metropolitan Art Museum was full of their beautiful works. I didn't see more than one or two works by women. The faculties at college were mostly men. The books I read for my classes were written by men. All the businesses I knew were run by men. The history books I read were all about men. And, of course, our imaginary God was masculine, and at least 95 percent of the stories in the Bible were about men. All the ministers, elders, and deacons were men. The teachers of adult Sunday school were men. Even the choir leader was a man, if a man was available to do it.

When I was about eleven years old, Dad thought Mabel, one of the church women, should withdraw her name for choir director at Hopefield as soon as Harold said he would do it. Dad's reasons were traditional old saws: She shouldn't have persisted in applying for that position. Women were supposed to do the things that men didn't want to do, or the things that required little authority or decision-making.

Women could lend soprano and alto voices to the choir, but they shouldn't lead it. They *should* make all the food for fellowship suppers, clean the church, teach and care for the children during Church functions. But when big decisions had to be made, they should shut their mouths. They weren't the right gender to have opinions that mattered!

After all, women hadn't been chosen to be Jesus's twelve disciples. They weren't male like Jesus or God. They weren't selected to be the head of any household. God very specifically instructed men to be leaders and women to be followers. He wanted women to obey men. He created them to be helpmates and supporters. He made men more intelligent, stronger, and more capable. These messages about a woman's place were consistent throughout my life.

If I dared believe these feminists—that women were equal to men—then God was wrong yet again: God should not be Father and male, and He should not have given men authority over women.

Feminist truth was not yet obvious to me, but I did know that cultures had a propensity to put down one group of people so that the powerful could use them to perform services and gain economic and other benefits from that exploitation.

One day in 1963, when I was thirteen, on Grandma Schrag's black-and-white TV I saw Bull Connor blasting the black children in Selma, Alabama, with a fire hose and beating up black men and women. I knew immediately that the mighty white culture was wrong, cruel, and abusive. When Grandma said she *didn't have anything against the Negroes but she didn't think they belonged in this country*, I restrained an urge to slap her. She said they should go back to Africa where they belonged! That stunned me: Didn't she know they were brought here against their will? Didn't she know that from the start it wasn't their idea to offer their labor night and day to the "superior" white race? Didn't she understand they didn't enjoy being slaves or servants—oppressed, beaten, and killed by whites?

Still, I shouldn't judge Grandma too harshly. She didn't understand that culture and religion could propagate huge lies about who is better than whom. These lies, repeated endlessly, pass for facts. Maybe that was what happened to women: men, with the help of their God, had generated demeaning falsehoods about women. I'd been as deceived as Grandma.

I decided that I'd read more about women's equality. Eventually I'd know if these women libbers were right.

My education major didn't fit my curiosity. I wanted to understand the internal world of people. What made us do the things we did? Was it possible to get inside the mind of a Ron or a Dennis and change a thing or two? I switched to psychology. Some students told me that the best psychology classes were taught by Jesuit priests. They were outstanding professors, many with degrees from the best schools in Europe. I broke my hard line against religious academics. I took a class from a priest.

I discovered these students were correct. The priests had a mindset that plugged into me. They didn't push religion. I appreciated the ethical consciousness they brought. I sensed a kinship with several of them. They didn't know me, but if they did, they would probably accept me, even without faith, even while I was on welfare. Like a stranger in a strange land, I was comforted that someone might be willing to know me. They appreciated how I processed information, and they wrote thoughtful comments on my papers. Grateful, I began to think of them as distant friends.

Of course, I was compelled to ask the omnipresent question. What if these learned men knew something I didn't? How could they believe in God? Why would intellectuals assassinate reason with a fairytale? Reconsidering faith and its potential place in my life was nothing less than ripping my heart out of my chest, throwing it on the ground, and stomping on it. Why did I consider betraying myself with *faith*? Why did I search for a reason to believe?

Like many a late-comer, I experienced the nineteen-sixties in the early seventies. Though I didn't have much time for protests, I attended one and held up signs about tricky Dick Nixon. I took a stand against senseless violence and war. I was like all the other kids in the street—I passionately condemned our actions in Southeast Asia. I shook my fists in the air and chanted with the crowd. Surely our country, which had power beyond measure, should stop killing the poor, hungry, and downtrodden. Why conscript and train good young men, most of whom were saner than Ron, and force them into positions where they would have to kill? Would their experiences make them as angry as I was? How would that affect their wives and families when they came home? What unrecognized and uncompensated price would American women and children pay? They wouldn't get veterans' benefits or the same chance to go to college or lofty speeches from government officials and preachers about their bravery.

I thought about women and children in Vietnam. They were dying by the hundreds of thousands, caught between warring factions. Was Nixon expanding the war so he wouldn't feel like a loser? No wonder Ron could justify violence, rape, and threats of murder. He was right in sync with the policies of this country. Right in sync with what he might have done had he joined the military. Would he have, like some did, used that situation to beat people up, exploit women sexually, and terrorize people at gunpoint?

Worse! Our government would have made him do the one terrible thing he hadn't done yet: kill people. Randy and I were the same kind of people that were killed in Third World crossfire—impoverished and vulnerable. Only in Vietnam, they were much poorer and more exposed. They had nothing—not even the option of talking to, no less soothing, the men who would kill them.

Christians who would gladly persecute me for blasphemy saw nothing wrong with justifying mass murder using the Lord's name. They blabbed this theology as naturally and compulsively as babies gurgled bubbles.

I felt proud of my Mennonite heritage that stood against killing in all its forms, and in the next moment began to feel like a coward: when some students wanted to move the protest to the BC campus, I resisted. I couldn't afford to get kicked out of school.

CHAPTER 39 – A NATURAL APPROACH

My search for an apartment I could afford produced no results. I was still on a waiting list with subsidized housing. When our lease ran out, I pivoted to Maggie, my friend and former landlady, hoping she would rent to me again. She knew the rough road we'd been on and agreed to take us for a month or two until I could locate a space. Fortunately this time we could use our car for transport to daycare and school. We could also move ourselves, with a little help putting our two mattresses on the roof of the car. Maggie and I babysat for each other again, which significantly supported fulfilling my psych field practicum requirements.

I was assigned as the recreational coordinator of Center House, a daycare facility for mentally ill patients, primarily those who had been institutionalized for many years and recently released, due to new drugs that somewhat controlled behavior. The patients spent days and evenings at Center House but slept in their cubbyhole apartments somewhere near the so-called Combat Zone—a rough, inner-city neighborhood near the Boylston Street subway station. I couldn't envision how to drive into the city and couldn't afford downtown parking, so I boarded the subway to and from my assignment.

Without much training, I rallied the troops and involved them in one activity or another. One evening I encouraged relay races. "Come on, Charlie," I said, walking through the gathering spaces. "You can do it. Let's meet in the gym. Nathan, Emma, and May, please join us."

After coaxing and cheering them and counting myself as one relay runner, I rounded up enough bored souls to create three teams of four. I explained the rules and ran my hardest. We laughed with each other about being out of breath and ready to collapse. They were amazed their legs still moved, because they hadn't run in years.

Some of the staff invited me to abscond with them after work. We arrived at a bedimmed bar in the Combat Zone, with red walls, diamond-patterned carpet, and dark, heavy wood trim. We huddled around the table and shared stories. Had we heard about Rosa Chimes? She said she received a telegram from President Kennedy asking her to come to the White House. Can you imagine? The thought brought guffaws around the table.

"Did anyone else see Charlie running? Leona, I can't believe you were able to get him to join the relay races," Bruce Wells, the night manager said. "He actually—now get this—put down his monstrous key ring to run the race. Do you know how often he lets go of that key ring?"

I shook my head. I hadn't realized he set his key ring down.

"Never before!" Bruce said. The rest of the staff nodded excitedly. "That was so unlike him to participate in anything. You must have put a spell on him."

"I just asked him."

I allowed myself one drink, knowing I couldn't afford more. I excused myself, saying I had to catch the subway home. They asked where I live.

"Wellesley," I said.

"I'll take you home," Bruce said. "I have to go to Newton. It's not safe for you to walk to the subway this time of night. Not in the Combat Zone."

"I've done it before," I said "I'm not too scared."

"No, I insist," he said. "I'll take you home. I should be leaving now anyway. I've got a paper due, with less than twenty-four hours to go from start to finish."

He made a show of protecting me from the drunks and crazies on the street. They freely commented when a woman walked by. He grabbed my hand to lead me safely to the garage where his Ford was parked. As he continued telling stories of his experiences at Center House, we laughed frequently. I acquiesced when he insisted on a bite at his favorite restaurant.

It was startlingly easy to converse with Bruce. He asked penetrating questions and seemed genuinely interested in my answers. It turned out he was a seminary student at Andover Newton Theological School and worked part-time as night manager at Center House. He was divorced and grieving his father, who died six months ago.

I admitted to being a welfare mom with a child. Surprisingly, that didn't curb his interest. I told him I must get home and relieve the babysitter. He kept pushing the envelope. Couldn't I stay a little longer? He craved this kind of conversation. It was rare for him to find someone with whom he could really engage. We drove around a deserted Jamaica Plain park and watched the moon. I, too, had not had a conversation like this with any man, ever. Somehow he elicited personal and meaningful stories, including a bare-bones review of my marriage to Ron. I told him more about me than anyone else knew. He managed to transform this introvert into someone who could talk the ear off an elephant.

For better or worse, I wasn't taking birth control pills since I had sworn off men eight months earlier, or further measures of intimacy might have been tempting. He certainly wasn't physically shy. Anyway, what happened to the paper he must write?

The next morning, an irritated Maggie listened to my reasons for being late. Her ears perked up as I told her I met the most amazing man. He wasn't turned off by anything about me or my history. Truly gifted and intelligent, he had a keen mind and was inquisitive. He was two years older than I. He sometimes stuttered, but that didn't seem to bother him. He kept talking. He had a unique way of understanding. I kept saying how amazed I was with this guy—a rare soul.

Maggie's eyebrows lifted and she patted me on the shoulder. "When do I get to meet him?"

With prodding, the Housing Authority finally came through. Randy and I moved to a small apartment in Newton. Finally, we had a place to call home! We didn't have furniture, but since we had a car we could gradually raid the streets on garbage days. I felt as giddy as the kid who hit a homerun.

I had Bruce's number, but I decided not to call. He might think I was desperate. Better to wait and not spoil the illusion. Besides, how would I grapple with him being a minister? What would *he* think if he found out what *I* think?

A few weeks after Dorthy's ordeal, Dad called to say that Mom suffered another stroke. She was at Moundridge Hospital, in a coma, teetering toward death. Crashed into panic again, Dorthy and Butch picked up more of the slack so Dad could be at the hospital. My urgent longing to go home and help languished as I contemplated Ron's formidable presence. The ball and chain of college also was an obstacle. Saving money for a trip required time and arduous effort. What if Mom died? I cringed at the inevitability, at the sadness drenching Dad's tone.

Dad called periodically during the next few weeks to report her unchanged status. Finally he said that, rather miraculously, after three weeks in a coma Mom had pulled through. But her bedsores festered, she couldn't move her arms anymore, and she was almost blind. Yet her mental acuity seemed fine, and

Dad could still understand her. He translated her words and needs for the medical crew.

Dad's description of Mom reminded me of a baby pig I once intended to save. Smashed underneath her mother's large body, with only her head sticking out, this piggy moved her mouth like a fish out of water and made weak pleading sounds. She died in my hands shortly after I chased the sow off the nest.

Mom desired to come home to her hospital bed in the living room, where she could listen to the kids playing, witness the energy of the family, and soak up Dad's love. In spite of the burden, he awaited her homecoming also.

I wondered, in light of my new feminist notions, if Mom thought about her identity as an individual person. She had been someone's wife for so long, birthing and raising children, and then a sad—and angry—person, losing her faculties one by one, day by day, until she was a shriveled, light-weight burden who could do nothing for herself, much less anyone else. If she needed to justify her existence, what did she tell herself? Was it important to her to know who she was, what her value was, or how she would be remembered? Had that ever been important to her? Did she still hold on to some part of herself that the rest of us couldn't know? Was *herself* even important to her anymore? What gave her the will to survive? She seemed to still have that. What is it, underneath everything else, that enables a bare soul to desire breath? What came into, through, and beyond abject helplessness?

Chapter 40 - A RELATIONSHIP UNFOLDS

Bruce and I continued to meet at Center House. He insisted on driving me home to Newton. Maggie's persistent clamoring to meet him was rewarded, and none of us could have imagined the conversations among the three of us. His charisma and relational charm impressed her, too. It was so easy, even compelling, to reveal things to him, to feel close.

I became more comfortable and subtly elated each time we met. As intimacy evolved, he showed interest in my well-being and my pleasure. Finally, sexual play ignited a joyful undulating passion, an urgent and slow unfolding, a tingling oneness that enticed abandon. It seemed too good to be true, and yet it seemed true. For the first time in my life, I was in love.

One night during that fall of 1972, Bruce and I were lying close to each other on the mattress we found for my apartment. Randy was asleep in his room.

"Leona," he said, touching my nose with his nose, "you are so naïve. Didn't you know that first night when I offered to take you home that I was crazy about you?"

"No—until you delayed taking me home."

"I fell in love with you the moment I saw you at Center House, rounding up the troops to run relay races. You were so natural, so unassuming. You were completely at home with the patients. You didn't distance yourself from them or act like you were better. I felt joyful watching you interact. Then when I saw you running with all your might, I couldn't believe it. You weren't acting. You were really there, one hundred percent. You enjoyed yourself with them. They responded to that. I knew then I was in love. I just had to figure out how to get to know you."

"Then you've fallen in love because I'm not sophisticated. If I had known there was another way to deal with the patients, I might have tried it. But I'm not that sophisticated."

"That's one thing I love about you. You're incapable of being fake. Anyone can see right through you. That's why people love you."

"You have a huge imagination. People don't love me. They don't know I exist."

Bruce twisted to his side, so we were turned toward each other. With little space between us, I put one leg over him and pulled closer. Since he was a foot taller than I was, I scooted up a bit to face him. He laughed.

He kissed with slow, deliberate emphasis, searching everything beyond our conscious knowing. We pressed into each other with a longing that words couldn't satisfy and melted into the assurance that each of us was what the other desired; that each gave freely, and gratefully received abundance.

I was so enamored with Bruce that my mind danced and twirled rather than concentrated and studied. I yearned to feel his arms around me. When I did, I felt secure, adored, and—finally—good for something. I trusted him implicitly. Because he was brilliant and a professional leader, I often deferred to his judgment about raising Randy. He played a symphony of knowledge, whatever the subject.

Bruce noticed that at night when I heard the slightest noise I immediately bolted up in bed. He reassured me, saying he would never let anything bad happen to me again. He said he would know I trusted him when my nightly startle reactions stopped. I said it was not about trusting him, it was about knowing Ron.

Because he wanted much of my time, Bruce offered to help me study. His mind somersaulted around mine. He didn't have patience for painstaking efforts. I fretted over sentences. Assignments reverberated endlessly in my mind, abating the fear of missing something important. He was the far-roaming fox, he said, and I was the deliberate hedgehog, digging down.

He wrote intelligent papers in a few hours. He didn't read a text from cover to cover. He scanned it, sucked up the author's intent like an elephant inhales water, and sprayed out an argument. He expressed himself artfully and competently. His professors respected him. But excellence in his studies was not his aim. He wanted to live it up, partake of daily pleasures, drink wine, smoke his pipe, and relish joy. When the present didn't delight, he created a distraction. How about a movie? We could drive to Maine this weekend, camp in pines, and pick up fresh lobster from beach vendors. It wouldn't cost much. He didn't mention black flies, and I learned the hard way.

Bruce and I ignored a reality that could become major trouble for me. Now that Bruce spent the night with me more often than he slept in his dorm room, I was breaking the rules. If the Housing Authority or the Welfare Office found a man living with me, I was toast.

At Thanksgiving, he flew home to Missouri to be with his mother. He made the trip as short as possible because he wanted time with me. Randy and I stayed in Boston. Finances, study time, and Ron's presence prohibited a trip to Kansas. Randy drew pictures for Lynnie and Carla, and we sent letters, asking mailed sentiments to stand in for full-bodied hugs.

Bruce came back from Springfield with stories about his mother. She had figured that he bounced into a new relationship because she couldn't ever catch him at home, though she called frequently. His anger flared when she indicated he shouldn't date a woman with a child, and certainly not a woman on public aid.

"I appreciate you standing up for me, but look at it from her side. Most mothers wouldn't want their sons dating welfare moms, would they?"

"She shouldn't presume she knows what's good for me. I'm a grown man. She shouldn't judge before she meets you."

I was beginning to see how Bruce hydroplaned on waves of anger. He insisted he knew better than I did how to raise boys, but I didn't agree with some of his approaches. He teased Randy. He resented Randy's intrusions. He thought I was too lenient. He suggested Randy and I should have more rules.

But Bruce's spontaneity made it clear to me that he himself couldn't possibly abide restrictions. He created family fun easily, naturally. He took us to movies Randy loved and treated him to toys. He drove us to the Stoneham Zoo to meet a giraffe named Leona. Playing Speed Racer, he let Randy pretend he was steering. He actively related to my little boy and became a significant force in his life.

Randy played in his room more, though, not totally comfortable with the changes in our family. Perhaps he felt I was too preoccupied with the new person in our lives. I was. Bruce positioned himself in the middle of everything. Suddenly our energy revolved around him. In most ventures he rose to the top. He was the leader directing an adoring swarm. He thought quickly and articulated what he wanted before I had inhaled. Whatever he wanted, he desired intensely, with heat. My wishes cropped up lukewarm in comparison. In my introverted style, I didn't formulate desires until I'd plunged into theories about them. Bruce was unafraid to believe his way was best. We typically did what he wanted, avoiding sour moods.

Bruce introduced me to the accoutrements of cultured, middle-class Bostonians. He sported a meerschaum pipe and aromatic tobacco. He aspired to be a wine connoisseur, a Charles Krug, on special occasions. We listened to John Prine, Van Morrison, and The Band on his stereo. He bought my first lobster dinner and showed me how to eat it. We laughed at my clumsiness that sent lobster juice flying across the table. The flavor was yummy!

We reveled in a live performance of *Jacques Brel Is Alive and Well and Living in Paris*. As a believer of existentialism, I liked the play more than he did. He teased me about my role as timid Frieda with her brave *fuck-you* stance. I said he resembled Jackie, who tried to be cute, cute, cute in a stupid-ass way.

Between the two of us, I was the simple realist, the one who was a focal point for love and a lightning-rod for reality. I could accept what must be endured and stay on my feet, could walk into truth without scrambling for ready-made illusions. I offered a strength that encouraged depth and groundedness. Bruce was playful, worldly, talented, active, energetic, funny, and full of mischief. And we both had enough anger to power a rocket around the world.

CHAPTER 41 – TO KNOW
AND STILL LOVE

Winter 1972

Late in the first semester of my second year, I struggled through papers and finals. Bruce zipped through his with time to spare for Christmas shopping. After much discussion about Ron, Bruce believed we should make the trip to Missouri and Kansas. Ron wouldn't know we were there, and if he showed up, Bruce had worked with crazy people for several years now. He knew how to handle rough situations. Besides, my mother had been in the hospital numerous times this semester; he wanted to meet her before she died. It would be a great opportunity to meet each other's family. "Come on," he said. "It'll be fun."

We stopped at his mother's house in Springfield, Missouri. Randy and I lagged behind Bruce as he greeted her and then introduced us. She was gracious, talkative, and welcoming. We might not meet her standards, but I hoped she would soften. I was astonished by her charming though small ranch-style home. The colors in her sofa and cushioned chairs highlighted the living room shag carpet. Every nook and cranny was thoughtfully appointed. She had artfully painted fruit and designs on some of her furnishings. She was a gifted person, intelligent, kind, and artistically talented.

We discussed how her job with the state, assisting unemployed people, was not fair to her. She was far too experienced and talented to be paid poorly, without much rank. The men were promoted to management positions—especially those who were veterans. They got extra points, promotions, and more money. I felt happy to have the bond of feminism with her.

We traded cars with her when it was time to head to Kansas. Our little Ford would not be proficient in the predicted snow. Furthermore, if Ron saw her Chrysler, he'd think we lived in Missouri.

I was excited for Bruce to meet my family. Though I had prepared him, I fretted that our living conditions might shock him. Randy opened the car door and hopped out the second we stopped. Dorthy, Butch, Lynnie, and Carla were genuinely thrilled and hugs abounded, before, during, and after introductions. Dad was not home but was expected back soon. We went inside to meet Mom. Lying in her hospital bed, she could not engage. Nonetheless, Bruce tried, and her eyes showed excitement, especially when we lifted Randy up to see her

Giving Dorthy a huge hug and telling her again how sorry I was that Ron terrorized her eased my pain, too. She still couldn't sleep at home, even though four months had passed. We professed gratitude that Ron hadn't shown his face since he abducted her. Just yesterday a neighbor said that he heard Ron went back to Massachusetts and somehow got in trouble in New Hampshire; he was reportedly serving jail time there. If that was true, Ron must have attempted to hunt me down.

Bruce noticed we had no Christmas tree. With his usual enthusiasm he proposed we chop one down. There were plenty around our fields. The kids jumped at the idea, so we left Mom, grabbed a saw and hatchet, and packed ourselves in the Chrysler. We found a perfect tree near the ditch next to Hopefield

Mennonite Church. After swinging a dull hatchet, we sawed. Excitedly we loaded the humongous tree into the trunk.

But take-off disappointed. Our Chrysler tires spun and spun. All but Bruce hopped out and pushed with Herculean might. Nothing worked. Bruce said he'd hightail it across the pasture to our house and petition Dad to help us. We rubbed our hands and sang Christmas hymns to stay warm in the Chrysler. We laughed about what story we might fabricate if someone found us here, with the incriminating evidence sticking out of our trunk.

Fortunately Dad had returned home. Bruce introduced himself and reported our pickle. Dad roared with laughter. They jumped into the truck and came to pull us out of Hopefield's lot.

With his usual charm, Bruce drew Dad into adult conversation. Dad relished the chance to engage. The kids and I strung popcorn and made construction-paper chains to decorate the tree. We laughed when our needles missed the popcorn and found our fingers or when our threads crossed and entangled. A few days of simple celebrations embedded us in the loving, gentle spirit of *home*.

Back in Boston, with family introductions behind us, our relationship seemed more solid, our future together more possible. It dawned on me that though Bruce lived what seemed a wildly extravagant life, with restaurant food, wine, movies, a stereo, and a nice selection of records, pipes, and tobacco, he didn't have much money. He was a graduate student working in social service jobs. His lifestyle, like his stories, was embellished.

The God problem inhabited our dialogue and our psyches, as big as a mountain between us. Bruce listened to and understood both my lack of faith and my anger at the God who *should* have existed. I listened to his theology. We didn't settle our differences. He swung between fascination with the challenge and frustration about our theological difference. How could he be a minister and I a minister's wife if I had no faith? The closer we came to planning a life together, the bigger this issue grew.

He said I was more like Jesus than anyone he knew. I should accept that God had chosen me for some purpose. If I wasn't infused with a faith tradition I would not be who I was—one Jesus would love and appreciate. Rather than driving me away, perhaps my suffering could bring me closer to Jesus. He surely suffered with me and with countless other people who struggled. Bruce saw that I lived a deeply spiritual life and that no rational construct such as pervasive doubt could remove the Mennonite from me.

I explained that I loved Jesus's message, whether or not He would approve of me. I thought He had no magic or supernatural power. It wasn't that easy for Him. He didn't embody the guaranteed superstar legacy of being God's only begotten Son. I thought He was a voice crying in the wilderness, like the rest of us, not knowing what difference His voice would make but daring to speak anyway. I believed in Jesus, the Prophet of justice, compassion, and love. No more. No less.

The Jesuits taught existentialism at Boston College. Their broad and encompassing way of imparting knowledge seemed right and comfortable to me. Since I took so many philosophy classes, I changed to a double major in psychology and philosophy. The Jesuits introduced a Christian spin to existentialism. I respected their version—but I had bought from that store before and came home with rags. I would feel ecstatic if I could see it their way, but I didn't. I still thought that humans compulsively constructed meaning, sometimes by imagining God.

Even so, I faced the fact that as I sped away from faith, I raced toward people who believed. These priests were among the instructors who understood me, the people with whom I shared a deeper connection. To make matters worse, these people I gravitated toward were intelligent men, far more edu-cated than I was. I didn't yet share their vast understanding or years of experience. I was just a twenty-two-year-old female student. Who was I to debunk the constructs of intelligent peo-ple who cared about me and the world?

Bruce had a whole theological school full of brilliant profes-sors standing behind him. I didn't have many people standing behind me. I could throw Jean-Paul Sartre at him and a few others, but I didn't believe what I believed because of Sartre—I liked Sartre because his atheistic constructions of meaning agreed with me. He articulated what I knew but couldn't for-mulate. Even then, I only understood a bit of his treatise.

I wouldn't abandon what I knew deep in my bones of God's non-existence, just to be aligned with Bruce. Still I had to ask myself, is what I know the whole story? Are there things I don't yet know that might change my perspective?

Bruce said I was hung up on theodicy—the question of how God could be good if all these bad things are allowed, created, or sponsored by God. In my simple mind, there was no answer. If God existed, His failure to help people was unforgivable. If God existed but wasn't good, why bother with faith? Why not curse the Bastard and replenish the bounce in our steps by our-selves? If He didn't exist, He wouldn't know it anyway. If He did exist, He deserved the jabs.

As the permanence of my relationship with Bruce became clearer, so did our arguments about God. "Science doesn't know everything, Leona. Even science admits that."

"Religion knows even less, Bruce, and religion doesn't admit that."

"Religion does admit it. That's why it's called faith."

"If religion truly admitted that it doesn't know, why would it attack people who say that God probably doesn't exist? Let religion admit it doesn't know and stay true to the admission."

"People relate to God because there's something there to believe in. The vast majority of people throughout recorded history believed in something."

"Bruce, I understand the *need* to believe. Who can bear to be alone, helpless, a random creature among arbitrary circumstances? It's easier if you believe. People have a compulsive need to."

"So why stand against them, as if you are better than the sum of history? Why not stand with them and search for the solution we all long for?"

"I know the longing. I don't like deception."

Bruce and I agreed to disagree, but neither could leave the subject alone.

CHAPTER 42 - MARRIAGE

October 1973

With his usual exuberance and passion for what he wanted, Bruce proposed marriage. I was deeply moved that he loved me, that he wanted to proceed. I was also cautious. By now I perceived some aspects of his character that didn't fit me. I wished *I* could be the one who knew what I wanted and persistently charged forward. I was not, but I knew I loved him.

Maggie helped me sew a beige linen wedding dress with seventy-three hand-covered buttons and light-blue trim. We also made a bonnet out of the light-blue fabric—a reminder of generations of Mennonite women working in gardens and fields. I brought my history and all of me to this event, though I was ambivalent.

Both Dorthy and I took a plunge. She married Grant a few weeks before I married Bruce. Bruce's mother came for the wedding. She adored Randy, who told her excitedly about his part in the wedding. He would join Bruce and me to covenant together as a family.

We married almost a year after we met. In the simple service at the Andover Newton chapel, with its stately crisscrossing wooden beams, we mentioned the people we loved and missed: my entire family, his brother and family, and his deceased father. We ditched the word *obey*, so I was not promising Bruce what he wouldn't vow to me. I swallowed hard to accommodate the Christian nature of the service.

Breathing a sigh of relief, I celebrated the end of my two and a half years on welfare. Randy would still receive some benefits, but I was no longer a welfare mom. Bruce would adopt Randy as soon as we could do so without giving Ron an address where we would continue living.

The next day we brought Randy and Bruce's mother with us to Vermont for a two-day honeymoon, promising ourselves we'd have a real one at some later date when we could afford it. I adored rolling hills, peaceful countryside, and farms with New England houses attached to barns. As we drove along a winding road, I insisted we stop and back up to view the antique manure spreader I spotted in a field. I walked as close to the spreader as I could without trespassing. The weather-worn, bare wood formed a rectangular box with metal teeth that resembled pitchfork heads situated on a turning pipe at one end. That piece shuffled the manure and turned it into a resource for crops the next year. I wished I could take that manure spreader home with me. I'd plant flowers in it.

Bruce, his mother, and Randy accepted my affection for the manure spreader with skeptical humor. We scoured the landscape for those precious manure spreaders just in case we came across another one that would thrill me to the core. Bruce's mother said she had not known anyone who was so loveable and sweet—and also had such a foul mouth! We decided we liked each other. I realized I was gaining a mother, and Randy a grandmother. With teary eyes, I translated our good fortune into my heart.

We settled into our two-and-a-half-room Andover Newton dorm apartment in Herrick House. The half room was a closet kitchen. Married student housing was quite charming. We had a great green as our front yard and a forest as our backyard.

Bruce thought Randy needed a dog. I was hesitant. What space did we have for a dog, and who would care for it?

Randy clamored for the idea, I softened, and Bruce found the Humane Society animal rescue. A young black-and-white border collie jumped up and ran to Randy. He petted her, she licked him, and he knew immediately. After some convincing that Jump might be a middle name, not a first one, Randy called his new friend Daisy Jump Wells. Immediately they become constant companions, and Daisy and Randy snuggled together at night.

CHAPTER 43 - A FEMINIST DIVINITY WIFE

Fall 1973

If I stampeded through another year of twenty-one-credit-hour semesters and a summer class, I would graduate with a bachelor's degree from Boston College. This was Bruce's last year as a Master of Divinity student at Andover Newton; he would graduate a few months before I did in 1974.

For the first time in my life I lived on a school campus. It was not my campus, but nevertheless I dwelled with professors and students—an apostate in a world of believers. But this time it was a world of smart believers; people of the real world, people with freedom, privilege, and know-how. They were learned book readers. They conversed in a strange and intriguing language. I continued to question how they could justify the things I could not. How could they be so smart and yet believe myths that seemed ridiculous?

Bruce served as a student minister in a suburban Congregational United Church. We worshiped there every Sunday to support his ministry. Bruce seldom preached, but he worked with the senior and associate pastors to establish programs for youth and other ongoing groups. After church we were usually invited to the senior pastor's house for lunch and drinks. They enjoyed Dry Sack sherry. We brought a bottle with us. I didn't have a frame of reference for church people who drank, especially not ministers, but they were delightful.

These ministers often railed against people using God in cruel and thoughtless ways: to justify mass murder, to prop up prejudices, to pretend that America is beyond sin or the need for self-reflection. This was not what God wanted nor was it God's fault. Some supposed Christians, the ministers concurred, would use anything to justify prejudice, violence, and cruelty: cultural beliefs and science when they could, economic theories, political rhetoric, the worst and most distorted testimonies of history, and they also used their sick conceptions of who God was. I listened attentively, remembering the Farm Bureau Camp.

Feeling sorry that he couldn't let me attend Camp Mennoscah earlier in my sixteenth summer, Dad had pulled off a minor miracle after the critical harvest weeks: he got me into the Farm Bureau youth camp. I was ecstatic. To feel free and like a regular teenager, I hid Ron's ring in my suitcase.

The American flag adorned all our lectures and meetings the way a cross might preside in a church camp. It was like a church camp for America; everything they said about America, we said in church about God. America/God was good. America/God was mighty. America/God needed our help. We were good when we worked on behalf of America/God. We were fortunate to have America's/God's protection. We owed what we are and what we have to America/God. It was good to sing songs of praise about America/God.

I upheld America and tried to count on God. I didn't believe in government interference or in its right to make people go to war. I disliked fancy people like Jacqueline Kennedy spending our tax money on dishes or other frivolous things. But I'd not felt that America and God were on the same level. I thought God was first and America a distant second.

When the larger group broke into smaller discussion circles, I raised a concern about the America-always-right theme. Much to my amazement, a young man, rather good looking, said that he thought America should not be involved in Vietnam. He thought the Cold War was a front for the military-industrial complex. I'd not heard these big words before. This guy, Lawrence, was smart. We ventured a few more comments and became fast friends.

Lawrence explained foreign policy and the mistakes our government was making. He knew! We became bantering rebels of the Farm Bureau camp, hashed out our ideas through lunch and dinner, and found excuses to chase and tease each other. The week felt like freedom and went by in a flash. I hoped Lawrence would write, though our connection never hit the pavement—not with Ron around.

I loved that experience with Lawrence—all the fun we had as the camp rebels—and now I realized that the theology and political discussion that Lawrence and I derided was the very theology that disgusted the ministers here. It is and was too simplistic. I wondered how Lawrence and I realized that, when we were just teenagers.

Ill at ease with upper-middle-class congregants, I didn't perceive our commonality. While I liked the social-justice message they derived from Jesus's ministry, I didn't resonate with their God-language. But what could one expect from a Church? They seemed like good people—much more like Bruce than like me. They knew how to read expectations and be appropriate, how to move smoothly on the stage of life, how to find acceptance without proving themselves. They shared a consensus that evaded me. I couldn't fathom how to see through their lenses or think their thoughts.

Feminist ideas, which I'd heard in a few classes, seemed to be noticed by more professors and discussed in more classes.

Like an evangelical, I jumped into that framework before I knew its adequacy. What I earlier suspected might be true ripened like summer fruit. Patriarchal culture and religion had kept women isolated, marginalized, and in a state of servitude, unable to think their own thoughts before they were circumscribed by male indoctrination. With their invisible labor and helper status, women had been largely unable to utilize resources and power to succeed in professional and business endeavors. Worst of all, because they ingested cultural and religious inhibitions, women had not esteemed their own ideas and well-being.

In fact, the work of women was often credited to men in insidious ways. I remembered that before her illness progressed, Mom insisted on two behaviors, both of which impeded our looking up to her: that her children waited for Dad to arrive before we ate, and that we prayed before we ate. After yelling across the yard numerous times—and still Dad did not respond—Mom sent a kid to the shed or barn to get him. He finished his task and then came, as if his important efforts should set the timing for the household. In the meantime, we grumbled and snitched food when Mom wasn't looking. She had labored for hours to put pot roast or sandwiches or homemade *knepp* noodles on the table, and then to protect her dishes until Dad arrived. When he sat down at the table, we bowed our heads and thanked Him for our food, saying that by His hand we all were fed.

Integrating insights from child development studies and feminist thought, I gained the sense that my soul's longing was actually for my mother. My infant being was entirely dependent on her ministrations. I would have died without her feeding, caring, holding, talking, and knowing me well enough to decipher my needs. Without her being bigger, better, all knowing, and nurturing, without her body's superlative work to conceive and to sustain me in the womb, without her birth pangs and anguish, I simply would not exist. I owed my being to her, who knew me before I could know, who gave me life, love, guidance, and connection.

But because I was a religious child, the birthing/nurturing aspect of my connection to her was shrouded in a replacement myth that removed her from my conception of those who created, loved, and sustained me. By the time I was a toddler, Jesus and God claimed my whole heart's allegiance. They became the Masters who created, birthed, nurtured, guided, and loved me. I sang songs of praise and kept Them close with gratitude and adoration. While my real nurturer vanished from my sight, I embraced the perfect and powerful Males who I believed created and held me, and the whole world, in the palm of Their hands.

Other female students told me about a feminist professor, Mary Daly. I hungered to hear her, but Bruce claimed he couldn't change his work schedule to watch Randy so I could attend an evening class. And on campus, some Jesuits—at odds with the strong feminist theologian who didn't want male students in her theology classes—sought her resignation. Though I respected the Jesuits, I hated what they did to Daly. In her book, *Beyond God the Father*, she had the courage to claim that the very image of God—as male—was duplicitous. I imagined that if God revealed Himself unequivocally to the world, so that everyone believed, I too would believe, but I wouldn't be satisfied. I'd have the same issues Daly expressed.

Since God didn't reveal Himself to be She and not just He, Goddess and not just God, He was at least partially responsible for half of humanity being demeaned, shamed, limited, and often enslaved. To make Himself moral and honorable, He'd have to strike all the misogynist texts from Scripture. He'd have to tell as many women's stories as men's. People would be shocked that God actually existed. They'd be even more surprised to discover that S/He models justice and love.

When a few other female students and I complained about the lack of feminist courses, we were asked to teach a reading and research class on feminism. I felt honored to be among the five female student teachers who assigned daring books and led discussions that pushed the envelope.

With energy and grace I faced the challenges of ordinary life—finding a jar for the bug that intrigued Randy, sitting up nights when he ran a fever, stretching each penny to cover what Bruce's desires warranted, forever cleaning, cooking, doing dishes and laundry, attending classes, and persistently studying in the nooks and crannies of my daily schedule. Finally I was in a marriage where I could express my opinions passionately, where I often felt known and loved, and where I was part of a team working together to create a better life. Still, no matter how many feminist manifestos I read or wrote, no matter how passionately I argued my case, no matter how much experience I had to back me up, I was still in a role of who I was supposedly created to be—a helpmate, a support, and a lover of the important man in my life.

Though I dissected every temptation to believe and scoffed at the obvious myths, I yo-yoed back and forth between what I thought I knew and what my gifted professors knew. My favorite Jesuits said I was a theological thinker. They encouraged me to explore faith from the perspective of modern Biblical scholarship. I'd find, they suggested, that my Mennonite notions about God were too simplistic. If I gave myself half a chance, I'd be able to resurrect the constructive aspects of my faith. Bruce also thought I would learn about God from an entirely different vantage point. I doubted that I could reason myself around what I already knew. But they might be right about one thing. If I could discover and reclaim a good God/dess, I could relax the part of me that had to shut down that naïve, faithful child in me who jumped towards belief at any opportunity. Without that internal struggle, I might bask in Light, loosen my grip, and sing in the shower.

Everything in me opposed this idea, except my banished childlike self—who still looked to find a reason to believe. If I could find a good God/dess who actually existed and offered capable love to humanity, I could also cradle my sunbeam self and feel whole again. I yearned to embrace that heart-wrenching reunion and deflate the loss and anger that kept us apart.

The years of tests, papers, readings, and studying, of spending thousands of dollars on tuition, and of reintegrating agony, grief, and rage might be the price I would have to pay for rapprochement, assuming I found it. I would investigate each deceit and strive to discover the transcendent kernel of truth that Bruce and my professors could somehow believe.

CHAPTER 44 - A TRIP TO KANSAS

Moundridge, Kansas, June 1974

I was essentially finished with my bachelor's degree in May of '74, though I would complete one more summer course—a reading and research class in theology. Bruce was graduating from Andover Newton with his master's degree. It had been almost a year and a half since our Christmas trip to the farm. Our graduation present to each other was to see my family and Bruce's mother. Shortly after the semester ended, we started the long trek to Missouri and Kansas.

Randy now loved a children's rendition of *Moby Dick*. Earlier we had visited a whaling museum in New Bedford, which brought a dimension of reality to that story. I read that version to him repeatedly on the trip. Randy also surprised us with his interest in a book about Harry Truman I read to Bruce as he drove. Randy listened as intently as we did. Truman became our Midwestern hero. Give 'em hell, Harry!

Randy and I couldn't wait for the last few miles to vanish. "Yes!" we heard Butch, Lynnie, and Carla say as we pulled in the driveway. They were standing close to the elevator building. Lynnie held a mama goat's head so Butch could milk her. Carla ran after our car. Lynnie and Butch were close behind her. Hugs went around, and soon Dad was with us also. Randy plunged his hands in his pockets and pulled out marbles and jacks with a red rubber ball to impress the girls. They ran across the yard to a mulberry tree and shade. We carried our luggage in and greeted Mom. Dad, Bruce, and Butch went outside to chore. I stayed in the house with Mom. Dorthy's absence reminded me that she, too, was a married woman.

Mom lay perfectly still in her hospital bed. I told her about our drive, how Randy and I relished the farms, fields, and animals we passed along the way, how we kept count of horses or silos. Knowing I wouldn't understand her answers, I didn't ask questions. I explained that I was almost finished with Boston College—just one more summer course—and I was accepted into Andover Newton Theological School, with classes starting in the fall. Bruce had helped me apply, and I was accepted and granted significant financial assistance. To raise money for school, we sold my car. Since I'd be living on the campus where I'd be attending school, we could manage with one car.

I told her I felt proud of these accomplishments, and I wondered if she understood enough to be proud, too. I hoped it brought her a modicum of satisfaction that her daughter was finding her way. Eventually I excused myself. She could rest while I cleaned off the table and washed dishes. I made a gallon pitcher of sweetened tea, Dad's favorite, and some Kool-Aid. After starting another load of laundry, I checked on Mom again. She was awake. I commented on the lovely yellow and purple irises in full bloom. I imagined those flowers brought her a bit of pleasure, if she could see them.

I ventured a little closer to our hearts by telling her that I was learning more about mothering children and becoming aware of the many loving ways she had helped her children, especially me. I wanted to say more, but a lump clogged my throat. It seemed that whenever I considered her full personhood, I cried uncontrollably with grief for all that she and we had lost through the years. I bit my lip and pinched my side to distract myself with pain while I managed to get out just one more thought. "I know you did your best, Mom, and I love you and am sorry for all the ways I didn't understand your care for us."

She didn't try to respond, but her tears said that she understood. I excused myself to find tissues for both of us. Imagining the throbbing in my head might be in hers, too, I sighed heavily and wiped the tears from her eyes and from mine. Together we had crossed some threshold, and we needed to let that be enough.

I wondered if I should say something to her about the strokes she'd had recently, the times she'd been hospitalized and in a coma. Her death loomed over us like smoke over a fire—inevitable, natural, and yet something that choked us and burned our eyes. What would the kids experience when she no longer resided with them? They wouldn't be lifting up her frail body and sliding the bedpan under her. They wouldn't be changing her diapers or fanning her or swatting flies away. And when she died, would they feel they had been motherless children for years?

I heard the kids screaming and running. They'd spotted Ron's Saab on the road, coming toward our driveway. I instructed them to hurry into the house while I ran to Dad and Bruce. Fortunately they were close to the house. Instantly they flew into motion, almost without a word. Dad walked into the driveway to meet Ron. Bruce jumped inside the house. He grabbed a baseball bat and held it tight, positioned to strike. He said he'd clobber Ron in the head if he came through the door.

"Don't kill him," I said, alarmed. "I don't want you to have to live with that."

"Phew!" he grunted, rumbling air through his lips. "That's exactly what I'll do if he comes in that door."

"No, Bruce. Don't!"

"I'm going to," he said, with solid determination. "You grab Randy and the girls and hide upstairs."

I hesitated, wanting to talk him out of his vicious approach. Of course, I had wanted to kill Ron before, but that was my rage talking after he hurt Dorthy. I didn't want to be more destructive than we absolutely had to be to stop him from hurting us. I didn't believe we were in serious danger right now.

"Get going!" he ordered.

"He's outnumbered here! Just disable him," I said as I ran toward the kids.

We hid in a closet upstairs. Our hearts pounded. I grabbed a wooden hanger, as if that would protect us. "Don't worry," I whispered. "Dad and Bruce will handle it. We'll all be OK."

We hardly breathed until we heard Bruce calling us from the stairwell. "It's OK now. He's gone." Bruce didn't use the bat. Dad had been able to assuage Ron's urgent need to find me and redirect him, partially with the message that I had a new husband. That startling message probably meant to Ron that some other man now owned my body.

After a while we all settled down. I played with the kids for a time, wanting to stay closer to them in case Ron came back. We all kept a lookout for him. He could park his car somewhere and walk to the farm, perhaps sneaking along the hedgerows.

That evening we shoved heavy furniture in front of all the doors. If he came in, at least we'd hear him. It seemed uncanny that he knew we were here. Would I ever be free of him?

Chapter 45 - HOSPITAL DAYS

Wichita, Kansas, July 1974

My eyes opened to discover I was positioned on the floor in the St. Francis Burn Unit reception area. Finally I was in Wichita, but I'd come too late. My father was dying. I was wrapped in a disaster that took my breath away, literally. I couldn't breathe, like long ago when the silage avalanched and I failed to jump quickly enough.

Relatives stared down as if I were dead, imagining the girl I used to be: a petite, feisty farmer's daughter, muscle-bound in leather work boots tied tight, jeans, and T-shirt—a girl who knew who she was and was proud to make the best of it, who loved by doing, and wore the calluses proudly.

"I'm OK," I said. "I must have fainted." I pushed myself up from the floor. It was the evening of July 14. Since the early morning of July 13 when I heard the hideous news, I'd been desperate to get here.

Bruce moved behind me. His pressed cotton shirt wrinkled as he reached around my waist. He planted a kiss in the middle of my part line. The fury I felt for him helped steady my waves of nausea. "What did the doctor just say?" I asked, to be sure I heard correctly just before I fainted.

"He said Dad isn't going to make it," LeAnn said in a flat tone.

"Can I go see him now? Can I see him?" I asked, sputtering at two nurses dressed in white, studying documents behind a partitioning counter.

"You need to sit down first. Put your head lower than your knees," one nurse said, shaking her Goldilocks curls. "You can't see him now. They're busy with him."

Bruce grabbed my shoulders. He turned me toward him, but I wouldn't look. I stared down at the commercial-grade, multicolored carpet. Dorthy extended a hand. She led me toward the waiting room. Her long legs and slight body wove through the hospital corridor like a weary apparition. Uncle Elvin and Aunt Neva removed themselves from a bench so Dorthy and I could sit down. We wrapped our arms around each other. We couldn't yet hug uncles, aunts, sisters, and brothers-in-law who lounged on waiting-room chairs and wooden benches, shoulders slumped in resignation. We nodded to them all but wouldn't reach out until after Dorthy helped me understand what happened.

Feeling woozy again, I lowered my head.

"It's been this way for several hours now," Dorthy said. "They've come out several times and said he wouldn't make it. Lonie, I've watched the elevator door since last night. What took you so long? Why didn't you fly into Wichita?"

"I'll be damned if I know. Bruce made the plane reservations. I've no idea why he made them for St. Louis. I'm furious with him. It's about a car. Ours died this weekend. Maybe the gravity of the situation didn't soak into his brain until after he made the reservations. It all happened so fast."

"Where's little Randy? Didn't you bring him?"

"No. We didn't think a hospital would be a good place for him, plus we didn't know if Ron would show up. So Randy is staying with some friends, Vicky and Russell. She's a seminary student and he's an engineer. They're so sweet. They said they'd keep him for now. Randy loves Vicky."

Bruce shifted his weight and rested against a wall a few feet away, holding my bulging canvas tote.

"Oh my God, Dorthy, Dad has to make it. I have to see him. He can't die now."

"I know, Leona."

"Where's Mom?"

Dorthy described how pitifully she lay in Mercy Hospital, in Moundridge. "She can't stand to be away from Dad. She's so afraid he'll die. Grandma checks on her and then leaves. Maybe she just can't stand it."

"I can't believe this is happening! It can't be true. Please tell me it's not true," I urged.

"Believe me, honey, it's all true. Wait till you see him. Black burns all over. His fingers are frayed. You can't find a spot on him that's not burned, except the soles of his feet. They said he has third-degree burns over a third of his body and second-degree burns over another third. Hideously painful burns!"

"He's been severely burned now *twice* in his life!"

Uncle Harley and Aunt Ruby hurried toward the waiting area. We hugged them. They made comforting sounds. We conceded shock and incredulous horror. Yes, we confirmed, they'd told us that he wouldn't make it.

Dorthy and I began to embrace the relatives filling the waiting rooms. I introduced my new husband. He engaged these introverts in small talk. Dorthy and I sat back down, like frightened groundhogs scuttling into interconnected holes.

"What happened, Dorthy?" I asked. "I don't know the story. Just bits I've pieced together. The fire started first thing in the morning?"

Dorthy shared what she had learned from Butch. Before dawn, Dad got up to light the hot water heater. The damn thing had stopped working the night before. He put on his overalls and shoes and went down into the basement. He didn't realize odorless propane had leaked into the basement all night. He struck a match to light the pilot, and whoosh—an inferno. Dad ran up the steps and outside, rolling in the dirt.

"At least he knew enough to do that. I can't imagine the anguish he was in—literally on fire all that way!"

"Leona, the whole thing is unthinkable. Wait till you hear the rest. Lynnie and Butch were waking up."

"Were they upstairs?"

"Yes. They heard the explosion and thought Dad was downstairs in the kitchen and had dropped a heavy casserole dish or something. They ran downstairs to where Carla slept. The blast woke her up, too. A large piece of glass blew over her bed. They heard Mom wailing. Mom, knowing that Dad had gone into the basement to light the hot water heater, immediately realized what happened. She made a noise for the kids to hear and waited for the fire to consume her.

"The kids rushed around, calling Dad. From outside, he yelled at them to get out, to get out of the kitchen. The explosion blew holes in the kitchen floor. Flames leaped through them. The kids didn't consider the back porch exit. Instead, they dodged flames and ran through the kitchen and out the chore room door."

A burning sensation traveled from my stomach to my throat. I imagined Butch, Lynnie, and Carla, full of confusion. They must have felt a gripping dread, wondering what happened to Mom and Dad. Outside, how long did it take them to accept the charred man as their dad?

Dorthy was crying as she continued, "Dad walked toward them with both his arms stretched straight out in front of him. From his fingertips hung the skin from the full length of his arms. The skin hanging down came all the way from his armpits and was attached only to the tips of his fingers, like clothes pinned to a clothesline. The kids were speechless in their horror. Dad told Butch to drive the pickup to the neighbor's house and have them call the fire station. Then Dad went back in the house to get Mom. Somehow he dragged her out of bed and lugged her into the old wooden wheelchair, and then he pushed her out of the house and down the back porch stairs. He did this with his hands and body burned to a crisp. It must have ripped the skin right off his fingertips."

"Oh, Dorthy. The thought of him lifting and dragging Mom!"

"Apparently it took the kids a bit of time to reach the Goerings up the road. Straining to grasp the reality of their situation, Butch blurted out a few goddamns. Carla's nine-year-old moral mindset couldn't abide swearing. She told Butch to quit saying bad words and accused him of not being a good Mennonite. Lynnett advised focus. They saw the barn lights were on. They honked, and Mr. Goering came out. Butch quickly related the explosion and drove back.

"Then another panic engulfed them. They couldn't find Mom or Dad. After Dad got Mom out of the house, he had pushed her close to the string buildings, away from the burning house.

"Dad walked toward them like a blackened ghost. He told the girls to stay with Mom and forcefully instructed them not to get near the house. Then he finally told Butch to drive him to the hospital."

"He doesn't even have his license yet, does he?" I said.

"Not even a learner's permit. Of course, he had driven around the farm, but never on the streets. And Dad told him to drive fast. He tried. Dad said to drive faster. Apprehensively, he did. Dad kept saying he didn't know what he would do. How could he take care of his family if he didn't even have a house? How would they all survive? He couldn't afford to buy a house. Butch reminded Dad of the little old house on the Halstead acreage, where they might move easily enough. This seemed to calm Dad's immediate fears. He was quiet for a moment. Then Dad said not to stop at Highway 81. Not much traffic that time of day, thank goodness," Dorthy said wiping her eyes.

"What did they do with him in Moundridge?"

"Apparently nothing. They immediately shipped him to Wichita in the ambulance. He was beyond their capacity. Butch said whoever the nurse was at the emergency room recognized Dad right away. 'What happened to you, Carl?' she asked. Butch said he was shocked that anyone could recognize him, because he nearly didn't recognize Dad."

"Where is Butch now?" I asked.

"Damned hospital rules. They won't let him come because he's not fifteen yet. In several weeks he will be, but that doesn't matter."

"He's old enough to handle this whole tragedy but not old enough to visit his father in the hospital? He's a hero, for Christ's sake." I shot an accusing eye toward the nurses' station, then turned back to Dorthy. "What happened with Mom and the kids?"

"Dad told Butch to go back to help them, so he started back. About two miles from the farm he rounded a hill and could see flames leaping up. He had to stop for a moment. He thought he'd be sick. He didn't think he could face it again. He said he felt so weird, like nothing he had experienced before. He felt terrible for delaying his return even for a moment."

Dorthy breathed heavily, as if enduring an asthma attack.

"When Butch got back to the farm a lot of people were standing around. He probably wasn't gone a full twenty minutes, yet it seemed like the whole community was there."

"And Mom and the kids?"

"There were people with them. Several were taking Mom to the hospital. Lynnie and Carla were waiting to see what Butch would do. Some men worried that the second propane tank would explode. The tanks were connected to each other and the propane kept feeding the fire. No one could turn them off.

Some guys sprayed water on the tanks to cool them. Finally someone turned off the second tank so it wasn't feeding the first. Then they sprayed the first for quite a while. Some guy jumped up on the first one. Others yelled at him not to do it, but he did anyway. He turned it off. Butch said that was scary as hell."

"God, Dorthy. Bravery or stupidity?" I asked.

"I don't know, but it takes damn good neighbors to do something like that."

I wondered if perhaps Mennonites really were special people. After overestimating their unique goodness in childhood, perhaps I had sunk to the opposite extreme. I yearned for Uncle Harley, our family historian, to tell again the virtues of our heritage. Hadn't our people suffered all things and survived? For centuries they lived in peace, even when violence was thrust upon them. That legacy was the strength behind Dad. Maybe he could suffer severe burns and survive.

Dorthy continued telling the story of the fire. "The house was long gone before the fire trucks arrived. Someone took Lynnie, Carla, and Butch to Grandma's house. I'm not sure where the kids went after that, but Butch has been back home. Foster's son and Butch went to the farm last night and this afternoon and did the chores together."

"Oh my God! After so much trauma, Butch had to do the chores?"

"That's what I said, too," Dorthy said. "But Butch just said somebody had to. You know how it is. He's the one who knows what to do."

"That makes me feel terrible! I'd offer to help, but I don't think I can leave the hospital. It took too long to get here, and now I can't abandon Dad."

"Butch said there was no need for others to do it. He knows how."

"Do you know how the relatives found out?"

"I don't know. Seems like everyone knew within minutes. Word just gets out."

"When did they call you?" I asked.

"Grant and I were out camping. They had a hell of a time finding us. Finally a policeman spotted our car and told us. I feel so bad that I wasn't there for the kids and for Mom and Dad. I *hate* that we were camping!"

"I know. I *hate* that we're in Boston, and then I end up going to St. Louis, for Christ's sake!"

"Apparently someone called LeAnn. The kids are at her house now. Maybe LeAnn called Debbie. I don't know the details."

"What will happen to Mom?"

"I guess they'll put her in a nursing home. She's not injured from the fire. No one else can take care of her the way Dad did. Basically no one can understand her."

"The last stages of MS are as dehumanizing and cruel as anything I've ever seen."

My loose stomach was doing flip-flops. I blew my nose and ran to the bathroom. On the toilet, I worried that Dad would die before I saw him. I seethed at Bruce. How could he fail me at such a critical moment? I held my breath, imagining him making the plane reservations to St. Louis rather than to Wichita. Why did I trust him? Why would he fly us to his brother's home in St. Louis when my father lay dying in Wichita? Just because his damn Ford died?

I pictured us rushing through the Boston airport. When I discovered we were going to St. Louis, I almost fainted. I was furious, hurt, completely dumbfounded. Could we change our tickets? Could I change the destination of the plane by sheer will power? I must! Sixteen extra hours, an eternity of loss, struggling to reach my father's bedside.

I felt clammy, sticky, and stinky, with dragon breath. I couldn't eat. If I weren't careful, I'd pass out again. With wet paper towels I attempted revival.

Bruce stood at the restroom door and caught me as I came out. He asked how I was. "Barely making it," I said.

He suggested getting something to eat. I retorted the obvious: I would not leave the hospital.

"I'm trying to help you, Leona. You don't have to be mean."

I snickered and walked a blind beeline to the seat beside Dorthy.

"How are you doing?" I asked.

"I'm not," she said. "We could have handled Mom dying. But Dad is our rock. We won't be the same again."

"I know." Tears rolled down my cheeks. "The house is gone. Everything in it is gone. No one can take care of Mom. I'm sure she'll die soon. And what will happen to the kids? They can't stay at LeAnn's house. She and Al have enough trouble managing LeAnn's drug problem and their own kids."

Dr. Littlefield, nervously stroking an Abraham Lincoln chin, emerged from the hallway and announced, "It doesn't look good for Mr. Stucky. His breathing has slowed. We don't expect him to pull through."

I pleaded again for a chance to see him.

"Not yet," he said. Dorthy explained that I was the daughter who just arrived from Boston. "Sorry, not now."

After that devastating announcement, Dorthy and I huddled with our tribe, listening to them tell incidentals about what they were doing when they heard about the fire. Most stories ended with platitudes from Scripture. We nodded appreciatively. They were offering compassion and love. They looked on me with sad eyes brimming with sorrow, knowing how close I was to Dad. It broke my heart to experience their tenderness, after all I had done to alienate myself. I sobbed silently, rocking back and forth with my hands covering my face.

Exhausted, I resumed questioning Dorthy. Had they seen Ron? She said there was no sign of him, and she heard he might be in prison.

"If he does show, we've got to do something to keep our husbands from killing him," I said.

"I know."

"We're in a burn unit, surrounded by our Mennonite relatives, and our pacifist dad is dying. All the while, we're worrying that our husbands might murder a goddamned fool right here in the hospital?" In all of my twenty-three years, I had never imagined a scene so bizarre.

I acknowledged that at times I'd wanted to kill him, too. "I have haunting dreams about it. One time I dreamt I could fly, and I had this laser-like gun. I shot Ron and all his skin fell off. He was walking around without skin!"

"That's about how Dad looks right now."

I pictured Dad lying between the hospital sheets. Weaker than ever. A small lump under the sheets, unimaginably different from the muscle-bound man who had worked the farm all our lives.

Debbie walked over and put her hand on my back. "Sis," she said. We embraced in a bear hug.

"Unbelievable," I said.

"I know," she said. "I know."

We looked at each other and managed to smile.

"I know you just arrived this evening and are straining to take it all in. I wanted to come over and hug you. It's a load to grasp the whole ordeal."

I nodded.

"I've been to see Mom," Deb said. "Of course she's devastated. So worried about Dad."

"Can you understand her?" I asked, surprised.

"You really don't have to understand her to guess that much. It's written all over her face. She keeps saying something that sounds like 'Dad.' I tell her over and over that he's here in Wichita, in the burn unit. She cries and pleads with the most pitiful eyes."

I teared up again, thought of Mom, and imagined her struggling to move any part of her body. She couldn't even bring her hand to her face to wipe her eyes. She couldn't look away. I could picture tears in her eyes and I was sure she'd silently pray. She still had that. Empty as it was, it was all she had.

At that thought, I sobbed. I took in three deep gulps of air. I tried hopelessly to calm myself. Bruce came over. He put his arms around me, and I leaned my head into his chest. He stroked my hair, held me close, and handed me fresh tissue every few minutes. *No one could make it better. I already understood that if God could, He wouldn't. He didn't.*

Sitting back down, I put my arm behind Dorthy's back and rubbed it slowly. Her long hair hung limply on her sagging shoulders. You could push her over with a feather, but she stayed upright on the bench. I could feel her heart pounding through her short-sleeved blouse. We sat in silence.

A hush in the air stirred my attention to a dark-haired technician wearing a long, white over-shirt. I held my breath. "Dr. Littlefield wanted me to tell you that he thinks your dad will pull through. At least for this evening. He's still finishing up some bandaging and when he comes out, you can come visit your dad," he said, now looking at me. "You don't want to stay long," he warned. "Your dad needs all the rest he can get."

Hearing that Dad would probably live through the night, the uncles and aunts gathered up their belongings and hugged us goodbye. Aunt Veralynn lingered with me. "Leona, I'm so glad you will get to see him. They've said so many times that he wasn't going to make it. Even in Moundridge, they didn't think he would make it to Wichita in the ambulance. He has some kind of staying power. God must be helping him."

"I hope so," I said, hugging her tight. "I hope so."

Before turning to leave she whispered, "We'll be praying for you all."

Dr. Littlefield entered the room, his face somber with exhaustion. We all gathered around him to hear any tidbit of hope. "He seems to have stabilized for now. His whole body is pretty shut down. Frankly, we didn't think he would make it this far. It's been touch and go since he got here yesterday, and we're all surprised that he is still with us. I'm sorry we keep telling you he's dying. That's what seems to be happening. Somehow he pulls through. We don't want to give you false hope, either. None of us thinks he will be here in three days. But we've been wrong before."

"Is there anything any of us can do for him?" Debbie asked.

"Be sure to wash up scrupulously before you go in there. Never go more than one at a time. Wear breathing cups, and don't touch him, except for the soles of his feet. Infection is a big risk right now. We'll have to get him into the whirlpool soon. I don't know how we'll do that. He's just too weak. I'll see you all tomorrow."

I hurried to the bathroom to wash my hands, arms, and face with soap, then asked the nurses for a nose mask. Nurse Swanson tied one snugly at the back of my head.

I breathed deeply. Whatever he looked like, I didn't want to wince. But I didn't know how I'd let him suffer in unscreamable pain and passively look on.

I pulled the heavy door.

He looked so small under the sheets, as if he'd lost fifty pounds in twenty-four hours. I wasn't sure if he was asleep. Then his head turned. Upon seeing his eyes, I burst into tears.

"Dad," I squeezed out. "I'm so sorry. I don't mean to cry. I don't mean to make it worse for you. I'm just so sorry. I don't even know what to say."

"Thanks for coming," he whispered hoarsely, each word speaking for a thousand other precious words he couldn't say.

"Oh my God! I wanted to be here sooner. I wanted so bad to be here sooner. I'm so sorry it took me so long."

He nodded his head ever so slightly.

"I just have to tell you, Dad. I love you so much. I love you so much more than I could ever tell you. You mean the whole world to me."

His eyes were a blurry gray-blue. He was behind them somewhere, but I couldn't quite see him in them. I wanted to cry out, "Come back! Don't leave us!" But I knew how selfish that would be.

"They told me not to touch you, but I wish I could just put my arms around you and hold you. I wish I could take away the pain."

"They gave me something," he said. He shook his head slightly, like it didn't matter what he said.

"I don't want to tire you out. I want you to rest. But if it's OK with you, I'd like to rub the soles of your feet."

"I'd like that," he whispered.

I cautiously and gently pulled the sheet away from his left foot. I grabbed the lotion on the tray and rubbed it between my hands to warm it up, and then gently applied it to every inch of his sole. My hands worked around and around. I didn't say a word. I hoped he might fall asleep. He was breathing heavily but regularly. I pushed love through my fingers into his foot. I imagined that each caress was worth a thousand pounds of love. I wanted him to know that I would help him stay alive for as long as he desired life. My fingers searched for any sign of satisfaction. If I sensed it, I rubbed exactly the same way over and over again.

He seemed to be resting better. The thought that I was not supposed to stay long kept returning. After some time I thought he was sleeping. I pulled the sheet over his foot and turned to leave.

"Don't go," he whispered.

His words lifted my heart. I looked at him and nodded.

"How about if I rub your other foot? Would you like that?"

He nodded without actually moving his head.

With another squirt of hospital lotion, I rubbed my heart into his right sole. I wanted him to feel the longing in my soul to know his soul, my hope against the doctor's knowledge, my bitter rage against anything that hurt him. I imagined I was oiling a baby's body.

As I pulled the sheet over his foot, he whispered, "I love you, Leona. Thank you." My heart stopped. I wanted to hear those words ringing in my ears forever.

"I'll be here for the night. Just out there in the waiting room. After the others have had a turn I'll be back to see you. If there's anything at all I can do, tell the nurses to get me. I'll do anything, Dad. Call on me any time. Please do that. I love you so much."

I closed his door behind me and rushed to the bathroom. Clasping the rim of the sink basin tightly, I rocked my whole body back and forth, sobbing ferociously. With gratitude in my heart, I knew that I would always love him.

CHAPTER 46 – THE ORDEAL

Feeling something crunchy under my cheek, I raised my head up from the hospital carpet and swiped the side of my cheek. Crumbs fell off.

Bruce turned over and put his arm around me. "It's early, Leona, just lie down again. You were so tired. Let yourself get a little sleep."

"No! I have to check on Dad. Did you bring our bathroom bag up?"

He pointed to the corner and I pulled myself out from under his arm and threw the cover off me. I rushed to the bathroom with the bag. Who was looking back at me in the mirror? Her eyes, like puffy toads, her swollen yet drawn face. I sponged myself off with paper towels and soap and brushed teeth, moisturized lips, and combed oily hair.

I faced the nurses and made myself smile. "What happened with Dad last night?"

"He's about the same as when you left. A little more rested, I think. He had a rough night, but he also slept a little. I wouldn't go in yet. I think he's still trying to sleep."

"How long should I wait?"

"I'll check on him in fifteen minutes or so and let you know then."

I thanked her and picked up cracker pieces bit by bit. I closed my eyes. My heart pounded. I must call Vicky and check on Randy.

They were enjoying our little five-year-old blondie. He wouldn't eat the meals Vicky made. He favored hotdogs and macaroni and cheese. He ate cereal any time of day. He was curious and loved attention. They were doing art projects, going for walks, and having a great time—not to worry. She was sorry to hear about the near-death circumstances. What a dear person she was. I felt grateful to Bruce for having friends like Vicky and Russell. I would not have known a soul who could have stepped in and helped on that scale.

The next day Dad faced another medical challenge. The burns on his body must be cleaned or they'd become infected. Also, they must pull off the dead or dying skin.

Bruce asked to be allowed to accompany Dad to his debriding whirlpool treatment. The doctor approved this. After the harrowing time, Bruce told me about it.

In his room they moved Dad from his bed to a gurney. He winced and struggled against the piercing attacks when his skin pulled away from or stayed stuck to the cloth under him. The technicians attempted to grab him where he was not burned. They helped him move. They knew they were causing unimaginable pain. On the way down the hall and into the basement, Dad asked Bruce to stop this treatment. Bruce told him he was sorry for the pain. Words were utterly inadequate.

I imagined Dad's body and mind absorbed the agony of being strapped, naked, into a halter and then lowered into the whirlpool. Water rushed into his massive open wounds. He managed not to faint. Two technicians with long tweezers were in the whirlpool with him. They picked dying skin off his body, bit by bit. He held on with all his might. He tried not to brace himself against the next stab; tried not to remain in his throbbing, pricked body losing its skin one pull after another. They saw his utter anguish. He noticed theirs, as they inflicted pain.

Finally they lifted him out, unharnessed him and positioned him on the gurney. As he left the whirlpool room, with each movement excruciating, he thanked each worker, the doctors, and nurses, for helping him heal. He knew this was horrifically hard on them, too. He thanked Bruce. He was grateful that this process was over for the day.

Maybe because the doctors and nurses knew what it meant to survive burn regimens, they were certain he would die any hour now. Perhaps they hoped he would die soon, so they didn't have to inflict more pain when they knew that no one in his condition could survive long.

The helplessness we felt was pervasive, so we used outside distractions as opportunities to release despair and "rage against the dying of the light." When Bruce returned from watching Nixon's impeachment hearings in another waiting area, I told him I'd seen Dad again. I felt grateful I could help him even a wee bit and that he looked forward to my visits.

We talked about Nixon. I thought the hearings were important but ill-conceived. "He should be tried for war crimes," I said, "and for telling voters he would get us out of the war and then expanding the war to Laos and Cambodia. He didn't stop bombing until Congress forced him to with the Case-Church amendment. He should be tried for murdering millions of peasants because he didn't want to lose political face. He should be tried for teaching young men to be murderers, pretending that his vainglorious whoppers can make their deeds honorable. He's a cold-blooded murderer. How unbearable that the only thing Americans can charge him with is petty burglary and a cover-up."

"At least Haldeman and Ehrlichman are gone and soon he will be, too," Bruce said.

"Yes," I said, ever ready to explore the worst. "But Kissinger isn't, and he won't be. Besides, at this point the war is over and we're too weak to fight another. A lot of good we're doing now. After his replacement takes office the Republicans have dramatically increased their chance to win the next election."

"Good God, Leona, are you ever satisfied?"

"I know I'm a cynic," I said, fighting back tears, guessing I sounded worse than an empty-glassed apocalyptic prophet. "I'm just strung out." But I remembered how I had learned that you can never be too cynical for this crazy world, and I wondered if perhaps I was right.

Days passed as doctors kept insisting that he wouldn't live another day, until they had been wrong so many days that they couldn't keep uttering those words to family. We believed Dad was stronger than any doctor could predict. They only knew his medical condition.

I dreaded going in to tell him, but I had to. I had told him I would do anything but I couldn't keep that promise. I noticed his crispy fingers curled unnaturally against the heavy air. First I rubbed his feet, then said I was grateful he was striving to survive, that I knew he endured unearthly pain every single moment. My heart was full of love for him. We all loved him. Was there anything any of us could do for him?

"Dad, I'm so sorry to do this, but we have to go back to Boston." His body stiffened, as if I had administered an electric shock. "I'm so sorry, Dad!"

"Leona, don't go," he whispered.

"Oh God, Dad, I wish so much that I didn't have to. I would love to stay here with you. I would give anything to stay here, but I can't. Randy needs me. He's been there for many days without us. I can't leave him longer."

Dad slowly moved his head.

I sobbed quietly. "Dad, I'm so sorry. I can't bear to leave you. I wish so much I could stay."

We were silent for a short while.

"Dad, I promise you I'll be back soon. I'll come as soon as I possibly can. I know I'll miss you so much. Please, know I'll be thinking about you all the time. I'll take you with me in my heart."

He opened his bleary eyes to look at me. "Please don't go."

"Believe me, I wouldn't if I didn't have to. The last thing I want to do is disappoint you. I have to go. I don't have a choice. I promise I'll come back quickly. I promise. Please be OK while I'm gone. Please hang on, Dad. I'll be back soon. I love you so much."

I stepped out of his room and rushed to the bathroom, straining to hold my sobs. I sat on the toilet and buried my face in my hands. How could I leave now? How could I do this? I pried myself from the toilet seat.

I splashed water on my face. I closed my eyes and imagined Randy's little smile, the way we all laughed when he said "bufflebull" rather than "buffalo." I imagined wrapping my arms around his sweet little body and holding him tight. I wanted to see his inquisitive eyes, his smile, his gentle little face. I'd let him guide me back to Boston.

Bruce and I said goodbye to the burn unit staff and thanked them for all their work. We hugged our family. We rushed to Moundridge to say goodbye to Mom. It was clear by her expression that she, too, didn't want us to leave. I told her how much I loved her. I promised to return. I cried all the way to our rented car and closed my eyes as Bruce pulled out of the lot.

I didn't open them again for five hours. We were still a few hours away from St. Louis where his mom would meet us. We turned in the car and spent the night at his brother's house. We checked all the ads. Hail-damaged Chevys seemed a good bet. We went there first thing in the morning. I dickered for a better price. Bruce's mother, grief-stricken for both of us, co-signed our loan.

I thought I had already lived the longest week of my life, but being in Boston, away from Dad, made an eternity of every day. Dorthy called to say that Dad had taken a turn for the worse. He did quite a bit better for about a week, but the doctors thought he was beginning the downward slide.

Bruce and I decided to drive back to Kansas. Betty, a seminarian's wife with a baby who lived two apartments away from ours, offered to take care of Randy. He could stay in his neighborhood and keep his dog with him. My boss offered to take over my switchboard job again at Andover Newton.

We gathered change to make long distance calls from pay phones. I was nervous the whole way back. Bruce saw I was pale and hoped I was not getting sick.

"No," I said, "I won't get sick. You can bet on that!" I felt invincible. Nothing and no one could stop me from seeing Dad. Germs didn't stand a chance.

When I could finally take a turn to visit Dad, I noticed his relief to see me. He looked smaller than ever beneath those sheets, like a bale of hay shrinking as the cows ate it. I couldn't imagine how much weight he had lost. Maybe they pulled it off him with those tweezers.

"Dad, we made it back. I'm so glad to be here with you."

He nodded his head and half smiled.

"I've missed you. You've been on my mind," I said.

"I'm glad you're here," he whispered in a raspy voice. He sighed heavily.

"I don't want you to strain yourself. You don't have to say anything. I will understand." I moved toward his feet, to start rubbing.

"Randy hugged us soundly and gathered up his rocket drawings and toys when we returned home. He did well, though, with Vicky and Russell. They're such great people. This time he's staying with a friend at Herrick House."

Dad nodded again. I could hardly bear to look at his profoundly sad eyes. Yet I couldn't look away.

I rubbed his feet, yearning to relieve mountains of pain with loving touch.

"Thank you," he whispered.

"I know you're in so much pain, Dad. I wish I could do more. I wish so much I could make it better."

He nodded knowingly.

After some moments of silence, he said, "I have to ask you, Leona." He paused and caught his breath. "Am I good enough?"

His words pierced my heart like a bullet tearing through. I couldn't believe I'd heard right. I moved closer to his face and said, "Are you asking if you're good enough?"

He nodded his head slightly, weary with pain, fatigue, and the burden on his heart. He blinked his eyes repeatedly, perhaps fighting tears.

"Oh my God! Dad, how can you ask that?" I burst into tears. "Dad, you're by far the best person I know. We adore you. You're our rock. You're so much more than good enough! You've done your best. You mean everything to all of us. There's no doubt in my mind that you're good enough!" These words clattered forward like a train barreling through a tunnel.

"Dad," I said, softer now, "it breaks my heart to think you doubt yourself. I know you pretty well. You are a good person. You've helped all of us to the best of your ability. You cared for Mom. You struggled through everything. You kept us all going. Dad, I know you have a good heart! That is all that matters."

I wondered how long he had been holding that question. Did he want to ask before I left? Did he worry about it while I was gone? Did he ask anyone else?

Before I left I said, "Dad, I love you so, so much. I think the world of you."

He looked concerned that I would leave him. "I'll be back, Dad. I know my time is up and I don't want to wear you out, but I'll be back soon. We aren't going back to Boston, not for a long time. I love you."

I told Dorthy and Bruce what happened. We wondered if he wanted absolution because he was who he was, or if someone had been judging him.

"One of the relatives might have told him he'd better make his peace with God," I said. "And a couple of them might have the self-righteous assurance to think they were doing him a favor. Goddamn them."

"It might be the new minister. He is one weird dude, and he's been up here a few times," Dorthy said. "He doesn't really know Dad. Nothing like Rev. Schmidt did."

Bruce said, "Maybe he just thinks he's going to die and wants to be reassured. It's not unusual to have doubts about yourself. I have doubts about myself."

"I guess Dad may review his life and see all the things he wishes he could have done differently," I said. "I just wish he wouldn't be so hard on himself. Imagine someone as good as he is, wondering if he is good enough!"

"If I find out that anyone has been putting the fear of God in him, I'll put some fear into them," Dorthy said.

"You can say that again!"

"You guys sound tough, but I can't picture either one of you saying one word to anyone," Bruce said.

We slept on the floor in the waiting area. If the nurses said Dad was awake, I went to visit during the night. Dorthy told us that Mom really wanted to come and see Dad. We asked the nurses if it would be OK to bring Mom here to see Dad. Could Dad endure the emotional pain? We couldn't decide if it would help him or hurt him. They didn't think it would be a good idea.

In the morning we drove to Moundridge to see Mom. We told her that the nurses thought he was not yet ready, that he needed to get better before she visited. She was not satisfied with that answer but knew it was all we could do. We weren't going to take her unless we had permission. Besides, how would we know that she would live through the ordeal? Of course, it wouldn't matter to her. She would rather see him and die than not see him at all. I felt like a cruel tyrant, denying Mom her last significant wish before she died.

We continued another three miles to the farm. A desolate place, forlorn and lost, confronted us. The house was a heap of ashes, wet now from a recent shower. From the road you couldn't see that it ever existed. Even with animals shuffling about and our Saint Bernard, Fred, wagging his tail, so happy to see human faces, the place seemed anemic, stagnate. We found some food for Fred. I showed Bruce the structures and hide-outs where we kids passed hours, completely engrossed in some creative effort, whether play or work.

Would Dad, by some miracle of determination, pull through his desperate condition and bring the kids home again? Maybe he could move a trailer house close to the old house foundation. Maybe he would sell the animals and just live on disability. It warmed my heart to think of Butch, Lynnie, and Carla playing on the farm again. I pictured them sliding down the barn roof, building campgrounds with bales and sleeping in the hayloft, and making fences and ladders in the shed. For Dad's birthday one year, they found some old boards, nailed them together, and gave Dad a ladder. They wanted him to have a way out if he fell into the elevator's open basement hole. They were thoughtful, sweet, and generous. They loved and needed Dad.

The kids were still living with LeAnn and Al, but it was not an ideal solution. With significant effort to find a time we all could convene, we gathered for a family meeting, with siblings, spouses, aunts, and uncles in a closed waiting room at the hospital. Uncle Harley explained that Dad asked him to see to the welfare of the children. He and Ruby had discussed it. They were willing to give the two youngest girls a home. I supported that, saying that none of us daughters was in a good position to take care of them. Uncle Elvin and Aunt Neva said they would open their home to Butch, who wanted to finish high school in Moundridge; he could do that if he stayed with them.

LeAnn was furious. She had resented me for some years. This situation was not helping. As the eldest daughter, she thought she should give the girls a home. Lynnie and Carla had responded well to her family. Perhaps she believed she'd kick her drug problem if she kept them. We wouldn't take that chance. I suggested that Dad would not want that, and Dorthy agreed.

After some haggling, LeAnn walked over to me, kicked me in the shin, and left in a huff. "Ouch!" I said, wishing I could belt her one. "She's obviously upset, but she'll probably get over it. I think we should move forward with our plan." I doubted that all the aunts and uncles realized she was addicted to prescription drugs. They were probably shocked at her behavior. Though I was not yet twenty-four, I felt somehow responsible for and embarrassed by her acting out. Perhaps as she once felt responsible for and embarrassed by my pregnancy before marriage.

The family also discussed whether the kids should see Dad. Butch, now that he had turned fifteen, had visited. He would have fainted and hit the floor if Uncle Elvin hadn't been there to catch him. It was shocking to see Dad. Butch said he knew that he was alone in this world. The man he had looked up to all his life would not be here much longer. He slept a lot, couldn't focus on much, and struggled just to bear the pain and breathe.

As for the girls, at ages nine and twelve, would it be better for them to remember him as he was on the farm? Would they feel betrayed if we didn't bring them before he died? We talked to the nurses. They suggested we might let them peek through the window in the door but not go in. That seemed like the best compromise we could muster.

Dorthy and I brought the girls to the hospital. We endeavored to prepare them, saying he was not well, was in a hospital bed, and didn't look as big as he used to be. They didn't have to look if they didn't want to. We just wanted to give them the opportunity if they did want to.

Dorthy and I decided to lift them up at the same time so they could see him. Dad was asleep and we hoped we would not disturb him. The girls took one look and started screaming. "That's not our dad! He doesn't look like that! What's the matter with him?" They wailed, and we quickly ushered them into the bathroom. We held them. Dorthy and I were crying, too. These two little sweethearts would be orphaned. And Butch, too. How would they survive without their dad? He was all they'd ever known.

"Will he die?" they asked, almost in unison.

"We don't know," Dorthy said. "He's very sick." On our knees on the bathroom floor, Dorthy and I looked them in the eyes and rocked back and forth with them.

They started wailing again, utterly distraught. Dorthy and I provided every honest reassurance we could generate. "If anything happens to him," I added, "or if he can't come home for a while, we'll make sure you have a home and are taken care of. You can count on that."

"We don't want a home. We want to go home with Dad!"

When they stopped crying, we brought them to the waiting area. Relatives invited them to come visit them. Did they know about the new puppies at Uncle Ernie's house? Guess what, Aunt Ruby made *bohne beroggi* for them. Didn't that sound good?

As one week wore into the next, I found myself sinking lower and lower. I felt like I was sweating all the time, even though I was sitting in an air-conditioned waiting room. I washed my hair in the bathroom sink and gave myself sponge baths, changed clothes and brushed my teeth, but nothing refreshed me. I worked constantly to keep my eyes open when I sat down. On occasion, I went to our car to take a nap.

Randy was OK with Betty. She said he was content to sleep with them. Playing with Daisy delighted him. He was quite enamored with their new baby, now three months old. Randy said he got an ice-cream cone for watching little Henry while Betty took out the trash. We told him we missed and loved him, that we'd come home in a few more days. We said that Grandpa and Grandma, Lynnie and Carla, and all the family sent their love.

Dad's kidneys were failing. When it was my turn to visit, I made sure that I told Dad that he was a wonderful person. I couldn't have asked for a better dad. Whatever his failings— and he had some—he loved us dearly and he lived that love. I hoped I could carry forward the love he inspired in me. I wanted to give to others, especially to Randy, the way he gave to me.

On our next visit to Moundridge Hospital we told Mom that Dad was getting worse. We saw the desperate way she looked at us. We understood that we were failing her. We didn't have it in us to go against our medical advisors, though we knew it was probably the last thing we'd ever do for her. Mom tried to accept this indignity also. She told us she'd see him in heaven, repeating herself many times before we understood. She was utterly exhausted when we left.

Chapter 47 - DEATH

Dad took his last breath on August 13, 1974. I sensed the chill. A kind of silence moved up his body. His monumental will to live brought him through painful day after day, thirty-two of them, each day one more than the doctors thought possible.

Relief tempered our ultimate letdown. We watched as doctors and nurses wiped their eyes. We expressed gratitude to all of them for their valiant efforts, for understanding our suffering.

"Your dad was a special man," one nurse said through tears. "He made such an impression on us. We will miss him."

For reasons we didn't fully understand, LeAnn went downstairs to the emergency room. It seemed that she, too, was a casualty of our suffering. Whatever they could do for her there, it wouldn't be enough.

Against proper etiquette, our family invited Reverend H. B. Schmidt to deliver the funeral sermon. He had left the Hopefield Church a few years earlier, but he knew Mom and Dad well and loved them. He had often come to the farm to talk with Dad. He seemed to like Dad's thoughtfulness, his unusual take on situations, and his engaging determination. He understood both the enduring anguish and the joy that made Dad who he was.

The service would not be at Hopefield Church but at Eden Mennonite Church, a mile or two away. Our uncles felt that Hopefield would not be large enough for the expected crowd of mourners. This surprised me. I thought I could count on one hand the families that seemed to befriend my family. Dad was right—people in our community were kinder than I had acknowledged.

We filed into a wing of the church in our dressed-up black, enveloped by grief, hearing *Amazing Grace*. Mom, propped and tied into her wheelchair, sat in the aisle next to us. A medical van brought her and would take her back immediately following the service. Before we headed back to Boston, we would visit her in the hospital and say nice things to her about the service. We'd say we were thankful she was able to come, that we understood it took all her strength and fortitude to be there. We'd say the people who packed the church were there to show her their support as well as grieve.

I cried too hard to sing *Just As I Am Without One Plea*, Dad's favorite hymn.

In the eulogy, Rev. Schmidt told the congregation that he often visited Carl and Deloris. He knew them well. He said that he and Carl had many challenging and in-depth conversations about a wide variety of subjects. He understood Carl's heavy heart, and yet he enjoyed his laughter, good spirits, curiosity, and compassion. Carl carried heavy burdens and still managed to live each day fully.

Rev. Schmidt continued the eulogy, "Sometimes we wonder why such painful and horrible things can happen to good people. Job is a prime example of the kind of suffering Carl endured. We will not know, any more than Jesus knew when He hung on the cross, why this cup cannot pass from us. We don't understand, any more than Carl understood, why explosions severely burned him twice in his life, or why trials and tests plagued him from his youth.

"Yet, as Carl did, we love the Lord. We know that God works all things toward the good. We understand that now, in God's home, Carl is blessed with new life. He is reunited with loved ones who passed before him. His questions and longings are supplanted with an all-encompassing love, with the peace that passes all understanding. Even though he is needed here and will be terribly missed by his family and friends, we can be thankful for his exceptionally courageous life. We can be grateful for his release to be with his Maker. He finally knows completely. He can now see face to face what he could only see through a glass dimly while he was here with us."

We followed the hearse for a mile or so to Hopefield Mennonite Church cemetery. With comforting words we lowered our father into the earth. A place next to him waited for our mother. Soon, multiple sclerosis coupled with unabated sorrow would take her, too.

In this ground, Dad was less than a mile from the place where he was born, grew up, and lived his entire forty-nine years. In this cemetery he was close to his parents and many ancestors before them. They were here, after years of toil, struggles with faith, and brave discipline to do the best they could. *Everyone buried in this cemetery was a remnant of a peaceful community of people who dared to believe that God led us to courageous acts of kindness in the face of danger, to an all-encompassing, compassionate love for the whole world and anyone in it—no matter what the cost, no matter who was lost.*

Chapter 48 - RESURRECTION

After the burial we took a few minutes to say goodbye and stop at the farm before our long trek back to Randy. Bruce and I walked hand in hand around the foundation of the farmhouse and stared into the heap of ashes in the basements. We stomped through the manure in the cow pen, petted a Holstein and a mixed-breed Jersey.

"I'm sorry for you," I said to the cows. "It will never be the same." They looked at me with sad eyes. The Jersey lowed a slow, mournful sound. She nearly convinced me she knew what was happening.

We continued to the faded white barn. I climbed into the sheep pen lined with straw where I used to take baby lambs and help them nurse. I turned to Bruce and wept uncontrollably in his arms, remembering a day when Dad and I were in this very pen. I woke him early that morning to help me with arithmetic, and we carried baby lambs out to their mothers in this barn.

Bruce and I headed toward the red barn. I told him I needed to be alone for a little while. I entered the barn by the door facing our vanished house. I felt the smooth wood next to the latch that my father's fingers had rubbed thousands of times, leaving an indentation. I longed for his touch, for one last chance to look into his eyes. I wanted to ask him if *I* was good enough. Could he forgive the ways I disappointed him? Could he pass absolution to a daughter too stupid to have asked for it when he was alive?

I imagined there would be many times when I realized the things I failed to question and could no longer ask. I could see now how he held all of us in his heart, even when he was powerless to make anything better. He continued to hope that what he couldn't do for his older daughters, he might do for his younger children still at home. Now that was lost, too. He would not do anything for his younger children that he hadn't already done.

The barn's particular pungent odor of manure and sweat made me know I was home. I looked at a shelf of dusty, heavy plastic bottles with long nipples on them, waiting for the next motherless calf. I climbed into the hayloft and spotted an abandoned case that once carried doll clothes and pretend medical instruments. I sat next to it on a row of hay bales and gazed at the light streaming through holes in the roof and the windows without glass.

I leaned back on the bale. Thoughts swarmed like bees close to a honeycomb. I could feel my chest open. I was conscious of giving way to the first whopping lie—a heavenly *home* prepared for him. It swooped into me like an uninvited but vivacious guest, offering favors and comforting stories from afar. I took the tales in whole. I didn't stop myself. Like Ron, unable to resist a salvific fabrication, I gathered the rest of the embellished religious sagas to my bosom—a heavenly *home* and so much more. I could feel it now, what I felt in childhood—a fullness, peace, a sense of sparkling lightness, almost floating like little angels riding on silage stalks. I held on until the experience escaped.

In this time of unendurable grief I needed to secure a second chance for my father. In spite of reason, intelligence, and everything I knew about God, I needed that *home* to be real—not words, not myth, but flesh-and-blood real. "OK, God. You've got him now," I breathed. "I have to go with your version. You didn't give me a shred of evidence, but suddenly I have to believe You will be there for my parents. *There is nothing for them but You.* They deserved so much more than You gave them. You better make up for it now!"

I stepped to the opening where we used the bale elevator to transport bale after bale from the loaded wagon below into the hayloft. I could almost smell the fresh hay and feel my muscle-bound arms lifting the bales to stack them, one on top of the other. I looked across the yard at the back side of the outhouse where I threw those baby sparrows. God didn't give a shit, but my dad did. Perhaps God didn't give a shit about violence or war, but my dad did give a shit, and I did, too, and so did that whole graveyard full of people. *I knew we cared, because if you care, you do something.* Perhaps God didn't care one whit if Ron killed all of us or if my dad died a grueling and hideously painful death. But I cared. Goddamn it, I cared!

I looked up to cloud-filled heavens, pointed my lecturing finger right at it, and though I knew on one level that I was being ridiculous, I nevertheless had to take a stand for Dad and Mom. I had to find them a home. I could not let Dad rot in the earth, and soon Mom, too. Surely they should be more important than fallen hedge apples! How could life be worth living if we become maggot-filled, bloated flesh? If there was nothing that resembled a fair chance, not in this life or beyond, why bother? The luck of the draw and you burn to death or your whole life is one, slow dying process with more and more taken from you each day. And what about all the people, millions and millions, who had it so much worse? So many worthy lives with too much agony.

The very reason why I knew God didn't exist—because people suffered too much and too unjustly—was now the reason why I realized He must! He had to! I needed that supernatural magic to make it right, somewhere, somehow in a life beyond this one! I craved God.

"So here is the deal, God, if by any bizarre stroke of luck You exist: I'll attempt to believe in You. I'll go to seminary, not just to ask questions but to find out about You. I'll hold You responsible, but I'll also rack my soul, because I hope so much that Reverend Schmidt was right."

My tears became sobs and I barely eked out the words, a prayer of my own making. "I'd give anything if Dad is with You right now, seeing You face to face. Please, please, let Reverend Schmidt be right. I know we see through a glass dimly now. Let there be something more after we die! This is the time, God. You'd better do it! Help him live again! When my mom finally gets there, put them together. Forever!"

CHAPTER 49 - CREASES OF THE PAST

D r. Craig, our New Testament professor, paused, his fingers curling at his side. "The text clearly asked people to believe in the physical reality of resurrection. The disciples saw Jesus's flesh and bones, they felt the holes in his hands and his side. Do Christians today, do we, believe that God intervenes in history? That God resurrected Jesus?"

In my own mind I added what Dr. Craig implied. If God did not raise Jesus, then what basis do we have to suspect that God uses supernatural power on behalf of humanity?

Again Dr. Craig wiped his forehead, "Presumably, the disciples continued their ministries because they became convinced that Jesus was raised again after death, and Paul's theology rests entirely on this belief." Students buzzed with opinions about its questionable nature. We already knew that Jesus's life did not match Jewish expectations for a Messiah, and Jesus's promise to return before the end of his follower's lives, to come in a blaze of glory and set the world right in a cataclysmic reckoning, didn't happen then or in the next two thousand years.

The oldest available gospel, Mark, and the one written closest to the time of Jesus, said that Jesus's last words on the cross were "My God, my God, why have You forsaken me?" They engendered a feeling of empathy for Jesus. After all His struggle to help people, to hope and endure, He felt betrayed by God, cried out, and died.

I listened for a while, pressing my heart against my mind like a pillow against breathing orifices. This was why Grandpa Stucky opposed higher education. Maybe you must choose to be fools for Christ, as Paul said. The more you knew, the harder that choice became. If death was the end, then this world was cruel beyond measure, and that was the end of the story.

Dr. Craig asked us to hold the tension and dismissed class with the assignment to reread the resurrection stories in the synoptic gospels and outline their differences.

Laden with books and heavy thoughts, I headed to Herrick House, walking through towering naked maple trees, filtering the New Testament discussion through visions of Dad's burned face, his gray, bleary eyes, and his burdened spirit.

I plopped onto our sofa bed and wondered how to exit these theological binds. In a haze of exhaustion and grief, my memory rifled to a day when I was about nine years old and Dad asked me to count goose eggs. I jumped up from the dinner table, slipped into sneakers, and we started at the shed, finding three nests there. On the north side of the red barn we counted another full nest. We tallied twenty-seven eggs by the time we rounded the house to the back porch.

"I'll watch for the goose. You crawl under there and count." He pointed down to the space between the ground and the underside of the porch. On all fours I entered darkness down under.

After my eyes adjusted, a squawking mother goose appeared out of nowhere and attacked. I screamed, jumped up, and my head hit the porch beams. I fell back down, almost into the nest of eggs. Mother goose hissed in my face. I scrambled, crawled backwards, and screamed again. I waved my arm to shield my face. She stopped chasing when I backed out into daylight.

Seeing I was OK, Dad laughed so hard he couldn't breathe.

"Da-a-ad!" I said. "You didn't do your job! You were supposed to keep the goose away!"

"I know," he tried to say but dropped to the ground and rolled sideways.

"What are you laughing about?" I asked, maintaining indignation.

Still he couldn't squeeze out words, so I rushed to him and pummeled his belly, which made him roar even louder. "I know, I know," he said admitting culpability. Finally, he leaned on his elbow and sat up. "You should have heard your squeal," he said, imitating my voice. "Honey, you've got a set of lungs! That's for sure." He wrapped his arms around me and squeezed tight, as if exercising a set of lungs was the best a person could do.

He checked if I had split my head open or shook-up my pupils, and we marched inside to share the hilarity.

I laughed then, as much at his delight as at the circumstance, and even now I smiled and folded myself into the comforting creases of the past. Sometimes we failed each other and loved every minute of it.

Most days I was glad to offer a day of hard labor to share a winked eye, a knowing glance, a bursting chuckle, or a long, all-out laugh. I would do just about anything to be with him now, feel his gaze, engage his humor, and trust his quiet courage. I still would do anything if only I could. I would even swallow everything I knew about God as if those doubts never occurred to me. I would guess the disciples weren't off-track to trust that Jesus was resurrected and therefore everything in the whole world had changed. I would ingest Biblical stories and treasure them as truth if I could know that Dad was laughing again.

I would love to be together traipsing through the greenish-brownish slush in the cow pen or chasing and killing rats under the pigs' shelters or rounding up the sheep to sort some for market or hooting at the almost-white barnyard owl or loading five-gallon buckets of feed and laughing at the surprise on his face when the handle broke and the bucket landed on his foot.

In that moment of laughter, neither of us would care what hurt or what time it was or what the price of wheat was or what anybody thought of us or if there was more work to do. In that moment we would be together, our spirits soaring free.

Inspired by memories of Dad's glee, I scrambled off the sofa and scrubbed the hibachi grill Bruce used yesterday. I tested the paint on Randy's picture—not quite dry. He had painted a clown's face on a sheet of cardboard. The clown wore an orange and black hat, had sad eyes, a multicolored face, and a huge, curvy smile, about to laugh—Randy's Mona Lisa with a crooked smile, both hiding and revealing the truth that, in time, we'd laugh again. What a beautiful representation of our realities! I'd save that painting forever. Perhaps the most important, timeless message could be found in a child's creativity, in the smile that produced it, and in the giggles that celebrated it.

Lynnett, Butch, and Carla, shortly after Dad's death

POSTSCRIPT

Families gradually find ways to adapt to tragedy and wrest some blessing out of the ashes. Our family was no exception. A few years after the fire and after our parents' deaths, Lynnett and Carla came to live with Bruce, Randy, and me. Their presence enhanced our lives. With struggle and gratitude, our family blended further as these girls became daughters.

Now their children and my son's daughter have become my grandchildren. They brought much joy, as we played with them and watched them grow. Every one of these children, grandchildren, members of my extended family, and dear friends are graces that transcend the story I have told.

My relationship with Bruce continued for twenty years. Together we nurtured our love, ventured to new vistas, exasperated each other, worked through disappointments, parented and developed our professional capacities. Still, we divorced in mid-life.

My siblings and I made special efforts to stay connected after my parent's died. Many times we failed and, with time, we prevailed. I have found aspects of Mom and Dad in family members and am gratified by their stamina, resilience, kindness, quiet courage, and artful productivity. Most of all, I love their humor. I call it our slapstick, red-neck, gut-splitting, pee-your-pants hilarity. It may not manifest often, but when it does, we know who we are. In the meantime, we smile knowingly with our flawed but abiding love, some with our traditional faith and some without, but with each other.

Ron continued to threaten our family periodically. He turned up at my mother's funeral. When LeAnn died in 1985, we asked for police protection and learned they had an inches-thick file on him. Each time he tried to make contact we had to brace for the worst, and without exception the police remained unable to protect us. He and his family also suffered devastating incidents, one when Ron killed their family pet and attempted to murder his mother.

Throughout my life, until about ten years ago, when police told us that Ron was too ill to pose much of a threat, I have fastidiously kept my whereabouts hidden from him. His obsession lasted more than thirty years.

I have been fortunate. My sometimes arduous and winding journey left room for me to learn, ponder, and grow spiritually and relationally. Integrating the diverse and sometimes opposite experiences of intuition and knowledge, circumstance and interpretation, struggle and joy has opened me to aspects of life and meaning I wouldn't have known otherwise. These personal expansions are helpful to my work as a psychotherapist and to my life as a human being.

Eric Fromm's *The Art of Loving*, a book I received from a salesman who had the grace to meet me as a human being when I felt more like a worm, became a guide for me, a resource to live by. Fromm promoted love based on mature relational capacities: self-awareness, a stable constancy to be fully present, and the quiet courage to be vulnerable. His influence was a part of writing this book.

Another treasured influence was my mother. After she fell, never to walk again, she gave up some of the tasks she had earlier attempted, and she found her meaning in holding her babies on her lap. She was grateful that she could do that. I can still visualize her sitting in her wheelchair with a droopy smile, welcoming her bundles of love, experiencing one measure of her worth that enhanced her contentment.

I like to think of her holding as a metaphor for my life's work. There are many things I couldn't and can't do well, but the emotional and spiritual holding I can do often leads to meaningful growth for myself and others. I can hold what has been and is my life; I can hold what others share honestly with me about their lives. Somehow in this holding, a kind of confessing, knowing, loving, forgiving, and learning happens— and we mature enough to tackle the next step of our journeys.

For more information about my current thoughts and beliefs and for some reflections about the stories in these chapters, please visit my website at WWW.FOGOFFAITH.COM.

Leona Stucky

QUESTIONS FOR REFLECTION, DISCOVERY, AND DISCUSSION

For personal reflection and small group discussion

Mental Illness

•Has mental illness touched your life? How has it influenced who you have become? Has anything in your life altered because you or someone close to you has suffered from mental illness?

•How would your life be different if all mental illness could be cured and no one suffered from it anymore?

Trauma

•Have you or someone close to you suffered a significant trauma? How did that experience invite you or them to reevaluate the meaning of life? Did you or they change? Abruptly or over time?

•Do you notice differences between how trauma feels in the immediate moment and how it can be experienced later?

Secular Ways of Seeing

•How do you make sense of fortune or mishap from a secular perspective?

•Does your secular view require things of you that you would not feel compelled to do if you had faith? What? When?

•In what circumstances are you most apt to use a secular world view? In what circumstances might you want a faith-based world view? What is the difference between the two? Why use one or the other world view?

•Since seeing through the lens of supernatural beliefs or through the lens of natural realism is often prompted by unconscious motivations and often is erratic or "plastic" within our minds, where would you place yourself on the spectrum between faith and atheism? Is one spot on this spectrum appropriate for you or would several places be accurate for you at different times or circumstances in your life?

•Studies show that people who are closer to the reality of death for themselves or for loved ones are more likely to make their beliefs fluid enough to include an afterlife. In these circumstances do you experience a pull to affirm a conscious afterlife or continuation of yourself into a new life after death?

•What aspects of yourself need to stay grounded in what is knowable? Who influenced you toward that direction?

•Have you always desired evidence to substantiate your beliefs or is that something that has developed within you as you have aged?

•What do myths mean to you? Do you like engaging them in your thought processes? Do you separate them from evidence-based ways of knowing? How do myths inform your life?

Religious Ways of Seeing

•Who among your family or friends were faithful? What did you see or experience with those persons that made them seem faithful?

•Was there a circumstance in which you moved closer to your faith or let go?

•Can you recall a time when you expected something from your Deity? What did you expect? How did you interpret what happened?

•Did your God/dess ever matter to you enough that you had to fight or struggle to change yourself or God/dess? If so, how? What? When?

•Have you used faith to reinforce your sense of security, safety, or well-being?

•Does your faith help you feel you are on the right side of issues? How? When?

•Does your faith implicate you being on the wrong side of issues? How? When?

•Does your faith require things of you that you would not feel compelled to do if you did not have faith? What? When?

•If you were to pray right now, what would you say or ask? Why?

•How much do your experiences and your interpretations of those experiences inform your beliefs? How much do your beliefs inform or influence your interpretations?

•How is the everyday meaning of lived faith—when faith really matters as a life or death issue—different from faith that simply involves beliefs and hopes?

Uses for Beliefs

•Do your beliefs provide an escape from reality?

•Do they help disguise or reveal the harsher aspects of reality?

•What is the role of complexity and contradiction in our lives? Our beliefs?

•Do you leave a space in your mind between what you *want* to believe and what you *actually* believe is true? Do you believe you have the right interpretation of your Deity's intentions and actions? Do you believe you will find life after death? How certain are you?

Characteristics and Understanding

•On what, in the final analysis, do you base your sense of good or bad? How do you know that basis is valid? What aspects do you debate within yourself?

•What characteristics and habits make a mother good enough to raise happy and healthy children? How does she interact with children? How do these qualities change as her children become teens? Adults?

•What characteristics and habits make a father good enough to raise happy and healthy children? How does he interact with children? How do these qualities change as his children become teens? Adults?

•What characteristics and habits make your God/dess good enough to help children become happy and healthy? How does S/He interact with children? How do these qualities change as children become teens? Adults?

•In what ways is your deity image impersonal? Personal? Generalized? Approachable? Alive? Inanimate? Part of everything? Distinct from everything? Only Good? Good and bad? Close? Far away? One who suffers with you? One who stays away? One who creates? One who guides? One who intervenes? One who relates specifically to you? One who relates specifically to others? One who helps you or others find or achieve positive qualities? One who punishes those who need punishment?

•How have you gained the wisdom that you now have? How important to you is that wisdom?

Authority

•Should vengeance be for God/dess and no one else? When? Why? How does your answer inform your behavior? In what circumstances should/would you fight back? Under what circumstances would you fight to the death? What would you leave for another authority? What would you leave for God/dess?

•When should you accept and follow what authority tells you? When should you question authority? When should you disobey authority? What authority can help you answer these questions? Under what circumstances do you become the authority for your life? When do you hand that power to another?

Cultural Themes

- List some of the cultural and religious norms that are commonly accepted. What norms do you question? What norms have you abandoned? What norms do you hold dear?
- What role does culture play in the ways humans define themselves and interact? Men? Women?
- What creates/sustains culture?
- What are some of the subtleties of growing up female in a male-dominated culture? Of growing up male in a male-dominated culture?
- Are male and female roles changing? Why? How do you feel about these potential changes?
- What types of humor do you enjoy most? How is your delight and laughter connected to your upbringing?
- Do you believe feminism was/is a necessary liberation movement? Why?
- How does poverty affect cultural perceptions? From the perspectives of poor people? From the perspectives of privileged people?

Values and Evidence

- How do adult wisdom, reason, and intellectual honesty interact with your childhood exuberant spirit, longings, trust, and beliefs in goodness/God/dess?
- How do faith and reality interweave? What does that woven "cloth" look like?
- How much do we allow evidence to influence our beliefs or decisions? Everyday decisions? Monumental decisions? Beliefs about the meaning of life? Beliefs about God/dess?

•What brain networks tend to support belief in God/dess? What brain networks desire evidence? What brain networks disregard evidence? When? Why?

Recent Scientific Studies

Neuroscience currently debates the ways various aspects of our brains work together; what aspects take charge in what situations and how much control or 'free will' does our conscious brain exercise. Some of the old debate between nature and nurture is now found in questions about the influence of epigenetics on the activation of genes. If you enjoy this kind of scientific discourse, you may want to address the following questions.

•What aspects of our brains tend to support belief in God/dess? What aspects of our brains desire evidence? Which aspects disregard evidence? When? Why? How does evolution influence this process?

•Are we as humans simply who we evolved to be? How much choice do/did we have in the matter? Do you have an opinion about the influence of genetics or epigenetics on who we are?

Leona Stucky

APPENDIX: POEMS

Moundridge, KS
For Leona

by William LaRue
© 2016, from *Desert Pilgrimage: Poems of Love and Liberation*

When I was a boy
Under blue prairie sky
And worn denim overalls
My body was mine

When I was a boy
Herding cattle bare back
Short legs clasped
My nimble horse

When I was a boy too small to see
Beyond the tractor hood
Plowing fields alone
I watched the furrow to my side

When I was a boy
Bucking bales till dark with Dad
I went to sleep on equations
My studies incomplete

When I was a boy
Under blue prairie sky
I was the strong daughter
Of a gentle farmer

When I was a boy
On hardscrabble farm
Working as a man
My body was mine

But I became a woman,
Married at 17, a desperate
Bargain to keep him
From killing my family

The police did not protect
Young women like me, so
I was forced to live as a sex slave
In the land of the free

As a woman I learned
A wife cannot be raped
Consent already assumed
My body was no longer mine

As a woman I learned
My place was where
He told me it was, or he
Violently put me there

As a woman I learned
I could not drive
Or use his money
Unapproved

As a woman I learned
To account for each minute
To ask permission, just
To go outside

As a woman I learned
To live in fear
To calm the raging beast
To save my life

As a woman I learned
Without escape
My body
Would never be mine

Carl's Accident

by Olga Laura Stucky
September 4, 1944

After the trials of many a day
Speak I am listening is all I can say
Lord yes Dear Lord praise be unto thee
That thou hast spared him I plainly now see

So my dear Lord when skies are still black
Teach me to follow right in your track
And what is calm comes o'er my soul
Still I can see the wild billows roll

Wait my dear soul yes wait do I hear
Teach me to trust in thy will and not fear
Only to what thou doth consent will befall
On thy dear loved ones yes on one and all

So teach me to trust in the day yet ahead
Even the hairs are counted you said (Luke 12:7)
And be not afraid for I am with thee
Even to the ends of the earth you will see

Take thou my hand and lead me always
Close to thy heart my Lord let me stay
And teach me to trust by night and by day
Lord thy will be done is all I can say

ACKNOWLEDGMENTS

As this is my first book and with no formal writing education, I needed assistance. In the more than ten years I worked on this story, people stepped forward. I'm gratefully humbled by their talents, wisdom, and their ability to be moved by my attempts to tell this story.

Each human life inspires awe, once you get to know it. My clients of the last thirty years, who have courageously confided in me, have taught me the delicate expanse of human strength. Their resilient stories have helped me understand my own and have emboldened me to tell it honestly and with the hope that others will benefit from it.

I've fortunately experienced insightful and encouraging writing teachers, including Robert Mayer, Ina Hughs, Sara Eyestone, Anya Achtenberg, and numerous others who led writing workshops. I've used Robert Mayer's profound book, *The Origin of Sorrow* as a barometer for excellent writing, and though I'll not write in his league, his stellar advice and belief in what I was saying made all the difference.

Elizabeth Trupin-Pulli, my literary agent and now a dear friend, has been a straight shooter, up front and honest, right from the start. I have appreciated her guidance on this project, every step of the way. Also Philip Spitzer was an early advocate for this memoir. His support of this work came at the right moment.

Several editors have offered their professional assistance, each making the document better along the way: Patricia de Andrea, David Colin Carr, Joy Waldron, Dr. Susan Waterman, and most recently, Mary Neighbour, whose capacity for checking detail while maintaining the focus of the big picture, brought structure and flow to the editing and publishing work.

She was able to create an integrated team and keep it on task to get the project done without a hiccup.

Several friends spent hours reading aloud with me and giving moment-by-moment corrections or thoughts about the content or style: the Rev. Dr. Ralph Milligan, Charlotte Cooke, and Dr. William La Rue. Others have read carefully and offered significant feedback. I won't name each of you here, but you have lifted my spirits and offered critiques that invariably made the work more coherent and complete. Thank you so much!

My dear friend, Dr. Ken Mayers has supported this effort from the beginning stages, and gracefully gave gentle tugs when I was bogged down. He read the memoir a number of times through these years and offered encouragement and access to resource persons each step of the way. My long-time friends and cohorts in creative endeavors, Judith Elfrink Weissmueller and Don Eaton, have also stood with me through rejection letters, writer's blocks, distractions, intense conversations, jubilations, and tough decisions brought by this long writing experience.

And finally, my family journeyed with me in incredibly supportive ways, helping me remember, getting critiques from their friends, reading even when it caused them grief, encouraging me from the beginning, offering delicate feedback, and loving me through various stages of my reactions. I could have accomplished little of this writing without the constancy of their support. To them I am deeply grateful.

ABOUT THE AUTHOR

The Reverend Doctor Leona Stucky has a thriving psycho-therapy practice in Santa Fe, New Mexico. When not working, she enjoys New Mexico landscapes, walking and driving in the open expanse, and exploring nature here and around the world with friends and family. Being a grandmother is one of the highlights of her life; she adores playing with the little ones and watching their relational capacities unfold. She revels in their joy and treasures moments together as they grow.

Dr. Stucky first received a degree in psychology and philosophy from Boston College, graduating summa cum laude, before plunging into seminary, first at Andover Newton Theological School and then at Eden Theological Seminary. She earned a doctorate from Southern Methodist University with honors, and a Diplomate certificate from the American Association of Pastoral Counselors—their highest credential—for teaching, supervising, and offering therapy services. She currently has standing as a Unitarian Universalist community minister. She values the UU principles that affirm loving engagement without requiring members to believe in God or bend to religious creeds.

After completing her formal education, she helped develop a post-graduate training center, The Southwest Institute for Religion and Psychotherapy. Her understanding of psychodynamic theory as well as other therapeutic approaches continued to blossom as she taught them to others. She has led workshops for clinicians in a number of states and several countries. She is a creative thinker and a life-long learner. She enjoys sharing insights with clients, students, friends, family, and fellow professionals—and now with you.

CPSIA information can be obtained
at www.ICGtesting.com
Printed in the USA
FSOW02n1621250317
32285FS

9 780998 647425